CIPS Study

C000182023

Level 4

Foundation Diploma in Purchasing and Supply

COURSE BOOK

Effective Negotiation in Purchasing and Supply

© Profex Publishing Limited, 2010

Printed and distributed by the Chartered Institute of Purchasing & Supply

Easton House, Easton on the Hill, Stamford, Lincolnshire PE9 3NZ

Tel: +44 (0) 1780 756 777

Fax: +44 (0) 1780 751 610

Email: info@cips.org

Website: www.cips.org

First edition October 2006
Second edition September 2008
Third edition April 2009
Reprinted with minor amendments October 2010

Contents

Preface

Welcome to your new Study Pack.

For each subject you have to study, your Study Pack consists of three elements.

- A **Course Book** (the current volume). This provides detailed coverage of all topics specified in the unit content.

- A small-format volume of **Passnotes**. For each learning objective, these highlight and summarise the key points of knowledge and understanding that should underpin an exam answer. Use your Passnotes in the days and weeks leading up to the exam.

- An extensive range of **online resources**. These include a **Quick Start Guide** (a rapid 40-page overview of the subject), practice questions of exam standard (with full suggested solutions), notes on recent technical developments in the subject area, and recent news items (ideal for enhancing your solutions in the exam). These can all be downloaded from the study resources area at www.cips.org. You will need to log in with your membership details to access this information.

For a full explanation of how to use your new Study Pack, turn now to page xiii. And good luck in your exams!

A note on style

Throughout your Study Packs you will find that we use the masculine form of personal pronouns. This convention is adopted purely for the sake of stylistic convenience – we just don't like saying 'he/she' all the time. Please don't think this reflects any kind of bias or prejudice.

October 2010

The Exam

The format of the paper

The time allowed is three hours. The examination is in two sections.

Section A – case study scenario, with two role play application questions based on the case study, each worth 25 marks.

Section B – questions to test knowledge and understanding. Candidates will be required to answer two questions from a choice of four. As with Section A, questions will be worth 25 marks each.

The unit content

The unit content is reproduced below, together with reference to the chapter in this Course Book where each topic is covered.

Unit characteristics

This unit is designed to provide students with the ability to apply a variety of theories relating to negotiation in respect of preparation, planning and participating in the negotiation process.

Students will undertake activities such as cost and market analysis, using information to support the planning of negotiation with suppliers to achieve value for money (VFM). Students should also apply their knowledge of various legal implications affecting negotiations.

Negotiating is often a finely balanced activity which also involves managing a range of complex relationships, and students should be prepared to manage those relationships effectively, avoiding conflict while maintaining the balance of power.

By the end of this unit, students should be able to plan and prepare how to undertake effective negotiations, and also to understand how they would be able to assess effectiveness.

Statements of practice

On completion of this unit, students will be able to:

- Plan and prepare for negotiations
- Apply a range of negotiation theories in order to achieve set outcomes
- Differentiate between a range of persuasion tools and techniques
- Explain the different approaches required when negotiating in different settings
- Understand how to analyse negotiation performance

Learning objectives and indicative content

1.0 Planning and preparing for negotiations
(Weighting 25%)

Chapter

1.1 Analyse the different phases of negotiation.

• Preparation	1
• Open	1
• Test	1
• Move	1
• Agree	1
• Finalise the deal	1

1.2 Identify and evaluate information required to understand the supplier organisation:

• Supplier information (supply, demand, timings, costings, budgets, readiness, capacity, account management structure)	2
• Competitor information, for example supplier competitors	2
• Oligopoly/monopoly/duopoly	2

1.3 Analyse market information to support negotiation

• PESTLE	3
• SWOT	2
• Supply and demand	3

1.4 Assess any legal information and implications for the purchase and supply of goods that might impact upon negotiations.

• Sale of Goods Act	3
• *Caveat emptor*	3
• Negotiating terms and conditions	3
• Penalties and damages	3
• Unfair Contract Terms Act	3

1.5 Undertake a risk assessment specifically relating to:

• Win-lose, win-win and win perceived win	3
• Generating variables and alternatives	3
• Risk assessment matrix	3

How to Use Your Study Pack

Familiarisation

At this point you should begin to familiarise yourself with the package of benefits you have purchased.

- Go to www.cips.org and log on. Then go to Study and Qualify/Study Resources. Browse through the free content relating to this subject.
- Download the Quick Start Guide and print it out. Open up a ring binder and make the Quick Start Guide your first item in there.
- Now glance briefly through the Course Book (the text you're reading right now!) and the Passnotes.

Organising your study

'Organising' is the key word: unless you are a very exceptional student, you will find a haphazard approach is insufficient, particularly if you are having to combine study with the demands of a full-time job.

A good starting point is to timetable your studies, in broad terms, between now and the date of the examination. How many subjects are you attempting? How many chapters are there in the Course Book for each subject? Now do the sums: how many days/weeks do you have for each chapter to be studied?

Remember:

- Not every week can be regarded as a study week – you may be going on holiday, for example, or there may be weeks when the demands of your job are particularly heavy. If these can be foreseen, you should allow for them in your timetabling.
- You also need a period leading up to the exam in which you will revise and practise what you have learned.

Once you have done the calculations, make a week-by-week timetable for yourself for each paper, allowing for study and revision of the entire unit content between now and the date of the exams.

Getting started

Aim to find a quiet and undisturbed location for your study, and plan as far as possible to use the same period each day. Getting into a routine helps avoid wasting time. Make sure you have all the materials you need before you begin – keep interruptions to a minimum.

Begin by reading through your Quick Start Guide. This should take no more than a couple of hours, even reading slowly. By the time you have finished this you will have a reasonable grounding in the subject area. You will build on this by working through the Course Book.

Using the Course Book

You should refer to the Course Book to the extent that you need it.

- If you are a newcomer to the subject, you will probably need to read through the Course Book quite thoroughly. This will be the case for most students.
- If some areas are already familiar to you – either through earlier studies or through your practical work experience – you may choose to skip sections of the Course Book.

The content of the Course Book

This Course Book has been designed to give detailed coverage of every topic in the unit content. As you will see from pages vii–xi, each topic mentioned in the unit content is dealt with in a chapter of the Course Book. For the most part the order of the Course Book follows the order of the unit content closely, though departures from this principle have occasionally been made in the interest of a logical learning order.

Each chapter begins with a reference to the learning objectives and unit content to be covered in the chapter. Each chapter is divided into sections, listed in the introduction to the chapter, and for the most part being actual captions from the unit content.

All of this enables you to monitor your progress through the unit content very easily and provides reassurance that you are tackling every subject that is examinable.

Each chapter contains the following features.

- Introduction, setting out the main topics to be covered
- Clear coverage of each topic in a concise and approachable format
- A chapter summary
- Self-test questions

The study phase

For each chapter you should begin by glancing at the main headings (listed at the start of the chapter). Then read fairly rapidly through the body of the text to absorb the main points. If it's there in the text, you can be sure it's there for a reason, so try not to skip unless the topic is one you are familiar with already.

Then return to the beginning of the chapter to start a more careful reading. You may want to take brief notes as you go along, but bear in mind that you already have your Quick Start Guide and Passnotes – there is no point in duplicating what you can find there.

Test your recall and understanding of the material by attempting the self-test questions. These are accompanied by cross-references to paragraphs where you can check your answers and refresh your memory.

Practising what you have learned

Once you think you have learned enough about the subject, or about a particular topic within the overall subject area, it's good to practise. Access the study resources at www.cips.org, and download a practice question on the relevant area. Alternatively, download a past exam question. Attempt a solution yourself before looking at our suggested solution or the Senior Assessor's comments.

Make notes of any mistakes you made, or any areas where your answer could be improved. If there is anything you can't understand, you are welcome to email us for clarification (course.books@cips.org).

The revision phase

Your approach to revision should be methodical and you should aim to tackle each main area of the unit content in turn. Begin by re-reading your Quick Start Guide. This gives an overview that will help to focus your more detailed study. Then re-read your notes and/or the separate Passnotes accompanying this Course Book. Then return to question practice. Review your own solutions to the practice questions you have had time to attempt. If there are gaps, try to find time to attempt some more questions, or at least to review the suggested solutions.

Additional reading

Your Study Pack provides you with the key information needed for each module but CIPS strongly advocates reading as widely as possible to augment and reinforce your understanding. CIPS produces an official reading list of books, which can be downloaded from the bookshop area of the CIPS website.

To help you, we have identified one essential textbook for each subject. We recommend that you read this for additional information.

The essential textbook for this unit is *Essentials of Negotiation* by Roy Lewicki, David Saunders, Bruce Barry and John Minton, published by McGraw Hill (ISBN: 9–78007–126773–1).

CHAPTER 1

The Phases of Negotiation

Learning objectives and indicative content

1.1   Analyse the different phases of negotiation, including:

- Preparation
- Open
- Test
- Move
- Agree
- Finalise the deal

Chapter headings

1   Preparing for a negotiation

2   Opening the negotiation

3   Discussing the issues

4   Finalising the deal

5   Collaborative and distributive approaches

Introduction

Many authorities on negotiation have seen the process as one that can be broken down into phases. The wording of your examination syllabus suggests that the examiner will be looking for this kind of analysis. In this chapter we discuss the various phases in the process of negotiation. You should bear in mind that the phases identified in your syllabus are not the only ones that might be identified; other authorities might prefer to analyse the process differently, and we will mention some of the alternative possibilities below.

1   Preparing for a negotiation

Why negotiate?

1.1   'Negotiation is applicable where there is disagreement or potential disagreement between suppliers and buyers. A good buyer will be sensitive to potential areas of conflict and will seek to resolve these before they arise by ensuring that the terms and conditions applicable to the purchase provide for such contingencies.' (Lysons and Farrington, *Purchasing and Supply Chain Management*)

1.2 In an ideal world, from a buyer's viewpoint, all of the materials and services required by a business would be freely available at cheap rates. From a supplier's point of view, the ideal world would be one in which he could charge as much as he liked for his goods and services. Somewhere between these two extremes businesses must find common ground. Much of the practical work of a buyer is concerned with finding this common ground. Often the means of doing so lies in negotiation.

1.3 This much is so obvious that negotiation might easily be thought of as an indispensable part of supplier relations. This is indeed so if the term 'negotiation' is understood in a broad sense. However, in purchasing contexts it is usual to define the term more narrowly. In its narrower sense, negotiation is not necessarily part of every purchasing transaction. The main alternative is usually seen as **competitive bidding**, in which suppliers are asked to quote on terms and prices, and the buyer chooses the best offer.

1.4 An analysis due to Dobler and Burt (*Purchasing and Supply Management*) establishes criteria for when competitive bidding should be used, and suggests situations when it should not be used. Clearly in cases where competitive bidding is inappropriate it is essential to use some form of negotiation. The analysis of Dobler and Burt is presented in Table 1.1.

Table 1.1 *The use of competitive bidding*

Five criteria for the use of competitive bidding	Four situations in which competitive bidding should not be used
The monetary value of the purchase should be high enough to justify the expense of the method	Situations where it is impossible to estimate production costs accurately
The specifications must be clear and the vendors must have a clear idea of the production costs involved	Situations in which price is not the only important variable
There must be an adequate number of vendors in the market	Situations in which changes to specification are likely as the contract progresses
The vendors must be both technically qualified and keen for the business	Situations in which special tooling or set-up costs are major factors
There must be sufficient time for the procedure to be accomplished	

1.5 Other authorities identify other alternatives to negotiation and competitive bidding. For example, Baily, Farmer, Jessop and Jones (in *Purchasing Principles and Management*) suggest the following alternatives.

- **Persuade**: encourage the other side to accept the merits of your case with no concessions on your side.
- **Give in**: accept the other side's case without reservation.
- **Coerce**: insist that the other side meets your demands, 'or else'.
- **Problem solve**: remove the difference, so that there is no need to negotiate.

What matters should be negotiated?

1.6   Not all transactions are conducted by means of negotiation or competitive bidding. For example, small-value branded items that a supplier maintains as part of his shelf stock and includes in his catalogue are not usually subject to negotiation.

1.7   The situation is different if the value of items is large. Negotiations may well be necessary if the terms of sale include many and varied clauses, or if the buyer suspects that the quoted price is unreasonably high. This could happen for example if the supplier has padded his quoted price in order to cover contingencies.

1.8   Other common situations where negotiations will be appropriate include the following.

- Contracts for capital items
- Projects with a large element of uncertainty in the eventual cost
- Contracts involving a learning effect
- Contracts involving a significant cost for tooling
- Contracts where the purchaser contributes expertise, materials etc
- Outsourcing agreements, and purchases of services in general

1.9   The terms subject to negotiation are of course very numerous. Price is the obvious matter: this includes the type of pricing agreement, discounts, terms of payment, contract price adjustment (CPA) clauses, transportation charges and so on.

1.10   Delivery and scheduling are also vital. The deadlines for delivery, the method of delivery, details of packaging and palleting are all relevant here. Remedies in the event of late delivery are also important.

1.11   Above all, negotiation must cover quality issues. This includes acceptable quality levels, methods and place of inspection, procedures in respect of rejected goods, site visits and so on.

Setting objectives

1.12   The above discussion establishes a starting point for the negotiation process: the buyer must decide whether negotiation is the correct approach at all. Assuming he decides that it is, the next step must be to determine his objectives. Many authorities on the subject have emphasised the importance of this preparatory step, while acknowledging that in practice it is often skimped.

1.13   A useful approach to setting objectives is given by the acronym MIL, originally coined by Gavin Kennedy. Kennedy distinguished between objectives we Must achieve, objectives we Intend to achieve (or which it is Important for us to achieve), and objectives we would Like to achieve. Must, Intend (or Important), and Like are the key words.

1.14   The MIL acronym identifies the relative importance of our objectives.

- The M objectives are show-stoppers. If we can't achieve these, the negotiation will fail.

- The L objectives are the icing on the cake. If we can achieve these we can feel that we have been very successful indeed.

- The I objectives occupy the middle position. While a failure to achieve one or more of these will not necessarily be disastrous, we will certainly be trying very hard to achieve them.

1.15 The main authority recommended for this module is Roy J Lewicki and others – their large text *Negotiation* and its abridged version *Essentials of Negotiation*. From now on we will refer to them simply as 'Lewicki'. Lewicki has an interesting discussion of how goals affect negotiations. The authors make four points.

- Wishes are not goals. A wish is a hope; a goal is a defined target.

- Our goals are often linked to the other party's goals. I want to buy the car; the dealer wants to sell it. We are both working to the same objective – the only (or main) issue is the price.

- There are boundaries to what our goals can be. It's no use expecting to get the car for £1,000 if the dealer's opening price is £10,000 – be realistic.

- Effective goals must be specific, and preferably measurable. Otherwise we can't easily communicate what we want, or judge whether what is offered meets our objectives.

1.16 Another important factor to address in the preparation stage is exactly what information we are prepared to reveal to the other party and the information we will be seeking from him.

Collecting information

1.17 To prepare for a negotiation, and in particular to help in establishing objectives, the buyer must identify necessary information and take steps to assemble it. Where an existing supplier is concerned, the buyer must ensure that he is completely informed as to the terms of the current agreement and on the supplier's performance to date. Other types of information (such as cost analysis) are important whether a new supplier or an existing supplier is concerned.

1.18 Buyers sometimes use a checklist to ensure that their background information is sufficiently comprehensive. An example is given in Figure 1.1.

1.19 Notice in Figure 1.1 the reference to the relative strengths of the bargaining parties. The buyer will attempt to maximise the strengths of his own position. This can be weakened by any or all of the following factors.

- Few alternative sources available (perhaps because the supplier enjoys a monopoly position, or because he has the advantage of a premium branded product or specialised equipment)
- Suppliers indifferent about obtaining the business
- Urgent demand for the material
- Option to make the product internally is not available
- Lack of knowledge of the supplier's cost structure
- Insufficient background information on the supplier – personnel, levels of authority, position in the market

- Unexpected arguments advanced by the supplier
- Inappropriate conduct of the buyer (eg too much talking and not enough listening, speaking out of turn)

Figure 1.1 *Negotiation planning checklist*

Fictional plc		Negotiation planning checklist
MEETING WITH:	*DATE:*	
		Reference
General	What are our objectives?	
	What assumptions have been used in framing our objectives?	
	How may these assumptions be challenged?	
	What are their likely objectives and arguments?	
	What are our strengths and weaknesses? What are their strengths and weaknesses?	
	How have they performed under the current agreement?	
	By what date must we reach agreement?	
	Which of our staff will take part in the meeting? Who will be the team leader?	
	How much do we know about the personnel on their side? What level of authority do they have to conclude an agreement?	
Financial terms	What is the current price (if applicable)? What is the range of prices that we can accept or hope for?	
	What are the general terms of payment, including credit period?	
	Are stage payments applicable?	
	Are there discounts for bulk orders or for early pament?	
	Are foreign currencies involved, and if so which?	
Quality and delivery	Has the supplier been given a complete specification? What feedback if any have we had?	
	How is conformance with specification to be measured?	
	Are any variations permissible in the terms of the specification? Has the supplier suggested any such variations?	
	What delivery date(s) will apply?	
	What will be the delivery quantities?	
	What arrangements should be made for packaging, palleting and transportation?	
Contractual terms	Are the terms of the contract clear, and have they clearly been accepted?	
	By which country's law is the contract to be governed? In which country's courts are disputes to be resolved? Is there any provision for arbitration?	
	Who is responsible for the various elements of purchase cost? Who is responsible for insurance?	
	Are there clear administrative arrangements for implementing the contract once agreed?	

1.20 Nearly all of these weaknesses can be overcome by careful preparation, which again reinforces the importance of this phase in the process. Sometimes the buyer needs help in this from colleagues; for example, demand will not be urgent if requisitions are placed in good time by user departments. However, if the supplier has a dominant influence in the market by reason of a monopoly or near-monopoly position, then the buyer's position will be weak no matter how carefully he prepares.

1.21 Buyers should be aware from the outset that the negotiations may not be successful. To cope with this, they should have a contingency plan (sometimes referred to as BATNA – the buyer's **b**est **a**lternative **t**o a **n**egotiated **a**greement). The stronger the BATNA, the less need a buyer has to persist with an unsatisfactory negotiation – he is more able to walk away if he has a good contingency plan up his sleeve. This strengthens the buyer's bargaining position.

1.22 A crucial point that should be mentioned at this point is the importance of **confidentiality** in the preparation phase. Buyers should be well aware that suppliers can become more confident, and less ready to make concessions, if they suspect that they are highly likely to obtain the business. Buyers therefore take care not to give them that impression. However, the point is less well understood in technical departments and unguarded communications from such a source can prove very expensive. There should be a firm policy that such matters are only to be discussed with the supplier by members of the purchasing function.

1.23 Another issue to determine at the pre-negotiation phase is who exactly is to represent the buying organisation. Should it be just one person or a team?

1.24 Finally, it is common in cases of very important negotiations to perform a trial run or rehearsal (sometimes called a 'murder court'). In this scenario, the team due to negotiate will play out their role before relevant experts within their own organisation. These attempt to 'murder' the buying team, ie to expose faulty arguments, unjustified assumptions and so on. The buying team use the experience to hone their preparation for the real meeting.

Subdividing the planning phase

1.25 To conclude this section, it is worth noting that Lewicki identifies several stages in the planning phase itself.

- Defining the issues: these will usually include one or two major issues and several more minor issues
- Assembling issues and defining the bargaining mix: the MIL acronym may be helpful in determining what issues are negotiable and which ones less so
- Defining interests: which may include short-term price reductions, but could equally well include maintenance of a long-term relationship with the supplier
- Defining limits: the minimum acceptable outcomes in relation to each objective
- Defining objectives and opening bids: ensuring that the opening bids are not so ambitious as to frighten away the other party
- Defining one's constituents: the people that must be satisfied by the outcome, eg one's boss, one's shareholders
- Understanding the other party: discussed in detail in the next chapter of this text
- Selecting a strategy
- Planning the presentation and defence: with use of effective argument and substantiating detail
- Defining protocol: eg where the meeting is to take place and who is to attend

2 Opening the negotiation

Alternative views of the negotiation phases

2.1   While most authorities would emphasise the importance of advance preparation, as discussed above, there is less consensus about the remaining phases of the negotiation process. Different commentators have analysed the process in different ways.

2.2   As an example, Gavin Kennedy distinguished eight steps.

- Prepare
- Argue
- Signal
- Propose
- Package
- Bargain
- Close
- Agree

2.3   Kennedy later simplified this to a four-phase approach.

- Prepare: what do **we** want?
- Debate: what do **they** want?
- Propose: what wants **might** we trade?
- Bargain: what wants **will** we trade?

2.4   By contrast, Leonard Greenhalgh (quoted in Lewicki) identifies the following seven phases.

- Preparation
- Relationship building
- Information gathering
- Information using
- Bidding
- Closing the deal
- Implementing the agreement

2.5   A feature these approaches have in common is that they appear to deal with a single negotiation meeting. The implication seems to be that one face-to-face meeting will be enough to wrap everything up. Other authorities have recognised that it is sometimes more complex than that. For example, Baily and others (in *Purchasing Principles and Management*) distinguish between processes based on a single meeting and processes based on multiple meetings: see Figure 1.2.

Figure 1.2 *The phases of negotiation*

(a)   Single meeting

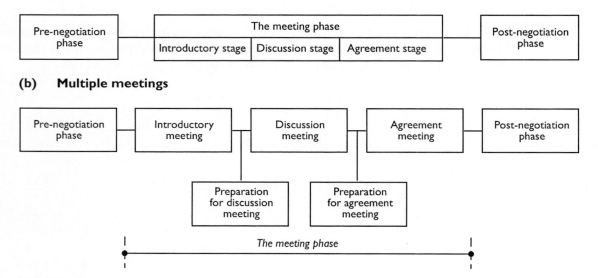

(b)   Multiple meetings

Getting started

2.6   The paragraphs above illustrate the difficulty of drawing hard and fast lines between the different phases of negotiation. Even so, it is possible to identify certain aspects that will always be relevant to the opening phase.

2.7   To begin with, it is important to establish the right atmosphere. Partly this is a matter of physical surroundings: a comfortable work environment is conducive to agreement. Partly it involves setting the right tone in what is said, perhaps beginning with social interchange and continuing with a statement of the matters that have already been agreed.

2.8   It is important to listen as well as to talk. The supplier may have new information to release, or may wish to clarify assumptions. His words and attitude may give clues as to his readiness to cooperate.

2.9   Frequently there will be an agenda agreed in advance. This prior agreement is important, because negotiators may refuse to discuss issues that confront them for the first time when actually in the meeting room.

2.10 It is often assumed that a negotiator should favour meeting on his own 'home ground'. Other authorities have disputed this. The issue will be discussed further in Chapters 6 and 10.

2.11 If it is likely that discussions will be lengthy it may be appropriate to discuss a timetable at the beginning (or even to agree it in advance). Details should include when to start, how long a discussion session should last, timing of coffee breaks etc.

2.12 Another point to establish early on is who will be recording what is discussed and agreed. This is an important role because later memories of detailed points agreed may be faulty. Lewicki points out that there may be an advantage in volunteering for this role: 'the person with the best notes may volunteer to draft the initial agreement ... this person may be able to take some licence in how the agreement is stated, and what points are emphasised or de-emphasised'.

3   *Discussing the issues*

Testing the ground

3.1   Most of the time taken by a negotiation process is occupied in debate. This is not to minimise the importance of advance preparation, but simply to emphasise how vital it is to conduct the spoken dialogue effectively.

3.2   A vital ingredient in this process is a clear statement of our own position. We must have adequately prepared ourselves to explain our perspective on the issues under debate, and to express what it is we are looking for.

3.3   Often we will be asking questions. In this context, Paul T Steele and Tom Beasor (in *Business Negotiation: a Practical Workbook*) distinguish between seven types of question.

- Open questions (eg 'What are your reasons for …?'). These are appropriate for encouraging discussion and gaining more information. They are not appropriate when more specific information is needed.

- Closed questions (eg 'Can you deliver by the 17th?') These are appropriate for checking specific facts and for clarifying the situation. They are not appropriate in cases when a 'No' answer would be unwelcome.

- Probing questions (eg 'What specific tests do you use to ensure consistent quality?'). These are appropriate if we are trying to tie down the supplier and force him to give the information we need.

- Leading questions (eg 'So there will be no problem in meeting our quality requirements?'). These are appropriate for gaining acceptance of our views. They are less appropriate if our aim is to find out more about the supplier's own opinion.

- Reflective questions (eg 'That causes you a problem?'). These are appropriate when we are encouraging the supplier to continue talking and to look deeper into the situation. They are less appropriate for checking facts.

- Hypothetical questions (eg 'Suppose we made you our sole supplier?'). The advantage of this is that it enables options to be discussed without either party committing themselves.

- Multiple questions (eg 'How do you ensure fixed prices, delivery and quality?'). This is useful for putting the supplier under pressure, but it is important to ensure that all parts of the question are answered.

3.4   Equally, we must **listen** carefully to the supplier's perspective and respond constructively to any difficulties they express. At the same time, there may be important benefits that we can enjoy simply from the fact that the supplier is talking. For example, a supplier may give away information that weakens his position or strengthens our position.

3.5   Another good reason for listening attentively is that we may become aware of misunderstandings on the part of the supplier. In such a case it is important to be open and honest about the mistake so that discussions can continue on the basis of mutual understanding.

3.6   Steele and Beasor are again useful in summarising characteristics of effective listeners. Their points form the basis of Table 1.2 below.

Table 1.2 *Characteristics of effective listeners*

Characteristic	Description
Non-verbal behaviour	The listener is attentive, with a positive and 'interested' posture, maintaining eye contact and responding when appropriate with nods and smiles.
Focus of attention	The listener ensures that the focus of the conversation remains on the speaker.
Acceptance	The listener accepts the ideas and feelings expressed by the speaker rather than rejecting them.
Empathy	The listener expresses understanding of why the speaker feels as he does.
Probing	The listener follows up interesting points in a constructive (but non-critical) manner.
Paraphrasing	The listener checks understanding by restating important points in his own words.
Summarising	The listener summarises conclusions from time to time.

Moving

3.7   A main aim of negotiation is to seek some movement in the other party's position. In the case of buyer and seller, the movement may relate (for example) to a price reduction: if the seller has opened the negotiation with an offer to supply at £X per unit, the buyer would like him to move to a (lower) price of £Y per unit.

3.8   Ideally, the buyer would like this to happen without having to make any movement in his own position. But of course the supplier has different ideas. He would like the buyer to accept a high price without himself having to offer any concessions in return.

3.9   It is easy to conclude from this that both sides must move in order to reach accord, but this is not necessarily the case. Of course, that may well be the outcome eventually, but before reaching that point the buyer should attempt everything legitimate to achieve **unilateral** movement from the supplier.

3.10   Steele and Beasor suggest three main methods for achieving this: emotion, logic and threat.

- With regard to **emotion**, Steele and Beasor cite lines such as 'My boss will shoot me if I go back with a deal like this', attempting to engage the supplier's sympathy.
- With regard to **logic**, this depends on identifying flaws in the supplier's position and convincing him that we are correct. It is best if we get our argument in before he can elaborate on the logic of his own position.
- With regard to **threat**, the obvious possibility is a subtle (or not so subtle) indication that we may take our business elsewhere.

3.11 If we don't succeed in inducing unilateral movement from the supplier, we are reduced to **trading concessions** (ie he will only move if we offer something in return). This of course is a situation that will occur in most negotiations, which makes it important to understand the appropriate techniques.

3.12 To begin with, preparation is vital. We **must** have worked out before entering the negotiation how much leeway we are prepared to give on each of the issues to be debated (price, delivery lead time etc). That indicates the maximum amount of movement we can contemplate, but naturally we would like to move less than that if possible.

3.13 The literature emphasises how important it is to induce a 'marker' from the supplier. This means leading the supplier into making an 'opening bid' on whatever issue is up for debate.

3.14 For simplicity, let's assume that the main issue for debate is price. We will have come into the negotiation with a firm idea of the maximum price we are prepared to pay, and with a target price significantly lower than the maximum. But it would be a mistake to mention either of these prices to the supplier. Instead, we jockey for position, trying to induce the supplier to suggest a price first.

3.15 In this particular situation – where price is the issue – the buyer will often have a readymade advantage, because the supplier's target price may be known already (eg from his catalogue, his price list, or his tender).

3.16 Once the 'bidding' has begun, the task is to make the supplier move his position to one that is more favourable to our objectives. If we have exhausted our efforts to obtain unilateral movement, now is the time to consider concessions. The trick is to make small concessions, and even then only in return for concessions from the supplier that are at least as valuable.

3.17 When a concession has been won, be sure to thank the supplier and then move on to explore the issue further, looking for means of achieving additional concessions.

Reaching agreement

3.18 We have simplified by assuming that only one variable is up for discussion, namely price. In practice, it doesn't work like that. When bargaining with a supplier you are interested in a whole range of variables: price, payment terms, quality, reliability, delivery lead times etc. This opens up the possibility of trading concessions on one variable for concessions on another.

3.19 As an example, suppose our preparation leads us to suppose that the supplier is stretched for immediate cash. It may be possible to obtain a more favourable price in return for a concession on speed of payment. If our own organisation is cash-rich, prompt payment may cause us no difficulty, and yet to the supplier it could be very valuable – enough to induce a significant price reduction.

3.20 Once all the variables have been discussed there comes a point when we may suspect that further progress is impossible. In other words, we conclude that the supplier has nothing more to offer. This is not a conclusion to be reached lightly, and certainly not just because the supplier says so. But if we really think there is nothing more to be gained in the negotiation it is time to make a decision.

3.21 If our objectives have not been met at this stage, the decision may be simply to walk away. While this may appear a drastic course of action, the ability to walk away from a deal is a vital tool for the negotiator. Without it, we risk being browbeaten into an unacceptable agreement.

3.22 On the other hand, if the overall deal – taking account of all the variables under discussion – meets our objectives, then it makes sense to shake hands and conclude the agreement. Dithering can lead to the loss of favourable deals, so if we are sure that we have got enough to satisfy our objectives, it is better not to delay.

3.23 Bear in mind that we may be dealing with the same supplier for years to come, so the outcome of the current negotiation is not the only consideration. If we are pressured into an unsatisfactory agreement, or if we impose an unfair deal on the supplier, the chances of good relations in the future are reduced.

4 Finalising the deal

Pressure ploys

4.1 In Gavin Kennedy's book *Kennedy on Negotiation*, the negotiation guru outlines a number of ploys designed to close off the deal. These typically take place when there is a good momentum towards agreement, caused by substantive agreement on a number (if not all) of the issues.

4.2 One ploy is referred to by Kennedy as the **quivering quill**. This is the tactic, frequently employed by sales persons, of beginning the paperwork before the deal is quite concluded. The buyer is nudged into thinking that agreement has been reached, and that only formalities remain. This can make it difficult for the buyer to resist when the sales person looks up from his paperwork and says 'As we discussed, I'm still a little unhappy about Point X. Can we agree my position on that so that I can sign off?'

4.3 Needless to say, a buyer facing such a tactic should not be browbeaten. The paperwork can wait if there are still substantive issues to discuss.

4.4 Kennedy also discusses the **now or never** tactic. The sales person makes it clear that there is an important deadline and that everything so far agreed may be jeopardised unless agreement is reached immediately. How credible this deadline is depends on how convincing a case the sales person has made in explaining it. Ideally, our advance preparation for the meeting should have uncovered any genuine reason why a deal is needed sooner rather than later.

4.5 Another ploy is **take it or leave it**. This is rarely a plausible technique in the early stages of negotiation, but if it comes after much discussion of a wide range of variables it may be more credible that the supplier simply has nothing more to offer. Even so, as in the case of 'now or never', the buyer should not be browbeaten. Is it really credible that no further progress can be made after the deadline, or that the supplier will refuse to re-enter discussions if we are unable to accept right now?

4.6 Finally, Kennedy mentions **split the difference**. When the supplier is insisting on a unit price of £2, and the buyer is haggling for £1.80, the seller may suggest splitting the difference and settling on £1.90. Often, this appeal to our sense of fair play may seem hard to resist. But it must still be handled with care.

4.7 Firstly, the buyer must ask himself whether the price of £1.90 will achieve his objectives. If not, then he has to decline, even at the risk of seeming unreasonable. Secondly, the appearance of fair play may be very deceptive. If the seller's original price of £2.00 was excessive, then even the reduced price of £1.90 may also be over the top. It might be more appropriate for the buyer to argue for 'splitting the difference' in a proportion other than 50: 50 – say, by asking for a price of £1.81.

4.8 There is a vast literature on techniques employed by sales persons in order to clinch deals. Buyers must keep a level head and not be rushed or browbeaten into accepting an unfavourable deal. We have more to say on this topic in Chapter 8.

The final stages

4.9 Assuming that all issues have been satisfactorily resolved, the time has come to conclude the deal. In many cases, it will be necessary to obtain final **ratification** of what has been agreed (eg from the Board of Directors), but buyers (and sellers) should avoid using the Board as a means of re-opening negotiations later. Provided the scope of the negotiator's responsibility was adequately defined at the outset, reference back to the Board should be little more than a formality.

4.10 The literature on negotiation emphasises the importance of avoiding misunderstandings in the closing phases. The usual recommendation is that negotiators should produce a written summary of what has been agreed, before leaving the meeting. This should be read out and agreed by the other party as a fair summary of the agreement.

4.11 In due course – and the sooner the better – the agreement should be embodied in a more formal document for signature by both sides. Once the written agreement is in place the buyer must ensure that it is implemented. This involves gaining commitment from relevant personnel in the buying organisation. For example, if the supplier is concerned about payment terms (and he always will be!) the buyer must ensure that finance staff are aware of what was agreed in this respect and able to comply.

4.12 Finally, it is important to monitor performance. It cannot simply be assumed that what was agreed will be implemented, on either side. Instead, a defined system of evaluation and reporting must be put in place.

5 *Collaborative and distributive approaches*

Two broad approaches

5.1   There are two basic orientations to negotiation.

- **Distributive bargaining** involves the distribution of limited resources, or 'dividing up a fixed pie'. One party's gain can only come at the expense of the other party: this is sometimes called a zero-sum game, or a win-loss outcome. If the buyer pushes the price down, for example, the supplier's profit margin will be eroded. If a trade union succeeds in securing a greater-than-budgeted wage increase for its members, the excess may have to be funded at the expense of shareholders (through reduced profits) or customers (through increased prices).

- **Integrative bargaining** involves collaborative problem-solving to increase the options available (or 'expanding the pie'), with the aim of exploring possibilities for both parties to find a mutually satisfying or win-win solution. This may also be called **added value negotiating** (AVN): the aim is to add value to the deal, rather than extracting value from or conceding value to the other party.

The distributive approach

5.2   The kind of tactics used in a distributive or transactional approach reflect a **push influencing style**.

- Presenting exaggerated initial positions/demands, in order to allow for expected movement and compromise

- Exaggerating the initial distance between the two parties' positions, and polarising conflicting viewpoints, in order to persuade opponents that their position is unrealistic

- Withholding information that might highlight areas of common ground or weakness in your bargaining position

- Using all available levers to coerce, pressure or manipulate the other party to make concessions

- Offering no concessions in return (unless forced to do so), even where they might be offered at low cost

The integrative approach

5.3   The integrative approach is now generally recognised as the most constructive, ethical (or principled) and sustainable approach. Negotiation gurus Fisher and Ury note that a 'wise agreement' is one that 'meets the legitimate interests of each side to the extent possible, resolves conflicting interests fairly, is durable and takes community interests into account.'

5.4   The foundation for win-win or integrative approaches in supply negotiations is the belief that cooperation along the supply chain can lead to elimination of waste at all stages, benefiting all parties. A buyer who focuses exclusively on one objective – say a 5 per cent price reduction – may miss opportunities to widen the discussion fruitfully. For example, by cooperating with the supplier in improved quality assurance measures the costs of assuring quality may fall for both sides. This may be enough in itself to achieve the desired improvement in profits without detriment to the supplier's margins.

5.5   Typical integrative tactics reflect a **pull influencing approach**.

- Being open about your own needs and concerns in the situation, and seeking to understand those of the other party: getting all cards on the table

- Collaboratively generating options (which may be more creative than either party could come up with on their own), seeking to find those with genuine mutual or trade-off benefits.

- Focusing on areas of common ground and mutual benefit, to keep a positive and collaborative atmosphere

- Supporting the other party in accepting your proposals, by emphasising joint problem-solving, offering additional information or help with follow-up etc

- Maintaining and modelling flexibility by making and inviting reasonable counter-offers and compromises

Principled negotiation

5.6   In their classic text *Getting to Yes*, Fisher and Ury note that negotiation has traditionally depended on **positional bargaining**: each side takes a 'position' on an issue, arguing in its favour and attempting to get an outcome as close to that initial position as possible. People may bargain hard (taking up an aggressive or extreme position and holding onto it, often eliciting an equally hard counter-response) or soft (making concessions readily in order to reach agreement, but often ending up with a negative result, based on the initial position having been compromised). Either way, the focus on positions fosters a win-lose or lose-lose outcome.

5.7   Positional bargaining tends to be unsatisfactory at best: 'Any agreement reached may reflect a mechanical splitting of the difference between final positions rather than a solution carefully crafted to meet the legitimate interests of the parties.' At worst, it can lead to a time-consuming and relationship-damaging adversarial process.

5.8   In contrast, **principled negotiation** sees the parties as working collaboratively to attack a shared problem or to maximise a shared opportunity. Fisher and Ury advocate a style that is both hard (on the problem: deciding issues on their objective merits and standing up for your legitimate rights and interests) *and* soft (on the people: looking for mutual gains and insisting on fairness both in the debate and in the outcomes).

5.9   Principled negotiation requires:

- Separating the people from the problem, in order to deal with substantive issues in a way that respects people and maintains positive relationships: acknowledging and addressing the emotions, values and viewpoints involved.

- Focusing on reconciling interests (each side's needs, concerns and fears) rather than positions. 'For every interest there usually exist several possible positions that could satisfy it [and] behind opposed positions lie shared and compatible interests, as well as conflicting ones.'

- Generating a variety of ideas and options rather than pushing for a pre-determined answer: expanding the pie before dividing it.

- Insisting that the agreement reflect some objectively fair standard. Neither party need concede a win to the other: both may defer to a fair solution dictated by market value, legal/customary precedent, the principle of reciprocity, professional codes of practice, shared criteria (eg ethics or efficiency) and so on.

Selecting the appropriate approach

5.10 When it comes to negotiating in complex situations, the most appropriate style may be analysed on a grid (devised by KW Thomas) matching the negotiators' concern for the outcome (winning) against their concern for the long-term future of the relationship with the other party (relationship). We discuss this model in more detail in Chapter 10.

Figure 1.3 *Model of conflict-handling styles*

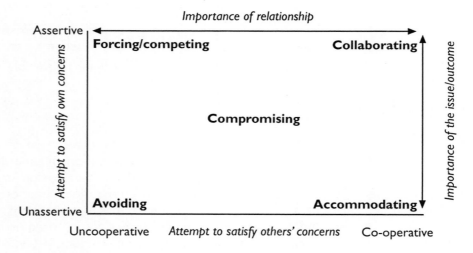

5.11 The diagram indicates the following possible approaches.

- Avoidance may be used where the issue is unimportant to both parties: it may be left unresolved.

- Competition/adversarialism may be used when a point is non-negotiable.

- Accommodation may be used to give soft concessions, in order to earn reciprocal concessions in other areas.

- Collaboration (integrative bargaining) may be used to explore win-win outcomes.

5.12 Another useful (and slightly different) model is *Andrew Cox*'s concept of **structural power**. Cox argued that there are inevitable inequalities of power between purchasers and suppliers, but that these need not present an obstacle to collaborative working relationships. Buyers should seek to create dominance, and use adversarial elements in negotiation, in order to wield influence over suppliers – with the mutually beneficial aim of achieving quality and cost gains.

Using concessions effectively

5.13 Concessions are a cornerstone of the bargaining approach, enabling movement from polarised positions towards the middle ground. There are two basic orientations to making concessions.

5.14 An integrative approach uses concessions to build trust. Unilateral or unconditional concessions send the message that ongoing collaboration is a priority, and there is an underlying belief in the potential for mutual satisfaction and gains over time. However:

- All concessions must be openly identified and acknowledged as concessions (ie of some cost to the offering party), so that the other party is placed under moral obligation to reciprocate.

- Unilateral concessions must be relatively low-cost and low-risk to grant (while being valuable to the receiving party) in order to avoid exploitation.

- The motives for making concessions (and demands) should be clearly explained where possible, in order to reduce suspicion: the more reasonable and justifiable your positions and expectations are, the less they will be perceived as purely political, adversarial or manipulative in nature.

5.15 A distributive, adversarial or transactional approach uses concessions as trading currency: they represent a cost to be tightly controlled, invested and leveraged for reciprocal gains. Such an approach leads to tactics such as:

- Avoiding being the first party to make a concession (a sign of weakness)

- Making concessions strictly contingent on gaining a concession of equal or greater value from the other party: no 'goodwill' concessions (which can simply be taken advantage of).

- Making concessions of least possible cost to you, while demanding concessions of greatest possible value to you (and/or cost to the other party)

- Giving the impression that every concession you make is a major concession: of great importance and cost (in order to earn greater reciprocal concessions from the other party)

- Making as few concessions as possible, in order to avoid creating an impression of weakness (or of excessive strength, raising the suspicion that the offer on the table is already biased in your favour)

- Getting the other party to make minor concessions in the early stages, in order to establish a pattern that can be applied to more important issues later.

Chapter summary

- The main alternative to negotiation is competitive bidding. Dobler and Burt analyse situations in which competitive bidding is and is not appropriate.

- Gavin Kennedy's MIL acronym is a useful basis for setting negotiation objectives: objectives we Must achieve, objectives we Intend to achieve, and objectives we would Like to achieve.

- A buyer's preparation for a negotiation will include research into the proposed supplier. This may be formalised in a checklist such as that in Figure 1.1.

- Various commentators have attempted to analyse the negotiation process as a series of stages. The analysis of Leonard Greenhalgh has been influential: preparation; relationship building; information gathering; information using; bidding; closing the deal; implementing.

- Once negotiation is underway, it is again possible to distinguish phases in the process: testing the ground; moving; reaching agreement.

- Listening is as important as talking. Steele and Beasor identify characteristics of effective listeners.

- Ideally, we aim to 'move' the supplier without granting concessions. If concessions are essential, we must always give as little as possible and obtain as much as possible in return.

- Often it is possible to trade concessions in relation to one variable in return for concessions relating to another variable.

- Kennedy lists a number of pressure ploys that sellers may use to close the deal: the quivering quill, the now or never tactic, the take it or leave it tactic, and split the difference.

- Once agreement is reached, it is important to summarise it in writing before exiting the meeting. As soon as possible, a formal written agreement should be prepared.

- There are two basic orientations to negotiation: distributive negotiating (zero-sum or win-lose) and integrative negotiating (win-win or added-value). Distributive approaches are appropriate in transactional and adversarial negotiations, while the integrative approach is used to develop long-term collaborative and mutually-beneficial relationships with supply chain partners and employees.

- Concessions may be used in different ways, according to whether the negotiation is distributive/transactional or integrative in approach.

Self-test questions

Numbers in brackets refer to the paragraphs where you can check your answers..

1   List Dobler and Burt's criteria for the use of competitive bidding. (Table 1.1)

2   What alternatives are there to the use of competitive bidding and negotiation? (1.5)

3   Explain what is meant by MIL objectives. (1.13, 1.14)

4   List as many questions as you can that should be asked about the potential supplier as part of the buyer's preparation. (Figure 1.1)

5   What is meant by BATNA? (1.21)

6   What are the four phases of negotiation identified by Kennedy, and the seven phases identified by Greenhalgh? (2.3, 2.4)

7   Why may it confer an advantage if a buyer volunteers to be the person recording the points discussed? (2.12)

8   What types of questioning were identified by Steele and Beasor? (3.3)

9   What three methods do Steele and Beasor identify for achieving unilateral movement by the supplier? (3.10)

10   Explain the 'quivering quill' ploy and the 'split the difference' ploy. (4.2, 4.6)

11   Distinguish between tactics adopted in a distributive approach and in an integrative approach. (5.2, 5.5)

12   What are the requirements for 'principled negotiation'? (5.9)

CHAPTER 2

Understanding the Supplier

Learning objectives and indicative content

1.2   Identify and evaluate information required to understand the supplier organisation:

- Supplier information (supply, demand, timings, costings, budgets, readiness, capacity, account management structure)
- Competitor information, for example supplier competitors
- Oligopoly/monopoly/duopoly

1.3   Analyse market information.

- SWOT

Chapter headings

1   Obtaining information about a supplier

2   Supplier SWOT analysis

3   Information about competitor suppliers

4   Market analysis

5   Market structure

Introduction

In the previous chapter we took a brief overview of the negotiation process, concentrating on the actual negotiation meeting. We noted the importance of advance preparation before entering the meeting. In this chapter and those that follow we look in more detail at the kind of preparation that should be undertaken. In this chapter our focus is on general information about potential suppliers and the supply market.

1   Obtaining information about a supplier

A note on terminology

1.1   For many authors, there is no distinction between the terms 'vendor' and 'supplier'. The latter term seems to be preferred, but the former appears to be used on occasion for no other reason than artistic variation.

1.2   However, a minority of authors do observe a distinction which seems useful, namely using 'supplier' to mean an **existing** supplier and 'vendor' to mean a **potential** supplier. Since this section relates primarily to existing suppliers, the term 'supplier' in the section heading is justified.

Why do we need information?

1.3   Our interest in information about suppliers arises because we need to know as much about them as possible in order to negotiate effectively with them.

1.4   Our aim as a buyer is to ensure that the potential supplier can perform the contract to the required standard. This means that the process of assessment is another element of quality assurance, which has been the theme of this chapter. It will be particularly relevant in cases where no third-party validation of vendor quality – such as ISO 9000 accreditation – is available.

1.5   This is a bewilderingly complex subject, and the most difficult task is to place some kind of practical limit on the number and variety of factors that could form part of the assessment process. Reference to standard purchasing textbooks produces many different lists of the relevant factors, some of which are quoted in Table 2.1.

Table 2.1 *Factors involved in vendor assessment*

Purchasing and Supply Chain Management by Lysons and Farrington	*Purchasing Principles and Management,* by Baily, Farmer, Jessop and Jones	*Purchasing and Supply Management,* by Dobler and Burt
Personal attitudes	Task variables, such as quality, service and price	Results of preliminary survey
Adequacy and care of production equipment	Financial stability	Financial stability
Means of controlling quality	Good management	Good management
Housekeeping	Results of site visits	Results of site visits
Competence of technical staff	Ability to support electronic data interchange	Quality of service
Competence of management	Just in time capabilities	Just in time capabilities

1.6   In this section we will adopt the following framework for discussion.

- Assessing financial stability
- Planning and conducting site visits
- Assessing task variables: quality, service, price, extent of automation, and just in time capabilities

Assessing financial stability

1.7 Potential benefits of this procedure include the following.

- Financial information, at least for UK companies, is easy to come by. It is a simple matter to access published accounts by visiting the Companies House website. Similarly, credit information can be accessed (for a charge) via agencies such as Dun & Bradstreet. (Although such information is even more important in relation to credit customers, its importance should not be overlooked even in the case of suppliers.)

- Published accounts provide useful information about the supplier, particularly if ratio analysis is used. By examining the accounts carefully, the buyer can obtain an insight into the company's liquidity, gearing (and hence financial risk), profitability, financial stability, asset backing, sources of funding, etc. The fact that comparative figures are also published (ie figures relating to the previous year as well as the current year) enables the buyer to spot trends over time.

1.8 However, financial information is not the be all and end all.

- The published accounts display the level of detail required by the Companies Acts and accounting standards. This may be far less than the buyer needs. For example, published accounts will rarely, if ever, give the buyer sufficient information about the supplier's cost structure. The buyer will undoubtedly want to supplement his enquiries by further questioning of the supplier.

- The published accounts display historical information, which may be out of date even when published, and in any event may not be a reliable indicator of future financial strength.

- By definition, the financial information is restricted in its scope. It says nothing about other points of vital importance to buyers: quality procedures, delivery times, reliability, etc.

1.9 The assessment of a supplier's financial position is often a very straightforward exercise, and should therefore be undertaken at an early stage. If there are doubts about financial stability, the vendor can then be eliminated from consideration without the need for more elaborate appraisal.

1.10 The importance of financial stability should be fairly clear. Dobler and Burt cite three typical nightmare scenarios that can arise if dealing with a financially weak supplier.

- You need to insist on maintaining quality, but the supplier is forced to cut costs.

- You have a financial claim against the supplier, but he does not have sufficient working capital to meet it.

- You need to insist on speedy delivery to meet a promised delivery date, but the supplier cannot afford to pay overtime.

1.11 The most accessible source of information on a vendor is their published financial accounts. This is not a textbook on financial accounting, but you should know enough to realise the importance of factors such as financial gearing (ie the extent to which the vendor relies on loan capital), working capital levels (ie the extent to which the vendor has assets in the form of cash and debtor balances, rather than tied up in long-term and inaccessible assets), and of course profitability.

1.12   Buyers should not resent a high level of profitability in their suppliers ('Your prices must be too high...'). On the contrary, unless there is evidence of definite exploitation of buyers, this should be regarded as an encouraging sign of reliable quality and sound management.

1.13   Of course, the vendor's financial accounts present only **historical** data, but supplemented by financial forecasting techniques (where appropriate) and comparison with the accounts of similar companies they are a most useful source of information to the buyer.

1.14   One other source of financial information is worth mentioning. In appropriate cases it will make sense to request information from credit agencies to enhance your knowledge of a vendor's financial standing.

Planning and conducting site visits

1.15   This is an important stage in the evaluation process (sometimes referred to as a **vendor audit** or **capability survey**), but it is important not to underestimate the amount of resources that it consumes. It will not be necessary in cases of small purchases where recurring business is not expected. And even in the case of potentially large contracts, it should be left until a late stage in order to eliminate as many vendors as possible by less laborious means.

1.16   Despite this note of warning, it remains true that in appropriate cases site visits are a most important source of information on such matters as:

- production equipment and operations
- operation of key materials management activities
- existence of adequate production capacity
- expertise and motivation of personnel
- technological know-how of supervisory personnel
- management capabilities.

1.17   To get the best from the site visit, advance planning is vital. In many cases, the exercise is based on completion of a comprehensive questionnaire, part of which relates to advance planning while the remainder is completed during or after the visit. Usually, the vendor will be asked for information on the organisation's history and current standing, its key management personnel, its products and markets, its attitude to quality issues etc.

1.18   During the visit it is important to speak to appropriate personnel, at the buyer's discretion, while the plant tour is in progress. Their contribution can often throw valuable additional light on statements made by management. In particular, it is worth bearing in mind that procedures managers genuinely believe to be in force are not always performed as they should be, or even performed at all. In addition, the general level of skill, knowledge and enthusiasm of operating personnel can be an important indicator for the buyer.

Assessing task variables

1.19 An important differential between one supplier and another is the quality of management. This is particularly true when the proposed purchase is of a custom-made, large-value item. In these cases the buyer needs reassurance that the managerial resource is adapted to cope with planning, problem-solving and implementation. This goes much further than an assessment of production capability, though of course that too is an essential ingredient.

1.20 Allied to this is the quality of service that the buyer can expect. Service is a broad term, and encompasses such variables as on-time delivery, prompt response to queries or problems, prompt communication, suitable credit facilities and after-sales service.

1.21 Buyers will also be interested in the extent to which a vendor adopts the best modern practices. Are they able to cope with electronic data interchange? Do they have adequate just in time capability? Do they adopt a total quality management approach? Do they use statistical process control?

Carter's 7Cs for supplier selection

1.22 The traditional 'five rights' of purchasing (right price, right quality, right quantity, right place, right time) may not provide a sufficiently broad framework for assessing suppliers. It is not that these have been superseded. Rather, buyers should adopt wider-ranging criteria in the selection of suppliers.

1.23 Ray Carter provided one possible list of such criteria (Carter's 7Cs). Subsequently, other authorities have added to this. The list below contains 10Cs.

- Competency of all staff all of the time
- Capacity of supplier (must have sufficient, flexible capacity)
- Commitment to quality, evidenced by quality systems
- Control of processes
- Cash (must be financially sound)
- Cost
- Consistency of output
- Culture (must be compatible with buyer organisation)
- Clean (ie environmentally sound)
- Compliance (ie sound policy on corporate social responsibility)

1.24 These criteria are particularly relevant in an age of 'mass customisation'. This refers to an environment where organisations seek fast, efficient, low-cost production of products tailored to the needs of individual customers. Such an ideal will hardly be attainable without the closest relationships between the organisation on one hand and highly flexible suppliers on the other.

Information needs at different stages of negotiation

1.25 It is possible to distinguish between different types of information required by the buyer at different stages in the negotiation process.

1.26 In the pre-contract stage, the emphasis is on obtaining knowledge of the market and the potential suppliers. Much of the discussion above has focused on potential suppliers and this will be developed in the next section of the chapter. Market knowledge is the subject of Section 3 in this chapter. The information we seek is concerned with the supplier's capabilities, management resources, financial stability etc, and with supply and demand factors in the market generally.

1.27 During the main negotiation the focus switches to the detail of the proposed contract. We will need to pin down exactly what is offered in terms of price, volumes, quality, delivery lead times etc.

1.28 Once the contract has been awarded, our information needs are centred on performance measurement. We need to evaluate the supplier's performance in the light of agreed service levels and key performance indicators (KPIs). We also need to evaluate the relationship between our two organisations: this is a topic covered in another Level 4 module, Managing Purchasing and Supply Relationships.

2 *Supplier SWOT analysis*

The nature of a SWOT analysis

2.1 A SWOT analysis (Strengths, Weaknesses, Opportunities and Threats) is a strategic tool designed to appraise the overall state of an organisation and indicate areas for concern and areas for improvement. In the normal situation we are looking at our own organisation to identify our own strengths etc. In the present context we are using the tool as a method of assessing our suppliers.

2.2 It is normal to distinguish between the **internal characteristics** of the organisation (its strengths and weaknesses) and the characteristics of the **external environment** (the opportunities and threats facing the organisation).

2.3 The factors involved in a SWOT analysis are wide ranging and include decision variables which strengthen or constrain the operational powers of the company, such as the size of its markets, the competitive forces in the markets, opportunities for new products, availability of skilled labour, control of vital raw materials and access to additional capital.

2.4 Although many elaborate techniques are used in the SWOT process in practice, these are never feasible within the limited data provided in an exam question. If a question asks you to perform a SWOT analysis you should simply work through the data provided, picking out factors that are obviously strengths, weaknesses, opportunities or threats, and present your conclusions in a tidy format.

2.5 A particular format for a SWOT analysis has been recommended by various CIPS examiners: see the two-by-two grid in Figure 2.1.

Figure 2.1 *A SWOT matrix*

The environment

The organisation's capabilities	O	T
W	Opportunities that may be exploited by our rivals	Need to do something about these
S	Opportunities that can be exploited by our firm	May give our firm an advantage over our rivals

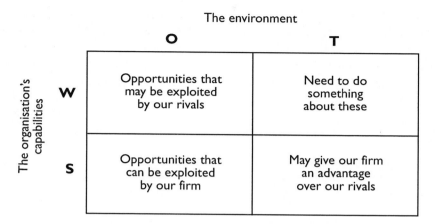

2.6 A similar grid is provided by the excellent MindTools website (visit www.mindtools.com). This is reproduced (with kind permission of the copyright holder) in Figure 2.2 The point of presenting the analysis in the form of a grid, rather than just four separate lists, is so that we can cross-reference strengths and weaknesses with opportunities and threats.

Figure 2.2 *SWOT analysis worksheet*

Strengths: What do you do well? What unique resources can you draw on? What do others see as your strengths?	**Weaknesses:** What could you improve? Where do you have fewer resources than others? What are others likely to see as weaknesses?
Opportunities: What good opportunities are open to you? What trends could you take advantage of? Looking at your strengths, how can you turn these into opportunities?	**Threats:** What trends could harm you? What is your competition doing? Looking at your weaknesses, what threats do these expose you to?

Obtaining the data

2.7   Of course, performing a SWOT analysis for a supplier is less straightforward than for our own organisation. In particular, we have less information available to work with. Even so, by asking the right kind of questions we may be able to steer ourselves towards useful insights. In the last resort, if we cannot answer important strategic questions about the supplier because of information shortage, we can at least pose the question directly to the supplier.

2.8   Here are some of the questions to which we might seek answers.

Figure 2.3 *SWOT analysis worksheet*

Strengths: What advantages does the supplier have as compared with their competitors? What unique resources does the supplier have access to? What resources are available to the supplier at lower cost than to other suppliers? What are the strengths of the supplier as perceived by others in the market (including the supplier's existing customers)?	**Weaknesses:** What aspects of the supplier's performance could be improved? What managerial, operational, technological or financial limitations constrain the activities of the supplier? What are the weaknesses of the supplier as perceived by others in the market (including the supplier's existing customers)?
Opportunities: Is the potential for doing business with our organisation a significant opportunity for this supplier? What changes in technology is the supplier exploiting, or could the supplier exploit, in order to improve performance? What favourable trends are visible in the supply market from which the supplier could benefit?	**Threats:** How well placed is the supplier to respond to competitive pressures from other suppliers? How well placed is the supplier to cope with technological advances? Can the supplier cope with increases in the level of environmental regulation? Does the supplier have any significant problems with cashflow (including likely bad debts)?

3 Information about competitor suppliers

Identifying alternative suppliers

3.1 Obtaining information about a supplier is clearly easier if we have dealt with the supplier before. We will have acquired much useful data in the course of our dealings, especially if the relationship has been a close one. In some cases we may even have dealt on an open book basis, exchanging detailed information that would not be publicly available.

3.2 Things are more complicated if we are thinking of dealing with a new supplier. The first problem is to identify suitable candidates.

3.3 A wide variety of information sources is available to assist the buyer in identifying potential suppliers. In fact, the main danger is of spending too much time researching the sources on occasions when it is not appropriate. In particular, the extent of research obviously depends at least partly on the monetary value of the business likely to be done.

3.4 **Past experience** is a good starting point. Most of the tasks in a purchasing department are to a greater or lesser extent repetitive. A well organised purchasing function will ensure that a good supplier database is maintained, usually nowadays on computer. This will enable buyers to locate suitable suppliers quickly from those known to the organisation.

3.5 **Salesmen from suppliers** are another common source of information. Many buying organisations tap this source systematically by displaying both their finished products and major components in public, in effect inviting visiting salesmen to deploy their knowledge to the advantage of both organisations.

3.6 **Contacts with other buyers**, both inside and outside the organisation, can help in keeping up to date with new developments.

3.7 **Published catalogues** are received by all purchasing departments as part of vendors' marketing efforts. They contain a mass of information, particularly for standard production parts, but this may be difficult to access unless there is a comprehensive system of indexing and filing. Some large purchasing functions employ staff just for this task of 'librarianship'.

3.8 **Trade directories** are also stocked by most purchasing departments, and contain lists of vendors organised in terms of the products they supply. In some cases such directories are available in electronic form which simplifies access to the information and enables more frequent updating by the publishers.

3.9 **Trade journals** provide information in the form of editorial, news items and advertising.

3.10 **Trade shows and exhibitions** enable vendors to display their wares and distribute product information and news of developments.

3.11 **Direct mail** from vendors is an increasingly important source of information, but again is likely to lose most of its value unless it is carefully indexed and filed.

3.12 **Formal requests for information**, often through the medium of questionnaires, can be used to elicit information from vendors who might be of interest to the buying organisation.

Other sources of information

3.13 Once potential suppliers have been identified the usual sources of information should be investigated. We have already mentioned many of these earlier in the chapter: the supplier's published financial accounts, credit agencies etc.

3.14 Another possible source of information is the existing customers of the potential supplier. Clearly we can approach these customers for information only if we have the prior permission of the supplier, but it is in the interests of the supplier to allow this. Even without a formal approach to the supplier's customers we may well have informal contacts to exploit.

3.15 We should be looking for evidence of financial stability, quality management systems, and reliability in delivery. If we find that existing customers are satisfied with the supplier's performance in these areas it provides us with substantial encouragement in our assessment of the supplier.

Evaluating suppliers and potential suppliers

3.16 Buyers must carefully evaluate potential suppliers before entering into business relationships with them. Even when suppliers are on stream, buyers should continually monitor their performance.

3.17 Dawn Carter has identified eight main areas of evaluation (gathered together under the mnemonic FACE 2 FACE, indicating that there are two factors corresponding to each of the letters F, A, C, E).

- **F** relates to Fixed assets (or physical resources) and Financial stability.
- **A** relates to Ability to deliver the goods or service required and Ability to work productively with the buyer.
- **C** relates to Cost and Commitment to quality.
- **E** relates to Efficiency and Environmental considerations.

3.18 The importance of adequate **fixed assets** (physical resources) is that without these the supplier will be unable to meet the buyer's requirements. The buyer can find information on this topic in the supplier's balance sheet. A point to look out for is the age of the supplier's main fixed assets: are they due for replacement soon, and if so is there finance available to replace them?

3.19 **Financial stability** is also important, and again the accounts of the supplier are an obvious source of information. Apart from the profit and loss account and balance sheet, the accounts will also include a cashflow statement, which contains important information on how successful the supplier is at generating funds from operations. Another useful source of information on financial stability is a report from a credit reference agency such as Dun & Bradstreet.

3.20 **Ability to deliver** can be tested by seeking references from existing customers of the supplier. The buyer will also want to look at some of the output produced by the supplier to ensure that it meets quality standards.

3.21 **Ability to work with the buyer** will depend partly on compatible cultures in the buying and supplying organisations. The buyer will form an impression on this point during negotiations and on site visits.

3.22 **Cost** is obviously vital. The supplier's prices must be competitive, but this should be seen in the modern perspective of total acquisition cost, not just basic purchase price.

3.23 The supplier's **commitment to quality** will partly be evident from the control systems they have in place (eg statistical process control, total quality management systems). Do they have ISO 9000 certification?

3.24 The buyer will also be concerned about the supplier's **efficiency**. The supplier's published accounts will contain information permitting calculation of efficiency ratios, eg speed of stock turnover, speed of collecting debtor balances etc.

3.25 Finally, buyers will want to examine the supplier's **environmental policies**. Modern thinking emphasises the importance of environmentally friendly production processes, and to some extent this is embodied in legal requirements.

4 Market analysis

The need for planning

4.1 It is possible to see the purchasing function in a very simple light: purchasing staff are there to react when a stimulus is received from production. When production staff realise they have a need for materials from outside, they raise a purchase requisition. From that point, the role of the purchasing professional begins. His job is to process the requisition to the point where the materials are made available to production. He then sits back and waits for another requisition.

4.2 This is a gross distortion of the role actually performed by modern purchasing functions. The main point is that the description omits any reference to the planning role of purchasing staff. In practice, purchasing liaises closely with production and other functions (such as marketing) to anticipate requirements. Merely waiting until the demand is urgent is a recipe for disaster.

4.3 The general change described here is from a view of purchasing as a mainly clerical and administrative function to a view in which it has an important strategic contribution to make to overall organisational objectives. A number of trends have contributed to this.

4.4 In developed economies there has been an explosive development in service industries; in many cases services outrank manufacturing in their contribution to gross domestic product. This has led to a greater appreciation of service functions **within** organisations, and a greater readiness to see manufacturing as just one element in a wider perspective.

4.5   This has been reinforced by a mode of thinking that underlies the now universal **marketing orientation**: to satisfy customers, all functions within an organisation have an important contribution to make, and none can be treated as somehow less important than others to the overall 'offering' that an organisation makes to customers. Of course, there have always been organisations that have recognised a strategic role for the purchasing and supply function; what has changed is that such organisations are no longer just a tiny minority.

4.6   Indeed, the point about marketing orientation can be developed further. Once it was recognised that **organisational** performance and effectiveness could be improved by placing the needs of customers first, it was a small step to realising that each **internal function** (such as purchasing) had its own 'customers'. Effectiveness of internal functions could be improved by exactly the same philosophies as had worked for the organisation as a whole. From this developed the notion that purchasing had a key role to play in satisfying its 'customers' (for example, production departments), and any question of a hierarchy of functions became meaningless.

4.7   At the same time as these changes in management thinking were taking place, a dramatic success story was unfolding in Japan. Western companies, threatened by the most serious competition they had ever faced, responded by trying to learn lessons from Japanese industry. Many of those lessons – just in time purchasing and production, zero defects etc – had a very important impact on purchasing functions. It was recognised that purchasing had a vital part to play in what has now become known as world class manufacturing.

4.8   A more recent development in world class thinking is the idea that quality cannot be achieved by an organisation in isolation. The concept of a 'supply chain' means that suppliers are regarded as an important contributor to quality. To get the most from suppliers involves a shift from traditional approaches to supplier management; the emphasis now is on partnership rather than adversarial relations. The impact for purchasing staff is that much more time must be spent on strategic aspects of supplier development, which means in turn that less time is available for clerical and administrative work.

4.9   This consideration leads on to another relevant trend. New strategic approaches leave less time for clerical work, but this luxury would hardly be affordable if old-style administrative procedures still had to be completed. It is developments in technology that have made the new emphasis possible.

4.10   A further group of recent trends relate to the transformation of the manufacturing cost base in recent decades.

4.11   In years gone by, the largest expense borne by a typical manufacturer, by far, was the cost of wages. Most manufacturing industry was heavily labour intensive; most manufacturing processes were carried out manually by skilled and unskilled workers. The result was a large workforce and a large wages bill. In this area of expenditure of course purchasing staff had little or no role to play.

4.12 Today the situation is very different. Many industries have seen a huge investment in automated production processes. In many cases this has been accompanied by painful cuts in manufacturing personnel. From being labour intensive, such industries have become capital intensive. The sums invested in plant and equipment, often computer controlled, are high in relation to the sums paid out to employees.

4.13 A related trend is a new focus on core activities – what Peters and Waterman in their management classic *In Search of Excellence* call a 'stick to the knitting' approach. Many businesses now see their strategic direction as being a concentration on certain core activities where they believe they hold competitive advantage. Many support activities, which previously would have been provided by in-house departments, are now outsourced – handed over to specialist external suppliers who provide the required service in exchange for a fee. In some cases this trend has been accentuated by regulatory pressures; for example, in many public sector concerns a regime of market testing and compulsory competitive tendering has been imposed.

4.14 This trend applies not just to the provision of services; manufacturing businesses have been increasingly ready to focus on just one part of the manufacturing process. Where previously they might have made Product X entirely from scratch, nowadays they buy the parts for Product X externally and confine themselves to the assembly process. Another organisation in the supply chain specialises in manufacturing the parts required for Product X.

4.15 Both of these trends point to the same outcome: organisations spend a much greater proportion of their income on buying in goods and services than they used to do. The impact for purchasing departments is obvious. Where previously the purchasing responsibility extended only to a small proportion of the organisation's total income, the proportion has now increased dramatically.

4.16 The increasing strategic role of purchasing brings pressure for buyers to **add value** in their negotiations with suppliers. According to Lewicki, the key to adding value (in the supply context) is to exploit the differences between the negotiating parties. Such differences are said to arise from four main sources: see Table 2.2.

Table 2.2 *Differences between negotiating parties*

Area of difference	Explanation and examples
Interests of the parties	Negotiators may value different items in different ways. Lewicki gives the example of a company negotiating with a potential employee on a remuneration package: the company may be willing to yield ground on a one-off joining bonus, but less willing to increase their offer in relation to the ongoing salary.
Judgements about the future	For example, the buyer may see no likelihood of a close strategic relationship in the future, whereas the supplier may be hopeful of achieving such a relationship.
Tolerance of risk	A buyer may be very concerned about supply risk, which may deter him from entering into a single sourcing relationship. The supplier, by contrast, may very well want all of the buyer's business, even if he becomes over-dependent on that particular customer.
Time preferences	A supplier may be anxious to conclude a sale quickly, whereas the buyer may have no immediate need to deal: he may be thinking of requirements that will arise in the future.

4.17 The pressures described above – leading to an increased strategic role for purchasing – suggest an increased need for forward planning.

4.18 The process by which such planning is formulated is well documented in both the purchasing literature and in texts on accounting and financial management. This is not surprising, given the crucial effects on cashflows that are involved. The usual model is of a hierarchical sequence of budgets, beginning with the sales budget and converting that first into a production budget and then into a materials budget.

4.19 Working with sensible estimates of materials requirements, purchasing staff can remove much of the uncertainty and risk from sourcing by advance planning. Although there will always be a need for purchases not contemplated in the annual plan, most materials requirements can be forecast. Purchasing can then choose suitable suppliers to meet the demand and put sourcing plans into effect well in advance.

Purchasing research

4.20 To achieve planning objectives, it is essential for purchasing to appraise the supply markets. This is a form of purchasing research, which can be undertaken by specialist staff trained to investigate such matters. This is the usual organisational procedure in large purchasing departments. In smaller departments there may be no dedicated purchasing research staff, and instead individual buyers may be expected to conduct their own research.

4.21 The research should cover the following major areas in respect of each material or class of materials.

- **Demand analysis**. Procedures should be operated to ensure that particular attention is paid to high-value materials. The objective is to estimate likely usage in the period ahead.
- **Vendor analysis**. Buyers must evaluate the performance of current suppliers, as well as giving consideration to potential suppliers not currently being used. Once the decision on suppliers has been taken, attention will shift to the type of buying agreement to be implemented.
- **Market analysis**. Buyers must appraise general supply conditions in the market. What is the likely availability of each material, and are any shortages possible or probable? What is the prevailing price of each material, and what fluctuations (if any) are likely?

4.22 The research into supply markets conducted by purchasing departments is of an ongoing nature (though there is sometimes cause for a defined project of research to supplement this). Its objectives are:

- to provide information on which the organisation can plan to adapt to changes in the supply environment, whether to take advantage of new opportunities or to take defensive action in the light of perceived threats
- to secure competitive advantage by means of early information on innovations in supply markets.

4.23 To begin with, purchasing staff must define the scope of the research work. If they identify trends with a potential to impact on the organisation a sensible next step might be to conduct a limited research project, perhaps by means of consultations with suppliers. The aim of course is to obtain early warning of anything that could have a serious impact, for good or bad, on the organisation's supply chain activities.

4.24 Actual consultations with suppliers are not the only sources of information. For example, a buyer interested in the possibility of price changes in a certain material may be guided by any or all of the following.

- Historical trends
- Published price indices for particular industries
- Economic models
- Information from specialist forecasting agencies

The structure of supply markets

4.25 A useful starting point in the analysis of supply markets is to examine the main structural features that can be discerned. These are features that a buyer is unable to influence – the market just happens to be that way – but which may be an important influence on the buyer. Examples of these include the following.

- The number of buyers in the market
- The number of suppliers in the market
- Methods of pricing in the market
- The degree of product differentiation in the market (are there many closely similar products or just a single product on which all buyers are dependent?)
- Technological developments in the market

4.26 In terms of demand, a market may range from a state of pure competition (where many buyers are active, and no one buyer is big enough to influence the price by his actions) to a state of **monopsony**. Strictly this would mean only a single buyer in the market, who would of course wield enormous influence over suppliers. In practice, the strict form of monopsony is rarely (perhaps never) seen, but close approximations exist. An example might be the railway industry in the UK: the number of buyers of rolling stock is very limited.

4.27 In terms of supply, a similar range of possibilities exists. At one extreme there is perfect competition: many suppliers exist, and no one supplier is big enough to dictate prices. The other extreme is monopoly. Public utilities such as the privatised water companies in the UK enjoy a position of virtual monopoly, though this is being challenged (eg by the introduction of competition in the gas supply industry).

4.28 The buyer must be aware of these characteristics in the supply markets, because they influence the strength of his negotiating position. For example, a buyer facing a monopoly supplier, in a market with little product differentiation and few substitute products, is in a weak negotiating position. If there are many suppliers, and many products of comparable quality, the situation is very different: the buyer's position is strong. In the next section of this chapter we discuss market structure in more detail.

Kraljic's grid

4.29   One way of analysing the supply markets and the organisation's position in relation to them is to use a version of Kraljic's grid. This is a tool of analysis that seeks to map the importance to the organisation of the item being purchased against the complexity of the market that supplies it. The approach that the organisation should take to sourcing the item is determined by the intersection of these variables. We discuss Kraljic's ideas in more detail in Chapter 3.

Figure 2.4 *Kraljic's grid*

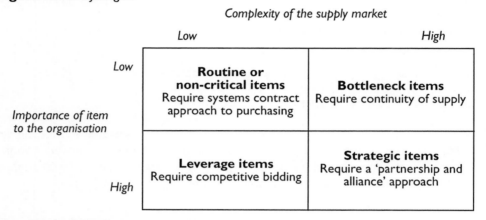

Stable and unstable supply markets

4.30   Market analysis is particularly important if supplies are of a type that is subject to instability. For example, purchasers of commodities such as metals or basic foodstuffs (wheat, vegetable oils etc) have to contend with severe fluctuations in both prices and availability. By contrast, purchasers of standard industrial supplies (valves, motors, nuts and bolts etc) have an easier time in this respect.

4.31   The analysis of a particular supply market as stable or unstable has an impact on the way in which a buyer will structure his buying plan, and in particular on the timing of his purchases. In stable markets, timing of purchases is usually not a critical matter. In unstable markets the situation is very different. If prices are fluctuating rapidly, the timing of purchases can have a dramatic effect on the total price paid.

4.32   If the supply market for a particular material is analysed as stable, a buyer may well decide, in effect, to ignore market conditions in timing his purchases. This reflects the idea that such conditions are unchanging and can therefore have no effect on the decision. Timing of purchases in this case is based entirely on current requirements.

4.33   On the other hand, if the supply market is unstable it is not usually safe to ignore market conditions. In this case, timing of purchases must be based on both current requirements and estimates of likely availability and price.

4.34   In some industries these considerations have given a new focus to traditional planning approaches. The conventional model of strategic planning (as mentioned briefly above) takes the sales budget as its starting point and then produces the operating budgets that must be achieved in order to meet the predetermined sales target. This is not quite sufficient in industries where supply markets are unstable or difficult to predict.

4.35 The point is that in such cases a sales budget may be quite meaningless if it is not supported by detailed analysis of materials availability. Setting a sales target of one million units of Product X, and building up an elaborate sequence of operating budgets to achieve that target, is a wasted exercise if materials likely to be available at reasonable price are sufficient only for 500,000 units.

4.36 The outcome is that, in industries dependent on unstable supply markets, the strategic planning process now involves an input from purchasing specialists much earlier than it would have done under the traditional model. This is in line with a more general increase in the strategic responsibilities of purchasing. Often the analysis results in decisions to secure supplies either by means of strategic long-term partnerships with selected suppliers, or by means of in-house production as an alternative to external purchasing.

5   *Market structure*

The spectrum of competition

5.1 The term market structure refers to the number of organisations competing in the market. The spectrum of competition is illustrated in Figure 2.5.

Figure 2.5 *Main forms of market structure*

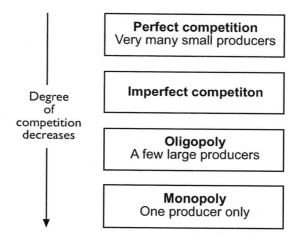

5.2 A perfectly competitive market is a theoretical device used to aid analysis. It exists when the following conditions apply.

- The market consists of many 'small' buyers and sellers. Each individual buyer or seller is so small relative to the market, that his actions cannot affect the market.

- In a perfectly competitive market, all individual consumers and producers are 'price takers' – they pay or receive the price set by the market. There is one market price.

- The goods being marketed are **homogeneous** (ie identical).

- Perfect information exists. The information is complete, so any relevant fact is known by everyone.

- There are no barriers preventing firms from entering or leaving the market in the long run.

- Consumers are utility-maximisers and firms are profit-maximisers.

- The effect of these assumptions is that the market consists of a large number of identical consumers, buying an identical good from a large number of identical suppliers. All consumers and suppliers know all relevant facts about the market and they all have freedom of choice, in the long run at least.

5.3   There are some markets which come close to being perfectly competitive. The stock markets and foreign exchange markets are examples. There are many operators in the market although some, such as the pension funds or insurance companies, do have a degree of market power; each company's shares and each country's currency are identical; information is very quickly disseminated to all market participants; transaction costs are similar for all operators; and it is safe to assume that everyone is trying to maximise profits or utility.

Implications of perfect competition for buyers

5.4   The theoretical model of perfect competition means that there is literally nothing to choose between one supplier and another. Buyers are perfectly able to desert a supplier whose costs are above the norm, and such suppliers will quickly have to come into line. Price is the only weapon with which suppliers can compete, and successful suppliers will be those who minimise their costs so as to make acceptable profit margins within the market price.

5.5   Even where a market is slightly less than perfect, there will be the same incentive for suppliers to compete on price, to the buyer's advantage. This is especially so if the market is contestable, by which is meant that new suppliers can enter the market easily. These new suppliers will push the market even closer to the state of perfect competition.

5.6   From a buyer's point of view, the downside of perfect competition is that there are many buyers as well as many sellers. Any individual buyer cannot dominate his suppliers: if they don't like his terms of business, they will sell their goods to other buyers instead.

Monopoly/duopoly

5.7   A perfectly competitive market is one of the basic theoretical devices of microeconomics, but, as we have seen, is rather unrealistic.

5.8   There are many possible imperfections, where the conditions of perfect competition are not met. For example, the number of suppliers could be small enough to allow them some market power; goods may not be homogeneous, so that suppliers again have market power, arising from customer loyalty; information could be imperfect, allowing suppliers to charge customers different prices for the same product.

5.9   In this section we look at one form of imperfect competition; namely **monopoly**. This lies at the opposite extreme of perfect competition and is also unlikely to exist in its pure form in the real world. Other forms of imperfect competition, examined later, represent stages in between the two extremes. They exhibit some degree of competition, but not to the extent to which it is found in a perfectly competitive market.

5.10 A monopoly exists when one producer supplies the entire market. (A duopoly is very similar – there are just two producers.) As with perfect competition, there are certain conditions which must be met for a monopoly to occur. These are:

- only one supplier of the good exists, and
- there are barriers preventing other firms from entering the industry.

5.11 Unlike in perfect competition, where every supplier is a price taker, a monopolist has power to set his prices at will: he is a **price maker**. It is this feature of monopoly in particular which can lead to consumers being over charged, and this is why monopolistic markets are usually regulated by government.

5.12 A monopolist may be able to operate **price discrimination**. Price discrimination occurs when a product is sold at different prices in different markets.

5.13 Price discrimination could not occur in a perfectly competitive market. There is perfect information, so those consumers who were charged the higher price would know that the good could be bought more cheaply elsewhere. With a monopoly, however, this does not apply, so price discrimination can be used to increase profits.

5.14 Imagine a supplier of jam who has two markets. One consists of corner grocery shops, (market 1) while the other consists of the food departments of the high-profile London department stores, such as Harrods and Fortnum and Mason's (market 2). Customers in market 2 are, on the whole, prepared to pay more for their jam than customers in market 1, despite the fact that the jam is identical in each market. They perceive the jam in market 2 to be of a higher quality.

Implications of monopoly for buyers

5.15 Monopolists enjoy **economies of scale** because of their size. Because of this, their costs may be lower than a firm in perfect competition and this may benefit buyers. This of course assumes that the monopolist passes on part or all of the benefits of lower costs by not charging excessive prices. This may be achieved by means of government regulations which dictate to some extent what prices the monopolist is allowed to charge.

5.16 Despite this possible advantage, there are of course obvious disadvantages in only being able to deal with a single supplier. Above all, most buyers will have little say in specifying exactly what they want from a monopolist supplier: the supplier has little incentive to tailor his product offering so as to suit a large number of potential buyers.

Imperfect competition

5.17 In Figure 2.5 we saw a spectrum of competition, from perfect competition at the top to pure monopoly at the bottom. Strictly speaking, anything other than perfect competition is imperfect competition, so this term strictly includes oligopoly and monopoly. However, in this section we are restricting the term imperfect competition to refer to the situation – very common in practice – where perfect competition does not exist, but where there are too many firms in the market to justify talking about an oligopoly or a monopoly.

5.18 The kind of market we are describing has fewer suppliers than a perfectly competitive market, but nevertheless exhibits some competitive characteristics. It is important to distinguish between the short run and the long run in the case of imperfect competition. Barriers to entry ensure that in the short run firms can operate in the same way as a monopoly; they can earn superprofits. But in the long run other firms can enter the market or develop substitute products and these super-profits can be competed away.

5.19 An imperfectly competitive market has the following features.

- It contains many suppliers, though not as many as in perfect competition.

- Goods are not homogeneous. Each supplier supplies a good which is slightly different from that produced by his competitors.

- Although there are barriers to entry, such as brand names and customer loyalty, these are insufficient to prevent other firms from entering the industry in the long run.

- Firms in the market have a degree of market power, as a result of the lack of homogeneity of output.

5.20 In fact, it may be possible in some circumstances to **increase** demand for one's product by increasing the price and mounting an advertising campaign to affect people's perception of the product, making it seem more luxurious and of a higher quality.

5.21 Similarly, a firm which lowers its price will increase demand a little, but many consumers will remain loyal to its rivals. This means that the demand facing the supplier is not very elastic and the firm can take advantage of this fact by raising its price and increasing its revenue.

5.22 If we draw the demand curve of an individual firm in imperfect competition, bearing in mind the characteristics just described, we will end up with something like Figure 2.6.

Figure 2.6 *An individual firm in imperfect competition*

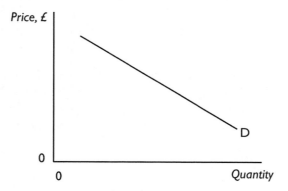

5.23 When the firm lowers its price, demand will increase a little. When it raises its price, demand will fall a little. In other words, the firm has a normal downward-sloping demand curve. Contrast this with the individual firm in perfect competition, which has a horizontal demand curve.

Implications of imperfect competition for buyers

5.24 The imperfectly competitive market is probably the situation you will face most commonly in your professional work. It is a more complicated market than either of the theoretical extremes, in that suppliers will compete along a range of different dimensions: price, quality, variety of product range etc. As purchasers you have to balance a large number of different factors to arrive at the best balance for your organisation.

Oligopoly

5.25 An oligopoly is a small group of firms which together dominate a market. The markets for petrol and car manufacturing are good examples. What makes oligopoly a distinct form of competition is that there are so few firms in the market that actions by any one of them have direct consequences for all the others because each has a significant share of the total market.

5.26 An oligopolistic market has the following characteristics.

- There are very few firms operating in the market. They have similar knowledge of input requirements and of their market, leading their cost structures to be similar, as well as their prices.

- The small number of firms means that firms cannot take decisions independently of decisions made by competitors. For example, a price cut will not necessarily lead to more sales, as competitors might react by cutting their prices too.

- Because of the danger of price wars, where the whole industry loses by the overall reduction in prices, competition often takes different forms, notably product differentiation supported by advertising, special offers and extra services offered at the point of sale, or after sale.

- Cartels often form. A cartel is a group of firms acting together to fix prices and/or output. These are discussed further below.

5.27 The difficulty of competing through price cuts means that the price in an oligopolistic market tends to be fairly stable, ie all firms charge more or less the same price.

5.28 There is a temptation for the few firms in an oligopolistic market to join forces and create a **cartel**. The cartel generally agrees on output of each of its members and the prices to be charged. It effectively creates a monopoly from an oligopoly. The most well-known cartel is OPEC, which controls most of the oil production in the world.

5.29 Anti-competition law in the UK forbids firms to form cartels, but informally buyers can often discern evidence of collusion in oligopoly markets. For example, if an oligopolist raises his prices, his rivals may do likewise. In a perfect market a firm that does this risks pricing itself out of the market, but in an oligopoly (even without any formal cartel agreement) the few firms operating will be watching each other closely and may decide simply to follow the leader, rather than competing. We say that they are colluding with each other, which does not necessarily mean that they have secretly discussed and agreed their plans: they may simply be watching each other and following suit.

5.30 For this reason, oligopolists normally do not compete on price. Instead, they compete by branding, supported by heavy advertising. By achieving brand distinction they can hope in turn to achieve customer loyalty, even if they then raise their prices.

Implications of oligopoly for buyers

5.31   The extent of competition in a market has important implications for purchasing. In one way, buyers may prefer something close to perfect competition, because if one supplier disappoints we can always find another. However, a perfect market also implies that we are just one buyer out of many, which tends to dilute our bargaining strength.

5.32   In a (theoretical) perfect market there are no costs involved in switching from one supplier to another. In real-life markets such costs exist and may be substantial, which means that we are tempted to stay with a particular supplier unless we have a strong reason to move.

5.33   In an oligopolistic market, formal or informal collusion gives bargaining strength to suppliers and reduces that of buyers.

Market structures: a comparison of their essential characteristics

5.34   We end this chapter by summarising the essential features of the market structures we have been examining.

Table 2.3 *How market structures compare*

Perfect competition	Imperfect competition	Oligopoly	Monopoly
Very many small suppliers	Many slightly larger suppliers	A few large suppliers	One supplier only
Homogeneous goods: suppliers' products are a perfect substitute for one another	Differentiated goods: suppliers' products are close substitutes for one another	Normally, differentiated goods: degree of substitution between products is variable	One type of product only
One market price	Price competition	No price competition	Price set by one firm. Possible price discrimination
Perfect information	Imperfect information	Imperfect information	Imperfect information
No barriers to entry in the long run	No barriers to entry in the long run	Barriers to entry	Barriers to entry

Chapter summary

- In assessing potential suppliers there are many factors that may interest a buyer: personal attitudes, production equipment, quality control, housekeeping, technical staff, management ability, financial stability, price offered, etc.

- In the case of large contracts, it may be appropriate to visit the potential supplier's premises. But this is a costly and time-consuming process which should be used with caution.

- A SWOT analysis is a useful tool to apply in the assessment of a supplier. It analyses the supplier's internal strengths and weaknesses, and external opportunities and threats.

- A buyer can use numerous sources of information to identify potential suppliers: past experience, supplier salesmen, contacts with other buyers, published catalogues, trade directories, trade journals, trade shows and exhibitions, direct mail etc.

- A framework for evaluating suitability of potential suppliers is given by the mnemonic FACE 2 FACE. This relates to fixed assets and financial stability, ability to deliver and ability to work with the buyer, cost and commitment to quality, efficiency and environmental policies.

- Modern views of the purchasing function emphasise the importance of strategic issues such as systematic forward planning. This has become increasingly important because external spending is an increasing proportion of an organisation's total costs.

- Purchasing research is often carried out by specialist staff. It should cover the areas of demand analysis, vendor analysis and market analysis.

- The structure of a supply market refers to the number of suppliers active in the market. This may range from just one supplier (a monopoly) to many different suppliers.

- Market analysis is particularly important if supplies are subject to instability.

- The term market structure refers to the number of organisations competing in the market. This ranges from perfect competition (very many small producers) to monopoly (just one producer).

- The essential features of each type of market structure are indicated in Table 2.3. You should study this carefully.

Self-test questions

Numbers in brackets refer to the paragraphs where you can check your answers.

1   List factors that may be involved in vendor assessment. (1.5)

2   What are the limitations of financial information in vendor assessment? (1.8)

3   List Carter's 9Cs for supplier selection. (1.23)

4   What is the point of presenting a SWOT analysis in the form of a grid? (2.6)

5   List sources from which a buyer may identify potential suppliers. (3.4ff)

6   What factors are included in the FACE 2 FACE framework? (3.17)

7   Explain what is meant by a marketing orientation, and how this can apply to internal functions. (4.5, 4.6)

8   What is meant by the concept of a supply chain? (4.8)

9   What three major areas of analysis should be included in a purchasing research exercise? (4.21)

10   What is meant by a monopsony? (4.26)

11   Explain the four categories of supplies distinguished in Kraljic's matrix. (4.29)

12   What conditions apply in a perfect market? (5.2)

13   From a buyer's point of view, what is the downside of a perfectly competitive market? (5.6)

14   Explain what is meant by price discrimination. (5.12ff)

15   Describe the features of imperfect competition. (5.19)

16   Why do oligopolists seldom compete on price? (5.30)

CHAPTER 3

Understanding the Environment

Learning objectives and indicative content

I.3   Analyse market information.

- PESTLE
- Supply and demand

I.4   Assess any legal information and implications for the purchase and supply of goods that might impact upon negotiations.

- Sale of Goods Act
- *Caveat emptor*
- Negotiating terms and conditions
- Penalties and damages
- Unfair Contract Terms Act

I.5   Undertake a risk assessment specifically relating to:

- Win-lose, win-win and win perceived win
- Generating variables and alternatives
- Risk assessment matrix

Chapter headings

1   Undertaking a market analysis

2   Supply and demand

3   The impact of legal regulations

4   Undertaking a risk assessment

Introduction

It helps the buyer to prepare for a negotiation if he is familiar with important factors in the market environment. In this chapter we examine a number of the environmental factors that are relevant in this context.

1   Undertaking a market analysis

PESTLE factors

1.1   A buying organisation does not operate in a vacuum. It interacts with its environment: its customers and suppliers, the general public, government and governmental agencies and so on. Negotiators need to be aware of the influences these factors have on their organisations, and of the influences their organisations transmit in the opposite direction.

1.2   Faced with examining 'environmental influences' your immediate reaction might be 'Where do I start?' There are so many factors to consider that some kind of framework is needed for organising our thoughts. One such framework is variously referred to as PEST analysis, or PESTLE, or STEEPLE. Your syllabus specifies the PESTLE version.

- Political factors
- Economic factors
- Sociocultural factors
- Technological factors
- Legal factors
- Environmental factors (in the sense of 'green' issues)

1.3   The importance of such issues has become clearer in recent years as the effects of changes in the external environment have become more sweeping and more rapid. It would be a mistake to regard environmental change as exclusively a bad thing. Although it does indeed bring problems, it is also a potential source of competitive advantage to organisations that react quickly and appropriately.

Political factors

1.4   The **political environment** embraces new social pressures and the attitudes of the party which is in power at the time, as well as the legislation that regulates the activities of organisations. Relevant factors include:

- the economic and social goals of the government
- the style of government adopted – centralised or decentralised
- the type and amount of aid given to industry in the form of capital provision, regional grants, assistance to small firms, export services etc.
- the role of pressure groups
- the political stability of the countries in which an organisation trades

Economic factors

1.5   The **economic environment** is important because every organisation and industry operates within a business ecosystem. The economic dimension for companies, then, can be considered by posing a series of questions.

   •   What are the essential economic characteristics of the industry?

   •   What is the level of industrial concentration (ie what percentage of total capacity is controlled by the five or six largest companies)?

   •   What are the prospects for fundamental changes in the industry's economic structure?

   •   What is the apparent relationship between sales and economic indicators (eg what degree of correlation exists between industry sales and gross national product)?

   •   What problems are likely to be created by fluctuations in the business cycle?

   •   What are the possible consequences for the company of fluctuations in business activity, government fiscal policy, and/or international events? How will these affect cost/profit/volume, return on capital employed on new investments or replacements of redundant or obsolete equipment, availability and utilisation of labour resources, cashflow and organisational structure such as flexibility and adaptability to swift or gradual changes in product/service output levels?

1.6   Making informed judgements and assumptions about future economic events is often crucially important for planning business strategy. The level of economic activity has a bearing on labour costs, interest rates, cost of capital, foreign exchange rates, inflation rates, sales turnover levels, unemployment levels, and so on.

1.7   Economic factors can:

   •   induce competition into an industry or force companies out

   •   encourage overseas investment or conversely inward investment by overseas firms

   •   prolong or shorten product life

   •   encourage companies to substitute automation for people, or to recruit more people and reduce machines

   •   make a very strong market relatively weak

   •   make a safe market risky.

Sociocultural factors

1.8   The **sociocultural environment** consists of demographic environmental characteristics, such as geographical distribution and population density, age and educational levels, as well as the norms, customs and values of the population within which the organisation functions.

1.9 Changes in consumer attitudes and expectations about such matters as purchasing on credit and home ownership have to be understood by organisations, as do changes in the age structure of the population, migration patterns and commuting habits. In the UK, and elsewhere, there is an increasing emphasis on improvement in the 'quality of life' through increased leisure time, a safe and clean environment, and freedom from discrimination.

Technological factors

1.10 The **technological environment** becomes more important every day, especially in areas such as electronics and mechanics. Technical barriers across national borders are easily overcome and it is as easy for a less developed country to produce high quality electronic products such as personal computers and television sets as it is for an advanced country.

1.11 A new generation of technologies is providing a sharp experience curve. It is possible for competitors around the world to offset capacity advantages with a relatively small production volume. It encourages local production through transfer of technology to other countries to gain cost advantages in local manufacturing and local assembly.

1.12 Life spans of technologies and therefore lifecycles of products are also getting shorter and shorter. It is therefore becoming necessary to recover capital as soon as capacity is installed. It is less and less desirable to think local first and global second when a business is about to invest in technology as that technology will rapidly become obsolete. Instead, businesses must think globally in relation to product design, manufacturing capacity, and marketing issues.

1.13 Traditional industries decline and others emerge as a result of technological innovation. For example, the long-established watch-making industries of Europe were damaged by digital watch technology. Traditional office machines were overtaken by PCs. Fresh food sales were damaged by frozen food. Examples such as this could be multiplied.

1.14 It is common to identify three broad ways in which technological development impacts on organisations (and departments within organisations).

- New technology can affect the way in which day-to-day operations are carried out. An important example of this in recent years has been the development of communication methods such as e-mail and the internet. For purchasing professionals this can be seen, for example, in the use of electronic data interchange, online auctions, etc.

- New technology can alter production methods, typically by replacing labour-intensive processes with automated processes. For example, many manufacturing organisations now use computer-integrated manufacturing systems that would have been unheard of 20 years ago. This development impacts on purchasing professionals, particularly in their need to stay abreast of their suppliers' cost base.

- New technology can lead to new products. Conspicuous examples in recent decades include computers, mobile phones, DVD players, and so on. This too has an important impact on purchasing, because product lifecycles become shorter, the range of inputs becomes more extensive, etc.

Legal factors

1.15   This is considered in a later section of the chapter.

Environmental factors ('green issues')

1.16   Recent decades have seen an unprecedented upswing in public concern over environmental issues. Pollution of the world's waters, damage to the atmosphere, and exhaustion of mineral and other resources, have all attracted the attention of pressure groups and the wider public. In many cases the blame has been laid at the door of large corporations, allegedly pursuing short-term profits at the expense of long-term damage to the environment.

1.17   These pressures have led many organisations to take direct action. Often the stimulus has come from organisations whose objectives are obviously wider than profit maximisation. For example, it is clear that local government authorities, though they are charged with observing tight financial disciplines, have wider obligations to the public.

1.18   Once any organisation takes on an environmental stance, it is likely that such attitudes will begin to spread along the supply chain. Similar commitments will be demanded from that organisation's suppliers, who in turn will pass on the philosophy to their own suppliers. A momentum towards better environmental policies is then underway.

1.19   This kind of reasoning does not begin and end in the purchasing department. On the contrary, it is often an overall corporate policy that leads to change and development. Even so, purchasing staff have an important role to play in giving effect to the environmental objectives.

1.20   Areas of environmental concern in which purchasing staff have a role to play are summarised by Malcolm Saunders in *Strategic Purchasing and Supply Chain Management*: see Table 3.1.

Table 3.1 *Environmental concerns relevant to purchasing staff*

• Recovery, recycling and reusing of materials and waste products
• Safe disposal of waste products that cannot be recycled
• Supplier selection policies to support firms that conform to environmental standards with regard to air, water and noise pollution
• Supplier and product selection policies that reflect concern for conservation and renewal of resources
• Safe testing of products and materials
• Concern for noise, spray, dirt and vibration in the operation of transportation facilities

Porter's five forces model

1.21   Another area of critical concern for purchasers is the general competitive environment. A key tool of analysis in this context is Professor Michael Porter's five forces model.

1.22   Porter states that 'competition in an industry is rooted in its underlying economics, and competitive forces exist that go well beyond the established combatants in a particular industry'. The problem for the purchaser is to determine which of these forces are relevant, and to what extent.

1.23   This approach to industry analysis, developed by Porter in 1980, is based on the concept of an industry being shaped by five forces. These are illustrated in Figure 3.1. The circle represents the industry sector in which existing organisations compete among themselves. The four arrows indicate threats from factors outside the group of competing organisations.

Figure 3.1 *Porter's five forces model*

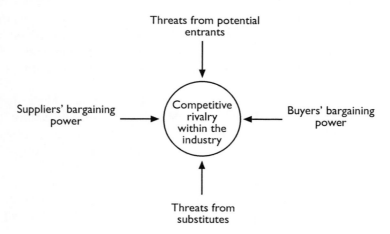

1.24   **Threats from potential entrants**. New competitors to an industry may make it more competitive in three ways.

- Expanding capacity without necessarily increasing market demand.
- Their need to penetrate the market to achieve critical mass and then build market share, which may include product and marketing innovations.
- Increasing costs as they bid for factors of production.

1.25   It is in the interests of existing competitors to deter new entrants. There are six main barriers to entry.

- Economies of scale – until new competitors have achieved a certain size their unit production costs will be high.
- Brand (or product) differentiation.
- Capital requirements – the high costs of acquiring premises, equipment etc in order to make the new business possible.
- Switching costs – existing customers may find that they incur costs if they wish to move their business elsewhere. Such costs include costs of certification, product redesign, costs and time in assessing a new source, or even the cultural problems of severing a relationship.
- Access to distribution channels – retailers must be persuaded to offer space previously devoted to other products.

- Government regulation (including legal barriers). Legal restrictions still prevent companies from entering into direct competition with some nationalised industries. Patents and copyright offer inventors some protection against new entrants. Governments also license the right to produce certain categories of products.

1.26 **Threats from substitutes.** These are alternative products that serve the same purpose, eg gas central heating systems in competition with solid fuel systems. The main threat posed by substitutes is that they limit the price that a company can charge for its products. There is also a danger that the threat of a substitute may not be realised until it is too late to arrest their entry.

1.27 **Threats from the bargaining power of buyers.** The power used by buyers in an industry may make it more competitive in three ways.

- Forcing down prices.
- Bargaining for higher quality or improved services.
- Playing competitors against each other.

1.28 All three of these are at the expense of industry profitability.

1.29 Porter claims that the power of the industry's buyer groups depends on the characteristics of its market situation and on the relative importance of its purchases from the industry compared with its overall business. He suggests that buyers are particularly powerful in seven situations.

- Purchases are large relative to sellers.
- Purchases represent a significant proportion of the buyers' costs.
- Purchases are undifferentiated.
- Buyers earn low profits.
- Buyers have the potential for backward integration.
- The buyer's product is not strongly affected by the quality of the suppliers' product.
- The buyer has full information.

1.30 **Threats from the bargaining power of suppliers.** Suppliers can exert bargaining power over companies within an industry in two main ways.

- Threatening to raise their prices.
- Threatening to reduce the quality of their goods and services.

1.31 The effect of this power will be to squeeze profitability out of an industry unable to recover cost increases by raising its own prices.

1.32 Porter suggests that suppliers are particularly powerful in six situations.

- There are few suppliers.
- There are few substitutes for their products.
- The industry supplied is not an important customer.
- The supplier's product is an important component in the buyer's business.
- The supplier's product is differentiated.
- Suppliers can integrate forward.

1.33 **Conflict among existing competitors** involves some form of offensive strategy. Tactics commonly used to implement such strategy include product innovations and improvements, price competitions, advertising battles and increased customer services.

1.34 Rivalry occurs because one or more companies feels threatened or sees a market opportunity to improve its position, although competitive moves by the initiator company usually result in counter-defensive strategies from its competitors. This interactive pattern of offensive and defensive strategies may not leave the initiating company and the industry better off, and on the contrary may leave all the companies in the industry worse off than before.

1.35 Porter suggests that there are seven main determinants relating to the strength of internal competition and rivalry within an industry.

- Many equally balanced competitors.
- Slow rate of industrial growth.
- Lack of differentiation.
- Capacity can only be increased by large amounts.
- High fixed costs in the industry.
- There are many diverse competitors.
- There are high exit barriers.

2   Supply and demand

What determines the level of demand for a product?

2.1 Demand is the quantity of a good which consumers want, and are willing and able to pay for. If you think about how you decide which goods to buy, you will realise that there are many factors entering into the decision. The main influences on the demand for goods and services are discussed below.

2.2 **Price** is probably the most significant factor. The higher the price, the less likely people are to buy it. For a particular product, economists can create a **demand curve** – a graph indicating how demand falls as price rises.

2.3 In general, the more **income** people earn, the more they will buy. The demand for most goods increases as income rises.

2.4 Two or more goods are defined as **substitutes** if they are interchangeable (or almost interchangeable) in giving consumers utility. For example, margarine is a fairly close substitute for butter. If something has a substitute, you will probably compare the price of the substitute with the price of the good you are thinking of buying. Butter is more expensive than margarine, so, apart from the health considerations, you may decide to buy margarine. On the other hand, milk has very few substitutes, so your decision to buy it will not depend heavily on the price of other products.

2.5   Suppose the price of margarine rises. Even if it is still cheaper than butter, some people will decide that the difference in price is so small that they would rather buy butter. Demand for margarine will fall, while that for butter will rise.

2.6   Conversely, if the price of a substitute falls, then demand for the good in question will also fall, as people switch to the substitute.

2.7   If good A and good B are **substitutes**, a **rise** in the price of one will cause a **rise** in demand for the other, and *vice versa*.

2.8   **Complements** are goods which must be used together. For example, a compact disc player is no good without any compact discs. The price of a good's complements is very important when considering whether or not to buy it. You may be able to afford the player, but if you will not be able to buy any compact discs, there is little point in the purchase.

2.9   If the price of a **complement** rises, then demand for the good in question will **fall**. Conversely, if the price of a complement falls, demand for the good will rise.

2.10   **Taste** is influenced by many different things. You may decide not to buy butter purely on health grounds, having been made aware of its high cholesterol levels. Or fashion may induce you to buy a new pair of shoes even if you don't really need them and cannot afford them. Of all the factors influencing demand, taste is the most difficult one to quantify.

2.11   Clearly, the size of total demand depends on the number of people who are aware of the good's existence, who are able to obtain it and who are likely to want it. **Market size** can be altered by changes in the size and structures of the population. If the birth rate falls in an area, this will have a long-term effect on the total population size and will have a more immediate effect in reducing the number of babies, hence influencing the demand for prams, equipment and clothing designed for babies. It will, of course, also affect the demand for school places, for schoolteachers and for people to train teachers.

2.12   It is not only the volume and quality of **advertising** that can influence demand for a product but also the amount of advertising in comparison with that for competing products. Advertisers cannot often increase total consumption; more often they transfer it from one good to another.

2.13   A change in the **quality** of goods or services will have an effect on how much will be demanded at a particular price. An improvement in quality will increase demand.

What determines the level of supply of a product?

2.14   **Supply** is the quantity of a good which suppliers (or a single supplier) are willing and able to produce in a given period. As with demand, the decision about how much to supply depends on many factors, of which one of the most important is price. In the suppliers' case, the cost of production is also of paramount importance.

2.15   The higher the market **price** of the product, the more the supplier will wish to supply because he will make a bigger profit. For a particular product, economists can create a **supply curve** – a graph indicating how supply increases as price rises.

2.16 In producing goods for sale, the supplier will incur **costs**. Clearly, these must be covered if the supplier is to stay in business. The supplier will therefore compare the market price with his costs to make sure that production will be profitable. Costs will change over time, as technology and production methods change.

2.17 Certain industries are particularly susceptible to **uncontrollable factors**, such as changes in the weather. The most obvious example is agriculture, where bad weather can diminish or even obliterate supply. If the farmer is lucky he can smooth out some of the fluctuations by storing produce during good times and releasing his stocks during bad times, but not all goods can be stored.

2.18 **The level of technology** influences the efficiency with which capital or machines and labour can be used to produce goods. Improved technology enables firms to produce more with a given input of resources, ie at the same cost, and can thus be expected to increase the amount that they are willing to supply at given prices.

2.19 Advanced technology may not be worthwhile in some forms of production unless a certain minimum level of production is desired by customers. Firms may not, therefore, be willing to supply at all unless this level is reached. Alternatively, they may only be willing to supply at high prices because at low quantity levels they have to use expensive methods of production. There may then be two sets of supply conditions – one for low production levels at expensive production costs and one for high levels of production where advanced technology can be employed to reduce the production cost per unit.

2.20 **New entrants** to the supply market increase the supply of goods or services in that market.

2.21 The availability of **complements** is also important. Many goods are linked to each other – for example, cameras and films. A reduction in the price of cameras will mean that more cameras are supplied (at a lower price); this increase in demand will have a knock-on effect on the supply of films without any change in their price.

The interaction of supply and demand

2.22 Consumers want to pay as little as possible, but suppliers want to charge as much as possible. The two sides of the market have to compromise at some price between these two extremes. When the demand and supply curves are put together, **equilibrium price** is at the point of intersection and is the result of the interaction of demand and supply. It also ensures that demand and supply adjust until the quantities which consumers want to buy just equal the quantities which suppliers wish to sell, in a compromise which Adam Smith in his *Wealth of Nations* (1776) called 'the invisible hand'. In fact, there is a two-way relationship: price affects demand and supply; and demand and supply affect price.

Price elasticity of demand

2.23   Price elasticity of demand is the degree of sensitivity of demand for a good to changes in the price of that good. Goods are described as 'inelastic' if the quantity of them demanded is relatively insensitive to the price charged. Typically such goods are basics, such as food, which people put at the top of their spending priorities. Conversely, demand is described as being 'elastic' where the quantity of a good demanded is relatively sensitive to a change in price. The phrase 'price elasticity of demand' is a bit long winded, so it is often shortened to 'elasticity of demand' or even PED.

2.24   Price elasticity is the proportionate change in demand divided by the proportionate change in the good's price. Although mathematically this can be defined in a number of ways, the most common formula is as follows.

$$PED = \frac{\text{Percentage change in quantity demanded}}{\text{Percentage change in price}}$$

Because an **increase** in price normally causes a **reduction** in the quantity demanded, the PED is normally negative. In fact this is so common that frequently the PED is stated without its minus sign, so beware!

2.25   As an example of this calculation, if PED for a certain good currently equals –2, how will sales be affected if price rises by 10 per cent? You should be able to see that there will be a fall of 20 per cent in the quantity demanded.

2.26   When PED > 1 (ie price elasticity of demand is greater than 1), demand is relatively elastic and the quantity demanded is very responsive to price changes; when PED < 1 (ie price elasticity of demand is less than 1), demand is relatively inelastic and the quantity demanded is not very responsive to price changes.

2.27   Note that if demand is said to be inelastic, this does not mean that there will be no change in quantity demanded when the price changes. It means that the consequent demand change will be **proportionately** smaller than the price change. If demand does not change at all after a price change, demand is said to be perfectly inelastic.

2.28   Price elasticity of demand will therefore be low for goods which are necessities or are habit forming because these have few substitutes in the perception of the consumer. Equally goods which have many substitutes and which represent a large proportion of consumer's expenditure have an elastic demand.

2.29   When demand is elastic, total revenue rises as price falls. This is because the quantity demanded is very responsive to price changes. A fall in the price gives rise to a **more** than proportionate rise in the quantity demanded. The net effect is that revenue (= price × quantity) rises.

2.30   Conversely, when demand is inelastic, total revenue falls as price falls. Here a fall in price causes a **less** than proportionate rise in quantity demanded, the result being a net fall in total revenue.

The relevance of elasticity to negotiators

2.31 It is not an easy matter to estimate the elasticity of demand for a product. The judgement of expert analysts may be a helpful indicator. Customer surveys may also provide useful information. Some companies use field testing exercises to assess the effects of price changes on demand. In the last resort, though, it is not an exact science.

2.32 Despite this, negotiators should not underestimate the usefulness of price elasticity. If a reasonable estimate can be formed of the elasticity of demand for a product, the information can be put to good use in a negotiation.

- If demand for a product is known to be inelastic, it may be unrealistic to hope for any price concessions from the supplier. The buyer should focus his negotiating effort on other areas.

- A buyer may be able to assess elasticity of demand for products of alternative suppliers. This can assist in making a choice between them.

2.33 Even if the supplier benefits from low price elasticity (enabling him to increase prices without losing business) it is not all bad news for the buyer. For one thing, the particular item may be only a small part of his total spend. For another, the buyer may be more interested in other factors, such as quality. Or the buying organisation may be so profitable that it can cope with price increases, and perhaps pass them on to its own customers.

3 *The impact of legal regulations*

The law of contract

3.1 The outcome of a successful negotiation will invariably be a supply agreement between buyer and supplier. This will form a contract governed by legal rules that have been developed over many centuries.

3.2 It is not a requirement of UK law that a contract should be in writing. In almost all cases, an oral agreement is binding on the parties. However, it is usually sensible to draw up a written agreement so as to reduce any possibility of disagreement or ambiguity as to what has been agreed.

3.3 The agreement will incorporate **express terms** agreed upon by the parties and specifically stated in the written agreement. However, it may also include **implied terms**: terms which a court will assume to have been incorporated into the agreement even if they are not specifically written down. For example, the Sale of Goods Act (see below) requires that certain terms are always to be included in contracts for the sale of goods, even if the contract between the parties is silent on the subject.

3.4 The contract should also contain terms governing action to be taken in the event of a dispute between the parties. It is usual for the parties to agree that some kind of arbitration or mediation will be undertaken, leaving litigation in the courts as a last resort.

3.5 Needless to say, buyers are not legal specialists. It is usual for organisations to take professional legal advice when drawing up a supply contract.

The Sale of Goods Act

3.6   Many of the contracts entered into by a buyer will be contracts for the sale of goods. Such agreements are governed by general principles of contract law, but are also regulated by Acts of Parliament. The main legislation is the Sale of Goods Act 1979.

3.7   As mentioned above, a key feature of this Act is that it lays down certain terms which will be implied into any contract for the sale of goods. Such terms will apply even if the contract between buyer and seller does not specifically include them in their contract. (There is limited scope for buyer and seller to exclude such terms, by mutual agreement, but this would usually be a bad move from the buyer's point of view.)

3.8   Here are some examples of the terms implied into contracts for the sale of goods by the 1979 Act.

- The seller is deemed to undertake that he has a good right to sell the goods (in essence, the seller must promise that he is the true owner of the goods).
- The goods must be of satisfactory quality and fit for their intended purpose – otherwise the seller is deemed to have failed in his contractual obligations.

3.9   The 1979 Act does not cover contracts for the provision of services. However, the Supply of Goods and Services Act 1982 fills the gap. Like the 1979 Act, it lays down terms which will be implied into any contract for the provision of services. These terms are closely modelled on those of the 1979 Act.

Caveat emptor

3.10   This Latin term means 'let the buyer beware'. This is the legal principle that a buyer is not protected in law for his foolishness or negligence in making a bad bargain. If the buyer regrets the price he paid, it is too late to look to the courts for redress: he should have been more careful in entering into the contract.

3.11   Of course, this does not mean that a seller can evade liability if he has deliberately misled the buyer, or if he has sold goods that did not belong to him, or otherwise breaches his legal duties. But if buyer and seller have both been straight with each other, then a buyer cannot ask the courts to rescue him from a deal that he later repents of.

Negotiating terms and conditions

3.12   Most of this book is concerned with the task of negotiating terms and conditions of supply. Once terms and conditions have been agreed, they will be incorporated in the legal agreement between buyer and supplier.

3.13   Every contract is different, but typical terms and conditions agreed in a supply contract include the following.

- The subject matter of the contract: what exactly the supplier is to supply
- The required standard or quality of the goods or services
- The price to be paid by the buyer, with details of payment dates, instalment payments etc
- The delivery date(s)
- The mechanisms for measuring, inspecting and agreeing quality
- In some cases, the damages to be payable in the event of any breach of contract (this is discussed further below)
- The means by which disputes will be resolved (arbitration, mediation etc)
- Any exclusion clauses, ie clauses which limit the extent of a party's liability in the event that things go wrong

Penalties and damages

3.14 When a party to a contract is found to be in breach of his obligations, the other party can usually claim a monetary remedy in the form of **damages**. The purpose of this is to put the injured party in the position he would have been in but for the breach. In other words, the purpose of damages is to compensate the injured party, not to punish the party at fault.

3.15 If the parties to the contract do not discuss the amount of damages that may be appropriate, and a breach arises, it will fall to the courts to assess the amount of damages. This is called **unliquidated damages**.

3.16 However, the parties may agree in advance on a sum of money to be paid in the event of a breach. This is a proactive form of dispute resolution and is referred to as **liquidated damages**.

3.17 A problem arises in some cases where a party to the contract tries to protect his position by insisting on a large sum of damages to compensate him in the event of a breach by the other party. In such a case, the courts may decide that the agreement is not a genuine attempt to estimate the appropriate amount of damages, but is actually a penalty designed to compel performance by the other party. The courts will not uphold a penalty clause, and the damages (if any) payable to the injured party will have to be assessed by the courts.

The Unfair Contract Terms Act

3.18 A party to a contract may seek to protect himself from the consequences of his own breach of contract by including an **exclusion clause** (or exemption clause) in the contract. This is a clause which attempts to limit the party's liability in the event of breach. For example, to take a far-fetched case, a supplier might want a clause excluding him from liability in the event that the goods he supplies are of unsatisfactory quality.

3.19 It is clear that there is scope for abuse in this area, particularly if the contracting parties are not of equal strength. The stronger party may bully the weaker party into accepting terms that are clearly unfair. To prevent this kind of abuse, the Unfair Contract Terms Act 1977 limits the circumstances in which this kind of clause may be used.

3.20 A person in business cannot exclude or restrict liability for death or personal injury caused by his own negligence. Nor can he exclude or restrict his liability for any other kind of loss, unless the exclusion is 'reasonable'. Any clause purporting to do this will be held to be invalid and unenforceable under the 1977 Act.

3.21 It is for the courts to interpret whether an exclusion clause is reasonable. The person seeking to rely on the clause must convince the courts that it is reasonable. If he fails to do so, the courts will presume that it is unreasonable and will not enforce it.

Other legislation relevant to purchasers

3.22 Guidance published by CIPS refers to other legislation relevant to purchasers, and also to details applying to tendering exercises. Although these issues are not specified in the syllabus, we follow the CIPS guidance by covering them briefly below.

3.23 Other legislation relevant to purchasers includes the following.

- The Data Protection Act 1998: this limits the uses to which organisations may put information held on their databases.

- Competition legislation: a number of Acts are designed to outlaw anti-competitive practices (eg supplier cartels), and to prevent abuse of monopoly markets.

Competitive tendering

3.24 Once a buyer has determined which vendors he is prepared to do business with, taking into account both his market analysis and analysis of specific vendors, an important decision is whether to enter negotiations with one or more vendors, or instead to use a competitive bidding (tendering) procedure. (In the public sector there is usually no decision to be made: competitive tendering is normally compulsory.)

3.25 To use a tendering procedure effectively the buyer may first screen the potential suppliers to ensure that the tender documents are addressed only to those who are technically capable of meeting the requirements.

3.26 Typically there may be from three to ten suppliers who are invited to bid, and in general the buyer will intend to choose the one submitting the lowest price. This is why prequalification of potential suppliers is so important: once the tendering process is underway it is difficult (and may cause ethical problems) to choose any bid but the lowest. The buyer does not want to become tangled up at that stage in discussions of technical capability.

3.27 The prequalification of potential suppliers should be objective. Certainly past experience will help if the buyer has dealt with the supplier before. Even then, a predetermined list of criteria can provide a systematic means of eliminating firms that should not advance to the tendering stage.

3.28 The kind of elimination criteria that could be used include the following.

- Lack of recent experience in the relevant kind of work
- Inadequate financial resources to complete the work
- Inadequate management resources to control the work
- Lack of the required facilities (eg lack of a strong design capability, or lack of production processes of a type to guarantee the required quality).

3.29 We have already emphasised the importance of prequalification of potential suppliers. This is part of the process of **selective tendering**. An alternative approach is simply to solicit bids from any supplier who is capable of doing the work: this is called **open tendering**. In this case it is normal to publish the invitation to tender in a way that will ensure widespread circulation. It is usual also to state that the buyer will not be bound to accept the lowest price quoted, though of course he would normally do so.

3.30 Table 3.2 sets out a checklist of the main stages in a tendering exercise which need to be planned in advance.

Table 3.2 *A checklist for tendering*

1.	Determine whether a tendering process is to be used, or whether some other process is preferable
2.	Determine the type of tendering process to be used – open or selective.
3.	Determine a realistic timetable. This should allow reasonable time for all interested parties to prepare their submissions. It should also allow reasonable time for the purchaser to make available any information that is required by the tenderers.
4.	Issue invitations to tender. In the case of open tendering this would be by means of a public advertisement. In the case of selective tendering it would be by means of a formal approach to each supplier on the shortlist, but the preliminary vetting should have excluded any that may not be willing to tender for any reason.
5.	Ensure that full specifications are issued to each potential supplier in identical terms and by the same date. It should be made clear to tenderers that they are to comply strictly with any timetable for submission.
6.	Arrange the opening of tenders on the appointed date. Return unopened any tenders received after the due date.
7.	List the tenders received and enter the main details of each on an analysis sheet for ease of comparison.
8.	Analyse each tender and select the best offer from suppliers who meet the tender criteria and who are judged capable of completing the contract to the required standards and within the specified deadlines.

3.31 Tendering is not an ideal solution to every purchasing situation. Indeed, it carries some quite serious disadvantages. Even where the situation appears suited to tendering procedures, care is needed to avoid potential pitfalls. One point often made in the literature is that once a contract has been awarded the contractor may have little incentive to perform to the highest possible standards. Since the contract award is a one-off benefit to the vendor, and leaves him with no particular reason to expect further business, he may be less motivated than a supplier who wins a contract by virtue of consistent quality performance during a long-standing business relationship with the buyer.

3.32 Another general criticism of tendering is that it tends to lead to an increase in the number of suppliers. This conflicts with the modern trend towards a narrower supplier base combined with long-term contractual relationships.

3.33 Finally, tendering is a cumbersome procedure and time schedules may be too tight to permit its use.

3.34 Sometimes, following tender evaluation and suppliers' presentations, it is not advisable to accept a supplier's tender without qualification. Equally, it may be advantageous, through **post-tender negotiations**, to find out whether any improvements in suppliers' offers are available. Such negotiations must be carried out by a trained buyer to ensure that other tenderers are not disadvantaged, competition is not distorted, and trust in the tendering process is not adversely affected.

3.35 Post-tender negotiations are rarely considered appropriate for tenders let under the EU Directives, which apply to buyers in the public sector. However, this exception does not prevent clarification of tenders, which is good practice.

3.36 If negotiation or clarification proves unsuccessful, it may be necessary to abandon the first choice preferred supplier and to select the second choice instead. The first choice must have irreversibly been eliminated from the process before any negotiations can commence with the second choice supplier

4 Undertaking a risk assessment

Kraljic's grid

4.1 The choice between competitive bidding and negotiation is not a straightforward one, and is not one that can be taken once and for all and thereafter applied to every purchasing transaction. On the contrary – the variety of purchasing transactions suggests that different approaches will be necessary in different cases. This idea is formalised in the purchasing product portfolio devised by P Kraljic (which we looked at very briefly in the previous chapter).

4.2 Kraljic's approach is to analyse the products purchased by a buyer in relation to two characteristics: their supply risk (ie the danger that the product will be unavailable when needed) and the impact of the purchasing function on overall financial results. This will be greater in the case of products of high value, or which are used in large volume, and lower in other cases.

4.3 This analysis is then summarised by means of a two-by-two grid (or matrix): see Figure 3.2.

Figure 3.2 *The purchasing product portfolio technique*

Complexity of the supply market

	Low	High
Low *Importance of item to the organisation*	**Routine or non-critical items** Require systems contract approach to purchasing	**Bottleneck items** Require continuity of supply
High	**Leverage items** Require competitive bidding	**Strategic items** Require a 'partnership and alliance' approach

4.4   Routine or non-critical products are those which are not critical, which have low supply risk in a straightforward market, and which have low financial impact. There are probably many alternative suppliers, many near substitutes, and probably also a low overall value.

4.5   Bottleneck products are similar to routine products, except that there may be expensive consequences if they happen to be unavailable. Bottleneck products and routine products between them probably account for a relatively small proportion of total purchasing spend.

4.6   For our present purposes, the main focus is on strategic and leverage products.

   •   Strategic products account for a high monetary value and also suffer supply risk, perhaps because of the small number of potential suppliers. These products are natural targets for a negotiation approach leading to a long-term partnership, perhaps with a single supplier or just two suppliers.

   •   Leverage products are also valuable in monetary terms, but their supply risk is low, probably because there are many possible suppliers. This category is a natural target for a competitive bidding approach. The main deciding factor is likely to be purchase price.

4.7   Notice that applying the matrix would give different results for different organisations, and even for the same organisation over time. For instance, for a large courier firm the sourcing of petrol and diesel for its fleet of vehicles would probably be a leverage item, whereas for a firm providing professional services online, the sourcing of fuel for the very small number of vehicles it is likely to have would be routine. However, if the services firm began sending its personnel out to clients on a large scale then the sourcing of fuel would become more of a leverage item.

4.8   Applying Kraljic's matrix to a particular context is a fairly straightforward process which often yields interesting results. It has some weaknesses though.

- It ignores the fact that not all the risk to the supply comes from within the relationship between the customer and the supplier; external environmental factors, especially competition and the PESTLE factor environment, can also have significant impact.

- It applies to products/services rather than to suppliers. A supplier of non-critical items may also be the supplier of strategic ones, for instance.

- While the buyer may perceive an item to be a leverage one, this is only perceived on the other side of the relationship by the supplier if the buyer's spend is significant. In other words, the relative sizes of the parties should also be taken into account

Evaluating supply risk

4.9 The use of Kraljic's matrix implies that we are able to evaluate the supply risk relating to the different items we purchase. CIPS have outlined a detailed risk management process, consisting of five stages.

- Identify sources of potential risk
- For each possible risk event, determine its likelihood and its impact
- Assess the overall impact of all risk factors
- Investigate risk reduction
- Plan, control and reduce risk

4.10 **Sources of risk** may be predictable or unpredictable. For example, it should be possible to plan for staff shortages during peak holiday time because this is predictable. On the other hand, if two or three key personnel leave the organisation unexpectedly to pursue other opportunities we may be caught unawares.

4.11 Some sources of risk arise within the organisation (like the staff shortages just mentioned). Others are external to the organisation (eg a movement in currency exchange rates or interest rates).

4.12 To identify sources of risk it is clear that past experience is a good starting point. But in appropriate cases this should be supplemented by research into particular sources of risk.

4.13 The **likelihood and impact** of each possible risk should be determined. If a risk is judged to be of low likelihood, and low impact even if it occurs, then there is not much point in worrying about it. But where the risk is very likely, or could have a damaging impact even if it is unlikely to happen, it will be appropriate to take action in advance.

4.14 The **overall impact** of several risk factors may be greater than their individual impacts. To cater for this, the buyer should tabulate all possible risks and attach a weighting factor to each, based on their likelihood and potential impact. By adding up all the weightings the buyer can assess the overall risk.

Generating variables and alternatives

4.15 To **investigate risk reduction** the buyer should consider the various possible things that could go wrong with a purchase and think of ways to reduce the risks. One possibility is to take direct action aimed at reducing the risk. Another is to transfer the risk to someone else by means of an appropriate term in the purchase contract. A final possibility is to take out appropriate insurance.

4.16 To **plan, control and reduce** risk is a task that should be assigned specifically to persons with appropriate responsibility. The task is carried out by careful monitoring of plans to ensure that actual outcomes are shaping up as they should. Use of technology is important in this area (eg in collating progress reports from suppliers, flagging when designated action is due to be taken etc).

Risk management matrix

4.17 Referring back to the discussion of risk in terms of likelihood and impact, it is possible to represent the possibilities on a two-by-two matrix (a procedure beloved of authors on management subjects). Here is what it would look like.

Figure 3.3 *A risk management matrix*

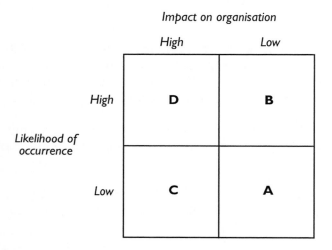

4.18 Outcome **A** refers to a risk which is not likely to happen and would have little effect if it did. The advice here is to ignore it. Outcome **B** is likely to occur, but will not have a big effect. The advice is to monitor it, in case it appears that its effects may be greater than expected. Outcome **C** is unlikely to happen, but will have a big impact if it does. The advice is to draw up a contingency plan just in case. Outcome **D** is the most serious case: this is something that is likely to happen and will have an important impact on the organisation. The advice here is to evaluate it and include your analysis in the strategic plan.

Win-win, win-lose and win perceived win

4.19　Your syllabus refers to these terms at this point. We have already discussed win-win and win-lose approaches at some length in Chapter 1. 'Win perceived win' is a phrase found in one of the recommended texts accompanying this module: *Business Negotiation* by Steele and Beasor.

4.20　To quote the authors:

Your objective should always be to achieve a fine result for yourself and a feeling on the other side that they didn't do too badly either. This is the difference between win-win negotiation and what this book advocates, that is win (by us)/perceived win (by the other party). You think you've won but you'll manage the situation to ensure that the other party feels good about the deal and will be happy to return.

Chapter summary

- To analyse the market environment it is helpful to make use of the PESTLE framework: political, economic, sociocultural, technological, legal and environmental ('green') factors.

- Bear in mind three main ways in which technological factors impact on organisations: they affect operational processes; they can alter production processes; and they can lead to development of new products.

- Once a buying organisation takes an environmental stance, it is likely that such attitudes will begin to spread along the supply chain.

- Professor Michael Porter identified five factors affecting the competitive environment: competitive rivalry within the industry; threats from potential entrants; threats from substitutes; buyers' bargaining power; and suppliers' bargaining power.

- The level of demand for a product is determined by such factors as its price and quality, income levels, availability and price of substitutes and complements, customer tastes, and advertising.

- A demand curve is usually downward sloping, meaning that the higher the price, the lower the demand.

- The supply of a product is determined by such factors as its price, cost levels, random uncontrollable factors, level of technology, new entrants to the market, and availability and price of complements.

- A supply curve is upward sloping, meaning the higher the price, the more suppliers are prepared to provide.

- Supply and demand interact to establish an equilibrium price.

- A contract between buyer and supplier will include both express terms and implied terms. Many implied terms originate in the Sale of Goods Act 1979.

- Typical contract clauses would cover issues such as price, quality, delivery time, payment dates and the means for resolving disputes.

- Competitive tendering is often compulsory for public sector buyers, and may be used also by buyers in the private sector. Selective tendering is based on pre-qualification of potential suppliers; without such pre-qualification we have open tendering.

- Kraljic distinguished between four categories of supplies: leverage products, strategic products, routine products and bottleneck products.

- CIPS outline a five-stage risk management process: identify sources of potential risk; for each possible risk, determine its likelihood and impact; assess the overall impact of all risk factors; investigate risk reduction; plan control and reduce risk.

Self-test questions

Numbers in brackets refer to the paragraphs where you can check your answers.

1   What do the initials PESTLE denote? (1.2)

2   List factors in the economic environment that may impact on buyers. (1.5)

3   In what three ways may technological developments impact on organisations? (1.14)

4   List environmental concerns relevant to purchasing staff. (1.20)

5   What is meant by 'barriers to entering' an industry? List some examples. (1.25)

6   In what situations does Porter suggest that suppliers are particularly powerful? (1.32)

7   What happens to demand for a product if the price of a substitute product rises? (2.5)

8   How might the total size of a market alter over time? (2.11)

9   Define 'supply' of a product. (2.14)

10 How can the supply of a product be influenced by changes in the price of complementary products? (2.21)

11 Give examples of terms implied into contracts by the Sale of Goods Act. (3.8)

12 What is meant by caveat emptor? (3.10)

13 Distinguish between liquidated and unliquidated damages. (3.14ff)

14 Distinguish between open and selective tendering. (3.29)

15 What type of supply arrangement is recommended in the case of leverage products (Kraljic)? (Figure 3.2)

16 List the five stages in the CIPS risk management process. (4.9)

17 Explain how we should manage each of the four possible situations indicated by the risk management matrix. (4.18)

CHAPTER 4

Analysis of Costs

Learning objectives and indicative content

2.1   Identify and calculate elements of fixed and variable costs associated with supply.

- Fixed costs
- Variable costs
- Suppliers' perspectives on fixed and variable costs
- Open book costing

2.2   Identify and calculate direct, indirect and standard costs.

- Difference between direct and indirect costs
- Standard costs
- Actual costs
- Budget costs

Chapter headings

1   Classifying costs

2   Standard costing and budgeting

3   Suppliers' perspectives on costs

4   Value chain analysis

Introduction

Perhaps the single issue most commonly negotiated is price. For a buyer to do well in this kind of negotiation he must have the fullest possible information as to his supplier's costs. This in turn makes it vital for the buyer to understand certain principles relating to costs, which are the subject of this chapter and the next.

1   Classifying costs

Direct and indirect costs

1.1   Classification is a means of analysing costs into logical groups so that they may be summarised into meaningful information for managers.

1.2   Managers require information concerning a variety of issues, each of which may require different cost summaries. For example, a manager may be interested in the total costs incurred in running a particular department, or he may want to know the cost of producing a unit of Product X. For this reason there are many different classifications of cost which may be used. We begin by distinguishing between direct and indirect costs.

1.3   A direct cost is expenditure which can be economically identified with a specific saleable unit of output. For example, the direct costs of producing the textbook you are reading might have included all the following elements.

- Direct materials, such as paper and ink
- Direct labour – the wages paid to employees directly working on producing this book
- Direct expenses. This is a less obvious category of cost. It might include, for example, a royalty payable to the patent holder of a production process used in printing the book.

1.4   **Prime cost** is a term sometimes used to describe the total of direct materials, direct labour and direct expenses.

1.5   Indirect costs (or overheads) are expenditure on labour, materials or other items which cannot be economically identified with a specific saleable unit of output. For example, indirect materials might include the oil used to lubricate the printing press while this book was being printed.

1.6   The reason this is called indirect is that it applies to various printing jobs, and is not specific to this one: the machine was still well oiled when this job was finished and another one began. Similarly, there might be a cost of indirect labour – for example, the wages of a production supervisor who keeps an eye on this printing job, but also on many others that might be in progress in the factory.

1.7   The position is summarised in Table 4.1 below.

Table 4.1 *Direct and indirect costs*

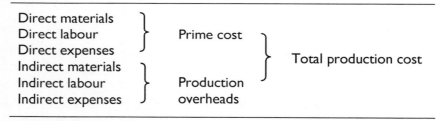

Functional analysis of cost

1.8   Overheads are usually categorised into the following principal activity groups, which relate to the different functions in an organisation.

- Manufacturing (or production) overheads
- Administration overheads
- Selling and distribution overheads

1.9   Prime costs are usually regarded as being solely related to manufacturing, and so are not classified in this way.

1.10 Developing the analysis shown above in Table 4.1, we can now build up the total costs incurred by a manufacturing organisation: see Figure 4.1.

Figure 4.1 *Total costs in a manufacturing organisation*

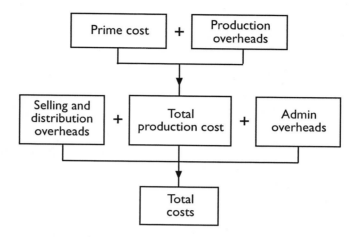

Fixed costs and variable costs

1.11 Cost behaviour is the way in which costs of output are affected by fluctuations in the level of activity. The level of activity usually refers to the volume of production in a period, though in some contexts another level of activity might be relevant (eg the level of sales).

1.12 To illustrate how total costs are affected as production levels vary we use a simple example. Suppose that when 10,000 widgets are produced in a period, a company's total production costs are £9,000, but when 20,000 units are produced total costs are £13,000.

1.13 Total costs have increased by less than 50 per cent although production has doubled. This is because some costs will not rise in relation to the increase in volume. For example, it may be that the production costs include simply the following two elements.

- Rental of a fully equipped factory, £5,000 for the period
- Raw materials, £0.40 per widget

1.14 When production doubles, the raw materials cost increases from £4,000 to £8,000. We say that this is a **variable cost**. However, the factory rental is unchanged at £5,000. We say that this is a **fixed cost**.

1.15 The way in which costs behave as production output changes is a key element in the way prices are set by suppliers. Consider Figure 4.2.

Figure 4.2 *Patterns of cost behaviour*

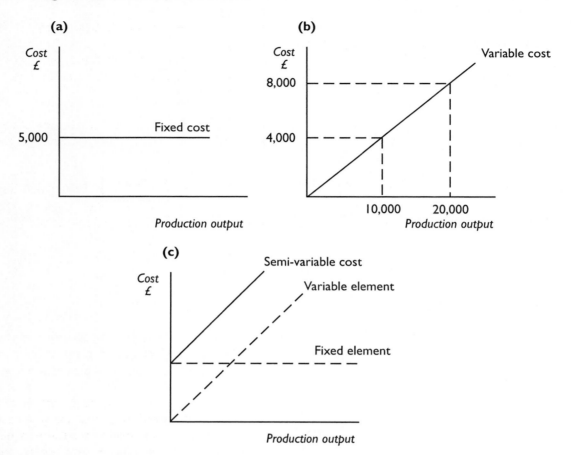

1.16 The first diagram shows the behaviour of a fixed cost. An example already cited is that of factory rental: no matter how much production output is achieved the rental remains fixed at £5,000 (per year, say).

1.17 As with many cost behaviour patterns, this assumption might break down in extreme cases. For example, if production expanded massively it might be necessary to rent a second factory and rental payments would double. But the descriptions given here are adequate for most purposes.

1.18 The second diagram shows a cost which is strictly variable with the level of production. An example might be the cost of raw materials used in producing widgets. If no widgets are produced, the cost of raw materials is zero; if 10,000 are produced, the total cost of raw materials is £4,000 (ie 40p per unit). And this **unit** cost remains constant: if production expands to 20,000 units, the **total** cost of raw materials rises to £8,000.

1.19 Some costs comprise a mixture of fixed and variable elements (see the third diagram). An example might be the cost of machine maintenance. Even if no production is undertaken, an element of standby maintenance will be needed and must be paid for; this is the fixed element. And once production begins the need for maintenance will increase roughly in line with how hard the machines are worked. Strictly this situation is to be regarded as two separate costs, one fixed and one variable.

Analysing semi-variable costs

1.20 In some circumstances (particularly when setting budgets – see later in this chapter) it is necessary to analyse the fixed and variable elements in a semi-variable cost. A common technique for doing this is the **high-low method**. The idea is to compare the level of the cost in a period of high production output with the level of cost in a period of low production output.

1.21 For example, suppose that for Quarter 1 of the year a certain production cost amounted to £2,500 and our production amounted to 20,000 units of output. In Quarter 2, the cost was £3,500 and our production amounted to 40,000 units of output.

1.22 Clearly this is not a fixed cost. It is also clear that it is not a strictly variable cost, because if it was our bill for Quarter 2 should be double the amount for Quarter 1. So we are dealing with a semi-variable cost. We can calculate the fixed and variable elements as follows.

	Units of output	Cost £
High activity level (Qtr 2)	40,000	3,500
Low activity level (Qtr 1)	20,000	2,500
Difference	20,000	1,000

1.23 The additional cost in Quarter 2 (the extra £1,000) must be the variable cost of the additional 20,000 units of output. This means that each unit of output has a variable cost of £0.05 or 5p. Looking at our total costs in Quarter 2, we conclude that the variable element is £2,000 (40,000 units @ £0.05 per unit). The fixed element must therefore be £1,500 to make up the total cost of £3,500.

1.24 This tallies with our Quarter 1 costs. In Quarter 1, the variable element would be £1,000 (20,000 units @ £0.05), and the fixed element is still £1,500, making up the total cost of £2,500.

Contribution

1.25 Contribution is the selling price less the variable cost of sales. We mention the concept briefly here, but we will return to this idea in the next chapter.

1.26 Suppose that the unit selling price of a widget is £1. We know that its variable costs are £0.40. Its contribution is therefore £0.60. What this means is that every time we sell a widget we earn a contribution of £0.60 towards covering fixed costs and making a profit.

- If we sell only a few widgets, our total contribution will not be sufficient to cover fixed costs and we will make a loss.

- If we sell very many widgets our total contribution will more than cover fixed costs and we will make a profit.

- Somewhere in between there is a sales level such that our total contribution exactly matches our fixed costs. In this case we make neither profit nor loss: we break even. We look at how to calculate this breakeven point in the next chapter.

1.27 You may care to calculate how many widgets we must sell in order to break even. Remember that our fixed costs amount to £5,000. But don't worry if you can't do this. We return to the example in the next chapter.

2 *Standard costing and budgeting*

Variance analysis

2.1 Managers use costing information to help them run operations more efficiently. An important technique in this regard is that of variance analysis. As the name implies, this is based on a comparison of what something **should have cost** with what it **actually did cost**, the difference being known as a variance.

2.2 In its usual form, variance analysis is based on the use of **standard costs**. Managers determine in advance what a unit of output should cost by drawing up standards for each of the cost elements comprised in it. For example, a company might determine that the standard cost of producing one blodgit is £4.40, made up as follows.

	£
Raw material X, 1.2 kilos @ £2.00 per kilo	2.40
Grade A labour, 20 minutes @ £6.00 per hour	2.00
Total	4.40

2.3 Suppose now that on a particular day 120 blodgits were produced, with costs incurred as follows.

	£
Raw material X, 150 kilos	285.00
Grade A labour, 35 hours	217.00
Total	502.00

2.4 Based on standard costs, we would expect 120 blodgits to cost £528.00 (ie 120 @ £4.40). In fact it has cost us less than that (good news). Variance analysis enables managers to pinpoint why.

2.5 The basic idea is to examine each input resource (in this case, raw material X and Grade A labour) and to compare actual results with standard, both in terms of the amount of resource used and in terms of the cost per unit of resource.

2.6   In relation to raw material X, the analysis is as follows.

120 blodgits should use	144 kilos
but actually used	150 kilos
Usage variance (bad news)	6 kilos

At a standard cost of £2 per kilo, the excess usage means bad news of £12.

	£
150 kilos should cost	300.00
but actually cost	285.00
Price variance (good news)	15.00

We have paid less than expected for each kilo of material.

2.7   Overall, the good news on material X (the purchase price) outweighs the bad news (the excess usage) by £3. Sure enough, in producing 120 blodgits we would expect to spend £288 on material X (ie 120 @ £2.40), whereas in fact we spent £3 less than that (£285).

2.8   A similar analysis applies to Grade A labour

120 blodgits should take	40 hours
but actually took	35 hours
Efficiency variance (good news)	5 hours

At a standard cost of £6 per hour, the improved efficiency means good news of £30.

	£
35 hours should cost	210.00
but actually cost	217.00
Labour rate variance (bad news)	7.00

We have paid our labour force £7 more than expected for the number of hours they have worked.

2.9   Overall, the good news on Grade A labour outweighs the bad news by £23. Sure enough, in producing 120 blodgits we would expect to spend £240 on labour (ie 120 @ £2.00), whereas in fact we spent £23 less than that (£217).

2.10   The advantages of standard costing are chiefly to do with the improved management control it offers. Each product's costs are carefully analysed and listed out, and an expected amount allocated. In addition, budgeted figures for expected production are calculated, so altogether the standard costing system has encouraged the organisation to plan very carefully. Once activities commence, standard costing requires regular and systematic comparison of actual with estimate so that variances are calculated. This should provide early warning signals regarding specific issues such as prices, efficiency and utilisation, which might go unregarded for a longer period were it not for standard costing.

2.11 The problems presented by standard costing are generally to do with the fact that the system is expensive to install and run effectively. In addition, a product's or service's standard costs can quickly become out of date, which renders the variances meaningless. Finally, while the system should mean that managers take more responsibility for the variances under their control, often the interdependence of variances means that direct responsibility cannot be taken on board by individual managers in quite such a straightforward way.

Budgeting

2.12 A budget is a plan expressed in monetary terms. It is prepared and approved prior to the budget period and may show income, expenditure and the capital to be employed.

2.13 Budgetary control is the establishment of budgets relating the responsibilities of executives to the requirements of a policy, and the continuous comparison of actual with budgeted results, either to secure by individual action the objectives of that policy or to provide a basis for its revision.

2.14 In general, budgets are set for specific periods of time in the future, for example the budget for the coming year. Sometimes budgets are constructed for specific projects that are to be undertaken, but again these can be analysed into the periods of time that the projects are expected to last. Thus, if a project is planned to last two years, the total budget for it can be split into that relating to the first year and that relating to the second year.

2.15 Budgets are plans expressed in financial and/or quantitative terms either for the whole of a business or for the various parts of a business for a specified period of time in the future. The budgets are prepared within the framework of objectives and policies that have been determined by senior management as part of its own planning activities.

Functions of budgetary control

2.16 Essentially the budgetary control process consists of two distinct elements.

- **Planning**. This involves setting the various budgets for the appropriate future period. Managers at the various levels in an organisation should be involved in the budgetary planning stage for their own areas of responsibility. In many medium and large businesses this activity can take a considerable amount of time. There is a need to coordinate the budgets of the various parts of a business to ensure that they are all complementary and in line with overall company objectives and policies.

- **Control**. Once the budgets have been set and agreed for the future period under review, the formal control element of budgetary control is ready to start.

2.17 This control involves comparison of the plan in the form of the budget with the actual results achieved for the appropriate period. Significant divergences between the budgeted and the actual results should be reported to the appropriate managers so that the necessary action can be taken. This should remind you of the process of variance analysis, used in standard costing.

2.18 It is clear that the budget process will involve the prediction of future costs. To do this effectively it is important to understand the nature of the costs in question, and in particular whether the cost is fixed, variable, or a mixture of the two. (Analysis of costs incurred in the past will help with this.)

2.19 A **fixed budget** is based on a particular estimate of activity levels. For example, it may assume that sales volume will be 200,000 units in the coming year. The revenue and costs shown in the budget will all be based on this assumption. The problem arises when the assumption turns out to be wrong.

2.20 Suppose that an unexpected opportunity arises to increase production by 50,000 units because of a sudden surge in sales demand. This is obviously good news for the business, but it means that the fixed budget is no longer much use as a control tool.

2.21 For example, it is likely that we are going to be overspending all of our estimates of costs. While this would normally cause concern, in this case it is just an inevitable consequence of the increased production. The budget is sending the signal that we are overspending, whereas the truth is that we are doing well.

2.22 To cope with this problem businesses use **flexible budgets** in preference to fixed budgets. A flexible budget is a budget which, by recognising different cost behaviour patterns, is designed to change as volume of output changes. In the example above, as soon as we know that sales are way ahead of target all of the variable costs of sales are automatically revised on the flexible budget. Fixed costs of course are not altered. That is one reason why it is important to be able to distinguish fixed from variable costs.

Calculation of budget variances

2.23 The following example illustrates the comparison of actual and budget results.

2.24 The differences between the budget and actual values are known as **variances**. Where they relate to costs (rather than revenue), if the actual cost is less than the budget cost the variance is described as favourable; if the actual cost is greater the variance is said to be adverse.

Example

2.25 Bug Ltd manufactures one uniform product only. The following statement shows the departmental overhead budget based on an average level of activity of 20,000 units of production per four week period, and the actual results for four weeks in October.

	Budget average for four week period £	Actual for 1 to 28 October £
Indirect labour	20,000	19,540
Consumables	800	1,000
Depreciation	10,000	10,000
Other overheads	5,000	5,000
	35,800	35,540

You are required to produce an analysis of the variances between budget and actual.

Solution to the example

2.26

	Average four week budget £	Actual results £	Variances favourable/ (adverse) £
Indirect labour	20,000	19,540	460
Consumables	800	1,000	(200)
Depreciation	10,000	10,000	–
Other overheads	5,000	5,000	–
	35,800	35,540	260

2.27 In this case, we see that we have underspent our budget for indirect labour by £460, whereas with consumables we are £200 over our budget.

Types of budget

2.28 There are various ways of establishing budget targets.

- With an **incremental budget** we begin by looking at the actual figures for the previous period. We then adjust in line with known changes to arrive at a budget for the current period.

- With a **zero-based budget** we ignore previous periods and start completely from scratch.

- With a **priority based budget** we allocate funds in line with strategic goals.

2.29 Whichever of these methods is used, it is important to keep the budget up to date. Two techniques are worth mentioning in this context.

- A **rolling budget** is usually maintained. For example, a 12-month budget may be constructed for the period January to December. At the end of January, we update this by adding figures for the following January. Our revised budget then still covers a 12-month period, from February to January inclusive.

- At intervals during the year it is common to revisit the budget and update it in line with new information. This is sometimes referred to as producing a **forecast**.

Using computers in budgeting

2.30   The nature of the budgeting exercise is that many of the resulting final values are dependent on the estimate made of sales volumes, together with a few policy decisions (for example stockholding policies, payment period policies).

2.31   It is also true to say that budgets are a planning device designed to assist in the achievement of an organisation's longer-term plans.

2.32   These two factors have the following consequences.

- There are likely to be a number of alterations made to the first draft of the budget to see the effects of such changes.
- The alteration of one value will cause many other values to alter.

2.33   It is these factors which have led to the preparation of budgets being computerised, using spreadsheet packages. A spreadsheet is a computer package which stores data in a matrix format where the intersection of each row and column is referred to as a cell. Columns are referenced alphabetically and rows numerically with the result that a cell reference is a combination of these.

2.34   Each cell within a spreadsheet may be used to store:

- a label (description), eg the title of the spreadsheet
- a value, or
- a formula.

2.35   The formula is used to carry out calculations on values entered in other parts of the spreadsheet. The benefit of using formulae is that if some value on the spreadsheet is changed – eg the forecast of sales volume may be amended – the computer automatically recalculates all the formulae. In an instant the effect of the new assumption is displayed in the budget without any manual recalculation.

3   Suppliers' perspectives on costs

Fixed and variable costs

3.1   From a supplier's perspective, the difference between fixed and variable costs is very important. We will look at this issue more closely in the next chapter (in our discussion of breakeven analysis) but a few remarks are appropriate here.

3.2   A sales person will always be seeking to generate at least enough business to cover his organisation's fixed costs. If the cost structure of his organisation includes a high proportion of fixed costs this puts pressure on him to achieve high sales volumes. Buyers may be able to take advantage of the seller's eagerness to do business.

3.3   Even if the seller has already generated enough business to cover fixed costs there are still opportunities for the buyer to obtain a good deal. In particular, the seller no longer has to worry about the level of fixed costs, so that any price in excess of his variable costs will be sufficient to make a contribution to profits. This means that the buyer can hope to obtain a relatively low price.

3.4   These ideas will be developed in more detail in the next chapter.

Open book philosophies

3.5 Open book management originated as the idea that a company should reveal financial information about its business to its employees. The purpose of this is to:

- develop the interest of employees in the performance of the company

- educate employees to understand that their own well-being (eg annual bonus) is linked to the financial performance of the company and

- educate employees to see a connection between the work they do and the financial performance of the company.

3.6 Open book management will, it is argued, encourage employees to associate themselves more closely with the company, and adopt a more collaborative and positive approach in their work.

3.7 A similar concept can be applied to the relationship between a company and its supplier. However, a distinction is made between:

- open book costing and

- cost transparency.

Open book costing

3.8 With open book costing, suppliers provide information about costs to the purchaser. Having cost information from the supplier will, it is argued, reassure the purchaser about getting value for money, and that the supplier will not be making excessive profits.

3.9 Open book costing is used in the automotive industry, and is also used in some service industries, such as facilities management, catering and logistics. It is also necessary with contracting work where the agreed price is based on some form of cost-related formula.

3.10 It has been suggested that open book costing is appropriate as part of a supplier development programme, so that:

- the customer can get to know more about the supplier's operations and processes, and

- the customer can identify areas where the supplier might be able to make improvements to reduce costs or add value in some other way.

3.11 In principle, open book costing can be a way for the customer to help the supplier, and creates a win-win situation. In practice however, open book costing is unlikely to appeal to suppliers, because the customer is dictating the requirements. The flow of costing information is all one-way, from the supplier to the customer. The supplier might be reluctant to divulge confidential information that the customer might pass on to another supplier, thereby reducing its competitive advantage. Faced with a demand from the customer for cost information and a reluctance to provide confidential information, the temptation for a supplier might be to provide inaccurate cost data.

3.12 Even if open book costing does result in added value, the supplier cannot be certain of enjoying any of the benefits. The customer might take all the benefit of cost reductions, for example, either to keep itself or to pass on to its own customers.

Cost transparency

3.13 The main drawback to open book costing is that the customer is in the driving seat and the flow of cost information is all one way. Cost transparency is something different. With cost transparency, the customer and the supplier share cost information, for activities where they have a common interest. The flow of information is two-way.

3.14 The objective of cost transparency is to reduce costs, because an understanding of the costs of the customer or supplier will help the other party to appreciate where the opportunities for savings might lie.

3.15 If the two organisations exchange financial information openly, they will also develop a better understanding of their concerns and objectives. For example, a company might want to buy a particular product on certain specifications, but for a price no higher than a stated maximum amount. Financial information from the company might help to explain to the supplier the reasons for the customer's maximum price requirement. Equally, a supplier might provide financial information to a customer to demonstrate that it is not making unreasonable profits on the items that it is supplying. An exchange of financial information could:

- promote greater mutual understanding, and
- encourage closer collaboration for mutual benefit.

3.16 Cost transparency is not currently adopted very widely, but might gain greater acceptance if strategic supplier-customer relationships continue to develop. However, there is still a strong tendency for managers to want to protect confidential information, such as profitability margins and technical details.

4 *Value chain analysis*

4.1 Guidance published by CIPS has emphasised the importance of value chain analysis. It is not clear what this has to do with the exam syllabus, but for safety's sake we cover the topic in this section

4.2 Value analysis is a method of gaining a deeper insight into customer needs. The value chain breaks down the firm into its strategically important activities in order to gain fuller understanding of the value of each.

4.3 The concept of value should be continually assessed from the point of view of the final consumer or user of the product or service. This may be overlooked by organisations which are distanced from their final users by intermediaries such as distributors, leaving them out of touch with the realities of their markets. The consumers' idea of value may change over time, perhaps because of competitive offerings giving better value for money becoming available.

4.4 According to Professor Michael Porter, the business of an organisation is best described by way of a value chain in which total revenue minus total costs of all activities undertaken to develop and market a product or service yields value.

4.5   All organisations in a particular industry will have a similar value chain which will include activities such as obtaining raw materials, designing products, building manufacturing facilities, developing co-operative agreements, and providing customer service.

4.6   An organisation will be profitable as long as total revenues exceed the total costs incurred in creating and delivering the product or service. It is therefore necessary that organisations should strive to understand their value chain and also that of their competitors, suppliers, distributors, etc.

4.7   The value chain, shown in Figure 4.3, displays total value and consists of value activities. Value activities are the physically and technologically distinct activities that an organisation performs.

Figure 4.3 *The value chain*

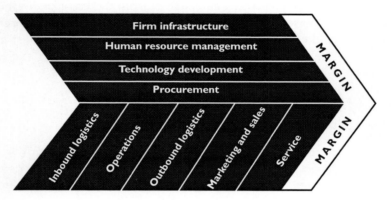

4.8   This schematic representation of the value chain clearly shows its constituent parts. The primary activities, in the lower half of the value chain, show in sequence the activities performed by the organisation in converting raw material inputs to finished products and the transfer of the product or service to the buyer and any after-sales service.

4.9   The primary activities are grouped into five main areas.

•   Inbound logistics are the activities concerned with receiving, storing and handling raw material inputs.

•   Operations are concerned with the transformation of the raw material inputs into finished goods or services. The activities include assembly, testing, packing and equipment maintenance.

•   Outbound logistics are concerned with storing, distributing and delivering the finished goods to the customers.

•   Marketing and sales are responsible for communication with the customers, eg advertising, pricing and promotion.

•   Service covers all of the activities which occur after the point of sale, eg installation, repair and maintenance.

4.10   Each of these may be a source of competitive advantage.

4.11   Alongside all of these primary activities are the secondary, or support, activities of procurement, technology, human resource management and corporate infrastructure. Each of these cuts across all of the primary activities, as in the case of procurement where at each stage items are acquired to aid the primary functions. At the inbound logistics stage it may well be raw materials, but at the production stage capital equipment will be acquired, and so on.

Chapter summary

- Direct costs of production are those costs that can be economically identified with a specific unit of production output. Indirect costs are those that cannot be so identified.

- A fixed cost is one that does not vary in line with changes in the level of activity. A variable cost is one that does change in line with activity levels.

- Contribution is the difference between selling price and total variable costs.

- Managers use variance analysis to help them control operations. This involves comparison of expected costs with actual costs.

- In a standard costing system, the benchmark used for comparison in variance analysis is the standard cost of producing an item.

- A budget is a plan expressed in monetary terms. It is normal for each budget to be under the responsibility of a designated manager.

- The budgetary control process comprises the two elements of planning and control. Control involves comparison of actual outcomes with the budget and investigation of material differences.

- For a supplier, the distinction between fixed and variable costs is very important, but we examine this in more detail in the next chapter.

- Modern ideas on relations with suppliers have emphasised open book philosophies, such as open book costing and cost transparency.

Self-test questions

1   What three categories of cost make up prime cost? (1.4)

2   Explain what is meant by an indirect cost. (1.5, 1.6)

3   Give an example of a fixed cost and an example of a variable cost. (1.14)

4   Define 'contribution'. (1.25)

5   What is a standard cost? (2.2)

6   Distinguish between a usage variance and a price variance. (2.6)

7   Define 'budget'. What main items are shown in a budget? (2.12)

8   Explain the two elements comprised in the process of budgetary control. (2.16)

9   What is meant by a flexible budget? (2.22)

10   What is the implication for a seller if his level of fixed costs is high? (3.2)

11   Explain what is involved in 'open book costing'. (3.8)

12   Distinguish between open book costing and cost transparency. (3.13)

CHAPTER 5

Margins and Breakeven Analysis

Learning objectives and indicative content

2.3   Identify total costs and margins.

- What total costs are
- What is meant by 'margins'
- Suppliers' margins vs market pricing

2.4   Undertake a breakeven analysis.

- How to demonstrate breakeven through economic charts
- Modelling using breakeven
- Suppliers' perspectives on breakeven
- Buyers' perspectives on breakeven

Chapter headings

1   Total costs and margins

2   Suppliers' margins vs market pricing

3   Breakeven analysis

Introduction

In this chapter we take a further look at the costs incurred by suppliers. As always, our focus is on the relevance of costing to the buyer engaged in negotiation. The buyer must have a good knowledge of his supplier's costs so that he is well prepared to negotiate on pricing issues.

1 Total costs and margins

Purchase cost and manufacturing cost

1.1   Retailers and wholesalers purchase finished goods for resale to customers. Usually, the retailer or wholesaler will not perform any work in transforming the goods to another form. The direct costs incurred are fairly simple to establish: they are simply the purchase price of the goods obtained.

1.2   With a manufacturer the situation is very different. Manufacturers purchase raw materials, components, subassemblies etc for incorporation into products. The manufacturer transforms the materials he purchases by acting on them with machines and labour. He may produce a large number of different product lines, for each of which he may produce many thousands of units each month or year.

1.3   To establish the cost of manufacturing one unit of Product X is not a simple matter. The cost of purchasing raw materials for incorporation into Product X is only a starting point, because the costs of converting those materials must also be included in the calculation.

1.4   Even the basic purchase price of raw materials may be difficult to establish. For example, a printer manufactured the textbook you are reading. How much ink was included in printing the cover of this one copy, and how much did it cost to purchase that amount of ink?

1.5   As we move beyond the raw materials the picture becomes even less clear. For example, the printer began the manufacturing process by making electrostatic plates from the originals supplied by the publisher. The cost of making the plates was, say, £200. How much of that £200 is attributable to the copy that you are reading, and how much to other copies? Suppose the book sells well and the publisher asks for additional copies to be printed; the printer will use the same plates he has already produced. Now how much of the £200 relates to each copy of the new print run?

The elements of cost

1.6   These questions are raised here to give you an idea of the difficulties that a cost accounting system is designed to deal with. Even in this preliminary sketch it may be apparent that manufacturing costs comprise three main elements: materials, labour and overhead.

1.7   Within these major cost elements, costs can be further classified according to the nature of expenditure: for example, raw materials, consumable stores, wages, salaries, rent, rates, depreciation.

Costs and margins

1.8   One reason why costing information is important is that suppliers must ensure that their selling prices more than cover their costs. To do this they obviously need to know exactly what their costs are.

1.9   Costs, profit and selling prices are related in the following fairly obvious way (using illustrative figures for clarity).

	£
Total costs	80.00
Plus profit	20.00
Equals selling price	100.00

1.10 It is often convenient to indicate the profitability of a particular business, or a particular product, by expressing the profit as a percentage. We may choose to express the profit as a percentage of total costs, or as a percentage of selling price.

1.11 When we express the profit element as a percentage of cost, we refer to it as a **mark-up**. In our example above, the mark-up is 25 per cent on cost (because £20 is 25% of £80).

1.12 When we express the profit element as a percentage of selling price, we refer to it as a **margin**. In our example, the margin is 20 per cent on selling price (because £20 is 20% of £100).

1.13 If you face a calculation relating to mark-ups or margins it is always helpful to construct a miniature 'equation' like the one above (total costs + profit = selling price).

Example

A supplier's margin on all products is 25 per cent. What is his mark-up percentage? If his total sales for the year amount to £2,000,000, what are his total costs and his total profit for the year in £?

Solution

For the first part of this question, we construct our 'equation', assuming a selling price of £100 for simplicity. We do not know what the costs are, but we can calculate the profit element because we are told that the margin is 25 per cent, ie 25% of the selling price, (£100) namely £25. It follows that costs must be £75 for every £100 of sales, and we can tabulate our results as follows.

	£
Total costs	*75.00*
Plus profit	*25.00*
Equals selling price	*100.00*

1.14 Since we now know both profit and total costs we can calculate the mark-up percentage, namely 33 ⅓ per cent (ie 25 divided by 75 and expressed as a percentage).

1.15 For the second part of the question, we know that his total profit is 25 per cent of his selling price, ie 25% × £2,000,000, or £500,000. This means that his total costs are £1,500,000.

Marginal costing and absorption costing

1.16 We have been looking at a method by which suppliers may set their prices: namely, calculating their costs, then adding on a mark-up or margin for profit. However, we have not yet looked at exactly which costs are included in this calculation.

1.17 Bearing in mind the distinction in Chapter 4 between fixed and variable costs, there are two main approaches that suppliers may adopt towards calculating the costs of their products.

- Under a **marginal costing** approach, suppliers concentrate only on the marginal cost of producing additional units. This essentially means that they cost their products on the basis of **variable costs** only. A supplier using this approach will have to add on a substantial mark-up in order to set his selling price. This is because the mark-up must be sufficient to cover fixed costs as well as earning a profit.

- Under an **absorption costing** approach, suppliers attempt to calculate the **total costs** of their products, both variable and fixed. To this total they add a mark-up sufficient to earn a satisfactory profit.

1.18 The problem with absorption costing lies in attributing a fair amount of fixed cost to each unit of production output. Historically, the approach to this problem has been to calculate the amount of some measurable resource consumed in a production period, and to relate the fixed overhead to this resource.

1.19 For example, a supplier might expect to require 5,000 labour hours in his assembly department during a particular production period, while expected fixed costs during the same period are £4,000. He might therefore conclude that for every labour hour worked he clocks up £0.80 of fixed cost. He would refer to an **overhead absorption rate** of £0.80 per direct labour hour.

1.20 Pursuing this logic, for any unit of product that is worked on in the assembly department for 30 minutes, say, an amount of £0.40 of fixed cost is incurred. This would be added to the direct costs incurred by the same unit of product, and by this means the supplier could eventually determine all the costs – both variable and fixed – relating to that unit of product. It is clear that this is far from being an exact science.

How suppliers set their prices

1.21 In practice, suppliers may well set their prices by estimating what the market will bear and charging the maximum they think they can get away with. We look at market-based approaches to setting prices in the next section of this chapter.

1.22 For now, though, we will stick with **cost-based approaches to pricing**. We have now seen the various costs that suppliers may factor into their calculations. How could they use this information to set their price levels?

1.23 An obvious approach is described as **full-cost pricing**. The supplier calculates the total cost of a product on an absorption costing basis, adds a mark-up to produce a profit, and the result is his selling price. A variation on this is to base the calculation on variable costs only; in this case, the level of mark-up evidently has to be greater if the supplier is to make a profit.

1.24 There are various ways in which the supplier might arrive at an appropriate level of mark-up. Some of these ways have been mentioned by a former examiner for this subject. In case this terminology is used in the exam, we explain below what is meant by each term described (which you will not find in standard texts on this subject – it is somewhat idiosyncratic).

- The supplier could add no mark-up at all – in the examiner's terminology, he uses a **minimum price**, meaning that he charges for a unit of product exactly the amount that it will cost him to replace it.

- The supplier could charge a **breakeven price** – ie he adds a mark-up just sufficient to cover his full costs at the budgeted level of production and sales. How this differs from the **minimum price** is not clear.

- He could charge a **mark-up price**. He determines the percentage mark-up he requires and adds it to total costs. In this case, selling price will be calculated as breakeven price divided by (100% minus the mark-up percentage). If the breakeven price is £150, and the supplier's desired mark-up is 25%, the mark-up price will be £150/75% = £200.

- He could charge a **target price**. He calculates the total cost of a product, including a 'fair' share of fixed costs, and adds a mark-up calculated as a percentage rate of return on the amount of capital he has invested. In other words, this is no different from a mark-up price: the only additional detail is that the required level of mark-up is specified as being related to the amount of capital invested.

Disadvantages of cost-based approaches to pricing

1.25 While cost-plus pricing has the advantage of being easily understood, it can lead to a number of anomalies and disadvantages. (That is why market-based approaches are more common in practice: see next section of this chapter.)

1.26 Cost-plus pricing ignores elasticity of demand, competition and other influences on pricing. It is also quite inflexible and does not take into account any changes or trends in the external environment. The problem of establishing fixed and variable costs is also much greater than it seems.

1.27 In some circumstances, the organisation may actually be ignoring potential profits. For instance, in a premium product such as perfume, the customer might be willing to pay much more than the price derived from cost-plus methods. Therefore, the organisation loses much potential profit.

1.28 Another anomaly with this method arises if an organisation pursues cost cutting objectives. If they are successful in reducing costs the result will be lower prices to customers and again profits will not be at their optimum level.

1.29 A final anomaly with cost-plus pricing is that the decision can become circular.

- The volume of sales affects the total costs of production.
- This in turn affects the unit cost of production.
- This in turn is used in calculating the unit selling price.
- This in turn influences the level of demand for the product.
- This in turn affects the volume of sales – and we are back where we started!

How does this affect negotiators?

1.30   From a buyer's point of view a problem with all of this cost analysis is that it is done by the supplier, who may well not wish to share it! In the case of a close, long-term supply relationship then a policy of open book costing or cost transparency may apply (see previous chapter), but in most cases the buyer will not easily be able to discover details of his supplier's cost structure. However, he may be able to derive information from a supplier's tender (if a competitive bidding approach has been used), or he may be able to estimate the cost of the supplier's products from his own knowledge of the industry.

1.31   If the buyer can ascertain the supplier's cost structure, it aids him in negotiating prices. He can assess whether the level of profit targeted by the supplier is excessive; if it is, there is scope for price reduction. He can also arm himself with other useful information in preparation for the negotiation.

- He can estimate the level of sales the supplier must achieve to break even.
- He can compare the level of profit targeted by the supplier with that earned by other potential suppliers.
- He can estimate how valuable his business will be to the supplier in terms of market share and profitability.
- He can estimate the lowest possible price the supplier can afford to charge.

2   Suppliers' margins vs market pricing

Target costing

2.1   In the above discussion we have assumed that companies set their sales prices by working out their costs and adding an amount for the desired level of profit. The total is then used as the price for selling goods to customers.

2.2   This is indeed a traditional approach to price-setting, and is referred to as **cost-plus pricing**, which means that the selling price is computed as 'cost of producing and selling the goods, plus an element for profit'. However, a problem with this method is that the selling price that emerges may be unacceptable to potential buyers.

2.3   A more modern approach, pioneered by Japanese firms, is referred to as **target costing**. This differs considerably from the cost-plus approach.

- The cost-plus approach builds up the cost of a product by analysing its components step by step. A profit margin is then added and the result is the selling price of the product. With luck, this will be a price that the market can stand; if it is not, the product will be unsuccessful.
- Target costing starts at the other end. The manufacturer first estimates the maximum selling price that the market will be willing to pay for a product with specific features. He then works backward to calculate the production cost that must be achieved in order to provide a reasonable profit.

2.4   The difference between these two approaches is crucial.

- The cost-plus approach accepts costs as given, and calculates a selling price that must be achieved. We must then hope that the market will be willing to pay.
- Target costing starts with what the customer will pay, and then attacks costs so that they are reduced to the required level.

2.5 Target costing is hardly achievable without close cooperation between members of the supply chain. Each member must work closely with the others to identify opportunities for cost reductions and progressively seek to drive costs and prices downwards.

Market pricing

2.6 The remarks above on target costing illustrate an important point about how suppliers set their prices. The method of cost-plus pricing sounds like common sense until one considers that this may not optimise the supplier's profit. A supplier clearly wants to charge his customers as much as they will be willing to pay – in other words, he wants to charge the market price. Certainly this must, as a minimum, be sufficient to cover his costs, but it may be much more than that.

2.7 A marketing-based approach to pricing is one that recognises the attitudes of customers and potential customers. A cost-based approach may lead to a supplier charging less or more than customers are willing to pay, both of which are likely to be unsuccessful strategies. It is preferable to see the pricing decision as being linked in to the whole range of marketing activity carried out by the business with a view to satisfying customers profitably. This allows flexibility to change prices in response to changes in market conditions.

3 Breakeven analysis

Costs, sales volume and profitability

3.1 In this section of the chapter we look at how changes in output and sales affect costs and hence profits.

3.2 To simplify matters, let us first consider a supplier (Y Limited) who produces just a single product. The normal selling price for the product is £15 per unit and the variable costs of production are £6 per unit. Again for simplicity, we will assume that all the supplier's other costs are fixed and amount to £630,000 per annum.

3.3 The table below shows the supplier's position on different assumptions regarding sales volumes.

Sales volume	50,000 units	75,000 units	100,000 units
	£'000	£'000	£'000
Fixed costs	630	630	630
Variable costs @ £6 per unit	300	450	600
Total costs	930	1,080	1,230
Sales revenue @ £15 per unit	750	1,125	1,500
(Loss)/profit per annum	(180)	45	270

3.4   The position is fairly clear: if sales of only 50,000 units are achieved, the supplier expects to make a loss of around £180,000; at a sales volume of 75,000 units a small profit is made; and at higher sales volumes profit increases quite nicely.

3.5   This has been a very simple example to illustrate the point clearly. In practice things will be more complicated. But the example does show the importance of what is called breakeven point: the point where sales volumes enable a loss to be transformed into a profit. We look at this in more detail below.

Contribution and profit

3.6   A firm's breakeven point is where it sells sufficient product to cover its costs exactly, so that neither profit nor loss is made. Breakeven analysis is the process of computing a breakeven point. Either arithmetic or graphical methods may be used, and both are illustrated below.

3.7   A key concept in breakeven analysis is that of contribution, which is the difference between sales revenue and the variable cost of making the sales. Another way of putting this is to say that it is the amount of selling price left over after variable costs have been paid for. It is this amount which must be sufficient to cover fixed costs and, perhaps, to make a profit. In fact, contribution is an abbreviated expression; in full, it should be **contribution to covering fixed costs and making a profit**.

3.8   Consider the example of Y Limited already given. The company sells its product at £15 per unit, but has to pay £6 per unit in variable costs. This leaves a contribution of £9 for every unit sold.

3.9   Now, for Y Limited to break even the company must earn sufficient contribution each year to cover its annual fixed costs of £630,000. This implies a target sales volume of $^{£630,000}/_{£9}$ = 70,000 units. Notice that this bears out the results in the table above. From the table it is clear that a large loss is made at a sales volume of 50,000 units, whereas at 75,000 units the company has just moved into profit. In fact, we can now see that the exact point where this happens is at a sales volume of 70,000 units.

3.10   The arithmetical approach we are developing here gives us further information. It is clear that once we have covered fixed costs, any contribution earned on additional sales volumes represents clear profit. So for Y Limited, a sales volume 5,000 in excess of the breakeven point leads to a profit equal to the excess contribution, namely 5,000 × £9 = £45,000. This is borne out by the calculations in the table.

3.11   As an exercise, use similar reasoning to check what profit Y Limited should make if a sales volume of 100,000 units is achieved. Check your answer by reference to the table above.

Margin of safety

3.12   The margin of safety is the difference between the planned sales level and the breakeven sales level. For example, if Y Limited plans to achieve a sales level of 100,000 units, the margin of safety is 30,000 units. This means that sales can fall short of the target by as many as 30,000 units before Y Limited begins to make losses.

Planned sales level – breakeven sales level = margin of safety
100,000 units – 70,000 units = 30,000 units

3.13 The margin of safety is often expressed as a percentage of the planned sales.

$$\text{Margin of safety} = \frac{30,000}{100,000} = 30\% \text{ of planned sales}$$

A loss will result if there is a shortfall of more than 30 per cent from the planned sales levels.

Breakeven analysis using charts

3.14 To show how breakeven analysis can be illustrated graphically we will again use the example of Y Limited. See Figure 5.1.

3.15 The diagram is simpler than it looks. To construct it just follow these steps.

- Mark a vertical axis for sales and costs in monetary terms, and a horizontal axis for sales volume in units. In the present case, the vertical axis is broken at the beginning to allow us to concentrate on the interesting part of the graph.

- First draw in fixed costs. This is a horizontal line at the level of £630,000, reflecting the fact that these costs are unchanged no matter what sales volume is achieved.

- Sales revenue rises in a straight line as sales volume increases. Just pick any two levels of sales volume, mark the relevant points on the graph and join them up in a straight line.

- Total costs also increase in a straight line. For a zero sales volume, total costs consist of fixed costs of £630,000; for a sales volume of 1,000 units, fixed costs remain the same, but variable costs of £600,000 have to be added, a total of £1,230,000. Now join up the two points you have calculated.

Figure 5.1 *Y Limited – breakeven analysis*

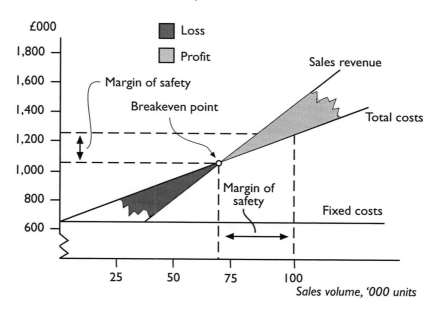

3.16   Notice how the breakeven point can simply be read off the graph: it is the intersection of the sales revenue and total costs lines. In other words, it is the point where total sales revenue is equal to total costs. In our example, this corresponds to the point on the horizontal axis representing 70,000 units of sales. This in turn corresponds to the point on the vertical axis representing £1,050,000 of sales revenue and total costs.

3.17   As an exercise, use the graph to estimate what sales level (in both volume and monetary terms) Y Limited would have to achieve in order to make a profit of £180,000. Check your reading by using the arithmetical approach. You should arrive at an answer of 90,000 units or £1,350,000.

Buyers' perspectives on breakeven

3.18   Of course in practice the situation is not as simple as we supposed for Y Limited. For one thing, we have assumed that the company produces only a single product. But despite these limitations, breakeven analysis has a number of important implications for buyers.

3.19   An important trend in modern manufacturing is the increased reliance of manufacturers on automated processes, and the consequent fall in use of direct labour. The use of automation has the effect of reducing variable costs (namely the cost of direct labour), while increasing fixed costs (the heavy capital costs of expensive plant).

3.20   To illustrate this, return to the example of Y Limited and suppose that the company has only recently automated its manufacturing. Before this happened its fixed costs were much lower at £250,000 per annum, while its variable costs were much higher at £10 per unit. With a contribution of £5 on every unit sold (£15 – £10) Y Limited had only to achieve sales volume of 50,000 units to break even.

3.21   Since automation, the task facing the company is much tougher. As we have seen, they will make a loss at all sales volumes below 70,000 units. This places great pressure on the sales staff of Y Limited: they must obtain substantial extra business to feed their hungry new machines. Other things being equal, they will be more prepared than previously to offer a tight selling price.

3.22   Another implication concerns the situation when the supplier has passed breakeven point. From then on his low variable costs mean high contribution and high profit. The supplier does not have to press too hard for optimum prices: even a comparatively low selling price will more than cover variable costs and so add to contribution and profit.

3.23   In the case of Y Limited, after automation and once the breakeven point of 70,000 units has been passed, any sales achieved at prices in excess of the £6 variable costs will add to profits. There is a wide gap between £6 and £15 for buyers to target in negotiations.

Suppliers' perspectives on breakeven

3.24   It is worth mentioning a further point about fixed and variable costs. Suppose that Y Limited had budgeted at the start of the year to achieve sales of 90,000 units. At that sales level the company's costs would be as follows.

	£
Fixed costs	630,000
Variable costs	540,000
Total costs	1,170,000

3.25 Dividing this total costs figure by the output of 90,000 units, a Y Limited salesman might be inclined to say that the cost of producing a unit of product is £13. In effect, he is spreading the total fixed costs over the 90,000 units at the rate of £7 per unit; added to variable costs of £6 this gives the 'total cost' of £13. It might seem very unfair of a buyer to ask for a price of, say, £10 per unit.

3.26 However, as we have already seen, this analysis would be quite misleading. Once the breakeven point has been passed fixed costs drop out of the equation – they have already been paid. The true benchmark is the **variable** cost of £6 per unit.

3.27 This example shows that buyers must be wide awake to what is meant by the idea of total cost. Otherwise, they will overlook opportunities for negotiating more favourable deals for their organisations. Of course, a buyer will not necessarily press his supplier for a selling price of £6 in this instance, especially if he is looking for a long-term relationship. This is because, for long-term, large-volume business the supplier cannot afford this kind of pricing (referred to as **contribution pricing** in guidance published by CIPS). He must, in general, price his products at a level sufficient to cover total costs and to make a profit. But the example shows the scope that a buyer may have for achieving a very good deal on a one-off basis, or when a supplier is looking to generate goodwill in the buyer as a basis for a longer-term deal.

3.28 In the previous chapter, we asked what is the breakeven sales volume for a company with fixed costs of £5,000 and unit contribution of £0.60. You should by now be able to calculate that the company must sell about 8,334 units to break even (£5,000 ÷ £0.60 = 8,334).

3.29 One final point about fixed and variable costs should have become apparent from the discussion above, but we will make it explicit here. That is that a supplier with a high level of fixed costs is at greater risk than one with relatively low fixed costs if the economy takes a turn for the worse. We can illustrate this as follows.

3.30 Suppose Company A makes annual sales of £1m, variable costs amount to 20 per cent of sales, and fixed costs are £600,000. Company A therefore makes a contribution of £800,000 per year (80% × £1m) and a profit of £200,000 per year.

3.31 Now suppose that trading deteriorates and sales drop to only £700,000. Contribution (80% × £700,000 = £560,000) is insufficient to cover the high fixed costs and the company suffers a loss of £40,000.

3.32 Contrast Company B, which also makes sales of £1m per year, but whose cost structure is different: relatively high variable costs of 50 per cent, but much lower fixed costs of £300,000. At this level of sales Company B makes the same profit – £200,000 – as Company A. But if sales fall to £700,000 Company B is much better placed. Contribution, at 50 per cent of £700,000 = £350,000, is still sufficient to cover the low fixed costs and the company remains in profit.

Chapter summary

- For a retailer the cost of goods sold is simply the purchase price charged by the supplier. For a manufacturer things are more complicated. Total cost includes both materials and conversion costs.

- The amount of profit is referred to as a mark-up when it is expressed as a percentage of cost. It is referred to as a margin when it is expressed as a percentage of selling price.

- Suppliers often set their selling prices by establishing their total costs and adding on an element for profit. This process is called 'cost-plus pricing'.

- Target costing is different. Instead of establishing costs and adding on a profit element to arrive at selling price, we set the selling price at what the market will stand. We then work back to establish what cost level must be achieved to ensure a viable profit is made. This is an example of a 'market pricing' strategy.

- The total contribution earned by a supplier must be at least sufficient to cover his fixed costs (otherwise he makes a loss). The sales level at which this is achieved exactly is called the breakeven point.

- The margin of safety is the difference between the planned sales level and the breakeven sales level.

- A business with a high level of fixed costs must work very hard to achieve a breakeven sales level. This gives opportunities to a buyer. Moreover, once the supplier has passed the breakeven level, the relatively low level of variable costs again enables a buyer to obtain a favourable price.

Self-test questions

1   What is meant by conversion costs? (1.3)

2   If costs are £160, and the mark-up is 25%, what is the amount of profit? What profit margin does this represent? (1.11, 1.12)

3   Explain what is meant by target costing. (2.3)

4   What is meant by market pricing? (2.7)

5   In the context of costing, what is meant by contribution? Contribution to what? (3.7)

6   Define the margin of safety. (3.12)

7   Why have fixed costs tended to increase as a proportion of manufacturers' total costs in recent decades? (3.19)

8   Why is a supplier with a high proportion of fixed costs at greater risk when the economy takes a turn for the worse? (3.29ff)

CHAPTER 6

The Meeting

Learning objectives and indicative content

3.1 Determine the objectives and strategies for negotiation meetings.

- Integrative vs distributive negotiation
- Negotiation strategies
- Developing ranges and targets
- Best alternative to a negotiated agreement (BATNA)

3.2 Identify and explain the key elements of effectively managed, resourced and timed negotiations.

- Opportunities for conditioning
- Room layout/surroundings
- Psychology surrounding away or at home
- The supplier's position

3.3 Establish the bargaining position of the supplier.

- Parameters for negotiation terms and conditions (purchaser or supplier)
- Who is attending the meeting, why, and the level of authority they hold
- Positions and interests
- Power base
- Strength of the purchaser vs the supplier
- Size of the organisation

Chapter headings

1 Objectives and strategies for negotiation meetings

2 Stages in a negotiation meeting

3 Managing the meeting

Introduction

In Chapter 1 we looked at the different phases in the negotiation process. It is now time to examine the crucial phase in more detail. This is the moment when the parties come together in a meeting to discuss the issues and attempt to reach agreement.

1 Objectives and strategies for negotiation meetings

Integrative vs distributive negotiation

1.1   The general approach to negotiations has undergone a change in modern times, similar to the changes that have occurred in approaches to supplier relations. There is now greater emphasis on long-term relations, which in negotiations suggests a need for cooperative 'win-win' strategies: both sides can gain by arriving at the best possible agreement. This contrasts with earlier ideas (sometimes referred to in terms of a 'zero-sum game') that a win for one party must mean a defeat for the other.

1.2   'Long-term relations' is the key phrase in this context. So long as buyers were content to shift from one supplier to another in search of short-term gains, it mattered less that a legacy of resentment was left behind. But with long-term relations a negotiation is not a one-off process. The buyer will be dealing with the same supplier again in a month's time or a year's time, and it makes sense to ensure that when that time comes both parties are happy with previous dealings.

1.3   How can both sides gain from constructive negotiation? The main point is that cooperation along the supply chain can lead to elimination of waste at all stages. A buyer who focuses exclusively on one objective – say a 5 per cent price reduction – may miss opportunities to widen the discussion fruitfully. For example, by cooperating with the supplier in improved quality assurance measures the costs of assuring quality may fall for both sides. This may be enough in itself to achieve the desired improvements in profits without detriment to the supplier's margins.

1.4   Despite this modern perspective on long-term relations, it is not the case that negotiators will always seek a collaborative strategy. In fact the choice of strategy is sometimes regarded as a balance between two different considerations: the importance of the negotiation's immediate outcome, and the importance of the long-term relationship. Lewicki shows how these considerations can be mapped onto a two-by-two grid: see Figure 6.1

Figure 6.1 *The dual concerns model*

Substantive outcome
important?

		Yes	**No**
	Yes	Collaboration	Accommodation
Relational outcome important?			
	No	Competition	Avoidance

1.5 This model indicates that where we regard the long-term relationship as important our approach to the negotiation will be collaborative or accommodative. In other words, we will seek an **integrative** negotiation. On the other hand, where we are interested in a good result from this particular negotiation, and not specially interested in the long-term relational effect, our approach may be more competitive: we will adopt a **distributive** approach. (Refer back to Chapter 1 for the distinction between integrative and distributive approaches.)

1.6 Lewicki pursues this analysis by identifying the main characteristics of three negotiation approaches indicated by the model above. Lewicki's analysis is the basis of Table 6.1 below.

Table 6.1 *Characteristics of different engagement strategies*

Aspect	Competition (Distributive Bargaining)	Collaboration (Integrative Negotiation)	Accommodative Negotiation
Payoff structure	Usually a fixed amount of resources to be divided	Usually a variable amount of resources to be divided	Usually a fixed amount of resources to be divided
Goal pursuit	Pursuit of own goals at the expense of those of others	Pursuit of goals held jointly with others	Subordination of own goals in favour of those of others
Relationships	Short-term focus; parties do not expect to work together in the future	Long-term focus; parties expect to work together in the future	May be short-term (let the other win to keep the peace) or long-term (let the other win to encourage reciprocity in the future)
Primary motivation	Maximise own outcome	Maximise joint outcome	Maximise others' outcome or let them gain to enhance relationship
Trust and openness	Secrecy and defensiveness; high trust in self, low trust in others	Trust and openness, active listening, joint exploration of alternatives	One party relatively open, exposing own vulnerabilities to the other
Key attitude	Key attitude is "I win, you lose"	Key attitude is "What's the best way to address the needs of all parties?"	Key attitude is "You win, I lose"
Remedy for breakdown	If impasse occurs, mediator or arbitrator may be needed	If difficulties occur, a group dynamics facilitator may be needed	If behaviour becomes chronic, party becomes negotiationally bankrupt

1.7 Notice that we avoid negotiation altogether if we are not specially interested in either the particular issue at hand or the long-term relationship (the bottom right quadrant of the dual concerns model). Once again, Lewicki is helpful on this point: he suggests that negotiation should be avoided altogether in any of the following circumstances.

- If one can achieve the objective without negotiating
- If the objective is not worth the time and effort of negotiating
- If we have compelling alternatives to negotiating (eg a very strong BATNA – see later)
- If we risk losing too much by negotiating
- If the opposite party acts in bad faith or unethically
- If waiting may improve our position

Developing ranges and targets

1.8   In Chapter 1 we outlined the MIL approach to objective setting: goals we Must achieve, goals we Intend to achieve, and goals we would Like to achieve. The MIL acronym originates with Gavin Kennedy, but Kennedy also emphasises an earlier stage in the process. His point is that before we can begin setting objectives we must identify our 'interests': for example, why do I want this problem solved?

1.9   Kennedy's analysis thus distinguishes between what we want (our positions or objectives) and why we want them (our interests). Our interests are a major influence on our objectives, but are not an exact mirror image of them.

1.10   Kennedy gives the following examples of 'interests' in a business context – both very relevant to buyers.

- Becoming more profitable is an interest because you decrease the risk of unemployment if you are more profitable.
- Satisfying your customers is an interest because satisfied customers decrease your risk of unemployment.

1.11   The buyer's priorities leading up to the negotiation are to assemble relevant information, to establish his objectives for the negotiation, and to plan the strategies and tactics he will adopt in order to achieve them. Successful negotiators devote a great deal of time and effort to this phase. Research evidence suggests that the causes of unsuccessful negotiations can often be traced back to inadequate preparation.

1.12   The objectives of a buyer will not be the same in every negotiation. In some cases, the priority may be to obtain better financial terms (lower price, bulk discounts, enhanced credit terms etc). Sometimes the issue of quality is the key area of negotiation: the buyer may want the supplier to work to tighter tolerances. In other cases again, the key issue may be delivery schedules: perhaps the buyer is moving towards a just in time philosophy.

1.13   Where a relationship is ongoing, it may be that one particular issue has come to the fore as needing attention. Often though there are multiple objectives, and this will especially be the case where negotiations are with a new supplier or potential supplier. In these circumstances the buyer should clarify his objectives by ranking them within the MIL framework. Most negotiations depend on concessions from both sides, and this ranking procedure will help the buyer to determine where he can best afford to give ground.

1.14 To clarify this still further it is helpful to determine two parameters in respect of each objective: the best that the buyer can reasonably hope for, and the worst that he is prepared to accept. Consciously or unconsciously the supplier will be defining similar parameters. Where the two acceptable ranges overlap there is scope for negotiation. This is illustrated in Figure 6.2, which uses the example of price; however, the principle is equally applicable to any other objective such as quality, delivery lead time etc.

Figure 6.2 *Defining the range of negotiation*

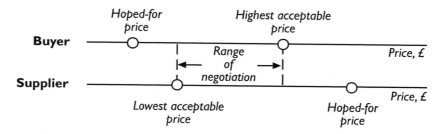

1.15 Figure 6.2 illustrates that negotiation is possible because the range of prices acceptable to the buyer overlaps with the range of prices acceptable to the supplier. If this were not so – for example, if the highest price acceptable to the buyer fell to the left of the lowest price acceptable to the supplier – then the negotiations would normally be doomed to failure. The only hope in that case would be that unexpected concessions elsewhere might alter the acceptable range of either buyer or seller. For example, the seller might offer new quality measures leading to lower inspection costs for the buyer.

1.16 This example reinforces the need for careful preparation. The fact is that good negotiators would not find themselves altering their range of acceptable prices as a result of such action on the part of the supplier. Instead, they would have anticipated some such possibility during their preparation and defined their range accordingly. The buyer who continually finds himself having to adjust preconceptions in the light of a supplier's proposals has probably not prepared sufficiently.

1.17 A further aspect of this same point concerns the assumptions that may be unconsciously built into a buyer's (or supplier's) arguments. The buyer must carefully examine what assumptions underlie the claims he makes. Unless he does so, he may find that the supplier brings such assumptions into the spotlight and challenges them, leaving the buyer unprepared.

Alternatives to a negotiated agreement

1.18 We have already seen one drastic alternative to a negotiated agreement: just don't negotiate! Refer back to the circumstances identified by Lewicki in which it is preferable simply not to enter a negotiation.

1.19 Assuming that we do decide to negotiate, we need to consider the possibility that we fail to reach an agreement with the supplier. To prepare for this, we must consider in advance what options will then be available to us.

1.20 **BATNA** stands for the 'best alternative to a negotiated agreement'. Buyers should always consider their best alternative before going into a negotiation. This enables them to be more assertive during the negotiation, because if they are not achieving objectives they have the safety net of a 'Plan B'.

1.21 This is an important consideration if negotiations reach a point where the supplier is saying 'Take it or leave it'. At this stage, you need to be quite certain of what your alternative is if you decide to 'leave it'. Otherwise, you can be bullied into accepting a deal that is unsatisfactory simply because you can see no valid alternative.

1.22 BATNA is closely related to the **walkaway position**. As Shapiro et al point out (in *The Power of Nice*) you must 'know where your bottom line is. How much will you give up to make this deal? If you don't face this hard question in advance, you may find yourself repeatedly lowering your expectations as the deal progresses. Be willing to walk at a certain point. But decide where that point is before you start negotiating'. This is sometimes referred to as the negotiator's **resistance point**, ie the point beyond which he will not be pushed.

1.23 Also relevant are **straw issues**. Steele and Beasor (in *Business Negotiation*) discuss this point. 'Have a list of things that will cost you nothing to give and bargain them for important items. You can talk up their value with effective use of emotion. Make a little seem a lot.'

1.24 Don't confuse straw issues with the **straw man ploy**. A straw man is an issue that is deliberately set up simply for the ease of knocking it down. As Kennedy explains, 'the straw man ploy alleges views that, in reality, are highly distorted from the truth or merits of the issue'. The negotiator refutes an argument that does not actually reflect the views of the other party. The other party has to be wise to this tactic, so that he can respond: 'Yes, so what you have proved is that X is not true. But I never said it was. My argument is that Y is true. You haven't addressed Y'.

1.25 Determining in advance what our BATNA is and what our walkaway position is can provide a safety net. If we stick to what we have decided, we avoid the risk of being carried away during the negotiation and agreeing a deal that in fact is unacceptable and does not meet our objectives. However, there is also a downside to this: we are unable to respond to new information coming to light during the negotiation meeting. To get the best results from BATNA, we should combine it with very detailed advance preparation. That way, the risk of surprise new information arising is minimised.

2 *Stages in a negotiation meeting*

Introduction

2.1 Various authorities have analysed the negotiation meeting as a process consisting of distinct stages. Representative of this view is the work of Baily, Farmer, Jessop and Jones (in *Purchasing Principles and Management*). We referred to their work in Chapter 1, but for convenience we repeat the diagram of their model below.

Figure 6.3 *The phases of negotiation*

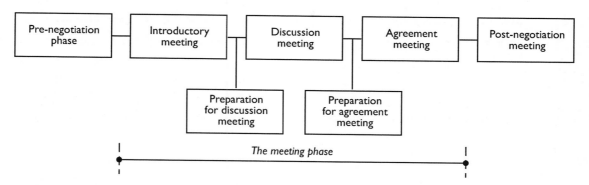

2.2 Lewicki goes further than this by distinguishing the stages in an integrative negotiation meeting from those in a distributive negotiation meeting: see Figure 6.4.

Figure 6.4 *Integrative and distributive negotiation meetings*

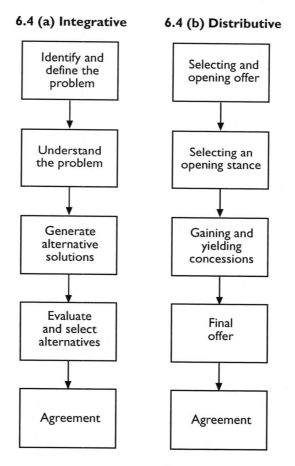

2.3 Lewicki also distinguishes between the tasks to be accomplished in each type of negotiation: see Table 6.2.

Table 6.2 *Tasks in integrative and distributive negotiations*

Tasks in integrative negotiations	Tasks in distributive negotiations
Create a free flow of information	Assess the other party's resistance points.
Attempt to understand the other party's real needs and objectives	Manage the other party's impressions: create an impression of your own position that will be favourable to your negotiation.
Emphasise the commonalities between the two sides and minimise any differences between them	Modify the other party's perceptions (eg by highlighting some adverse consequence that he has overlooked).
Search for solutions that meet the objectives of both parties	Manipulate the deadline so as to put pressure on the other party.

Integrative negotiations

2.4 Returning to the stages in integrative negotiations identified by Lewicki, we now give brief notes on each stage.

2.5 **Identify and define the problem.** According to Lewicki, there are five elements involved in this.

- Define the problem in a way that is mutually acceptable to both sides. 'For positive problem solving to occur, both parties must be committed to stating the problem in neutral terms.'

- State the problem with an eye toward practicality and comprehensiveness. Focus on the core problems and avoid distractions.

- State the problem as a goal and identify the obstacles to attaining this goal. The parties should focus on the goal to be achieved rather than on the solution process (how the solution is to be reached).

- Depersonalise the problem. Aim for dispassionate thinking, and don't assume that our viewpoints are inherently superior to the other party's.

- Separate the problem definition from the search for solutions. In distributive negotiations, the parties frequently work towards a preferred outcome. This can inhibit accurate definition of the problem, which is a primary aim of integrative negotiation.

2.6 **Understand the problem.** Refer back to the earlier distinction made by Kennedy between interests and needs. In integrative negotiation, it is important to identify the interests of each party.

2.7 **Generate alternative solutions.** This can be achieved by group techniques such as brainstorming. However, negotiators should also be alert for opportunities to redefine the problem as a means of creating new solutions.

2.8 **Evaluate and select alternatives.** Once again, Lewicki identifies the elements involved in this stage.

- Narrow the range of solution options – focus on those that are strongly supported by one party or the other.

- Evaluate solutions on the basis of quality and acceptability.

- Agree to the criteria for selecting an option in advance of evaluating the options.

- Be willing to provide justification for personal preferences.

- Be alert to the influence of intangible factors (such as gaining recognition, feeling like a winner etc).

- Use subgroups to evaluate complex options.

- Take time out to cool off.

- Keep decisions tentative and conditional until all aspects of the final proposal are complete.

- Minimise formality and record keeping until final agreements are reached.

2.9   **Agreement**. This will often be achieved by bundling together different issues so that all sides will have some issues on which they feel they have reached a good deal.

Distributive negotiations

2.10   Turning now to distributive negotiations, we again follow the analysis of Lewicki (refer back to Figure 6.4(b)).

2.11   **Opening offer**. Setting the level of the opening offer is difficult. Research cited by Lewicki indicates that negotiators do better to start with an exaggerated opening offer rather than a modest one. For a buyer, this might mean suggesting a very low purchase price, well below what he is actually prepared to pay. This leaves room for manoeuvre later in the negotiation.

2.12   **Opening stance**. The choices range from a belligerent, competitive attitude (fighting on every point) to a more moderate approach, with willingness to make concessions and compromises.

2.13   **Gaining and yielding concessions**. As Lewicki explains, 'Concessions are central to negotiation. Without them negotiations would not exist. If one side is not prepared to make concessions, the other side must capitulate or the negotiations will deadlock'. The pattern of concessions can reveal much about a negotiator's position. If successive concessions become ever smaller in amount, the inference will usually be that the negotiator is reaching his resistance point.

2.14   **Final offer**. Eventually a negotiator must make it clear that he is not prepared to go any further. He may do this by stating the fact explicitly, or by simply declining to make any further concessions until the other party realises that no more movement is being offered.

2.15   **Agreement**. Once a final offer has been made and accepted, the parties have an agreement. The task then is to implement it with commitment by both sides.

Resources for negotiation

2.16   There are three main resources needed to support a negotiation.

- Personnel. We must have sufficient staff, with the right experience and skills, for all stages of the negotiation. We must ensure that all personnel are fully briefed on their roles in the negotiation.

- Money. There must be an adequate budget for the essential costs that will be incurred as a result of the negotiation.

- Time. The negotiation meeting will itself require a possibly major investment of time, but this is likely to be dwarfed by the amount of staff time needed for full preparation beforehand.

2.17 The requirement for each of these resources will be partly determined by what Lewicki refers to as the **protocol** of a negotiation. This includes the following elements, each of which is briefly discussed in the paragraphs that follow.

- Agenda
- Location
- Time period
- Fallback position
- Keeping track of the agreement
- Assessing the agreement

2.18 **What agenda should we follow?** Negotiators sometimes prepare unilateral agendas as a means of preparing themselves for the main issues to be discussed. However, this raises the risk that the other party will have his own – different – unilateral agenda. For this reason, it may pay to negotiate the agenda ahead of the actual meeting.

2.19 **Where should we negotiate – home or away?** Most commentators appear to think that negotiating on home territory confers an advantage. The 'home' side feel comfortable with their surroundings, and have access to support from their own people and systems. To avoid conceding this advantage to the other party, it may be necessary to agree on some neutral venue for the meeting.

2.20 **What is the time period of the negotiation?** If the negotiation is expected to be a long one, it may be appropriate to agree in advance on the timing and duration of sessions, as well as arrangements for breaks.

2.21 **What might be done if negotiation fails?** One possibility is to invoke the assistance of a neutral third party.

2.22 **How will we keep track of what is agreed?** There is some advantage in being the party to keep the minutes. While this should obviously be done as objectively as possible, there is a certain latitude in framing the eventual agreement and a possibility of wording it slightly in our favour.

2.23 **How do we know whether we have a good agreement?** There should be a systematic means of appraising the outcome of the negotiation.

Opportunities for conditioning

2.24 The literature on negotiation covers a number of ploys designed to condition the opposite party in such a way that they are more amenable to accepting our position. This often happens in the initial stages of the negotiation.

2.25 The following examples are taken from Gavin Kennedy's book *The Perfect Negotiation*.

- 'Domination' behaviour. For example, we insist on preconditions before negotiating, or we insist that certain items are non-negotiable, or we attempt to fix the agenda unilaterally.
- Shaping behaviour. For example, using the 'tough guy/soft guy' approach we show personal willingness to accommodate the other party's point of view, but we make it clear that others in our organisation may take a sterner view.

Room layout/surroundings

2.26 As was mentioned in Chapter 1, a comfortable work environment is conducive to agreement.

The supplier's position

2.27 We always attempt to analyse the supplier's position before the negotiation begins. This was the subject of Chapter 2.

2.28 It is worth adding at this point that there are certain circumstances when a supplier's position is particularly strong. These are listed by Lysons and Farrington in *Purchasing and Supply Chain Management*.

- The buyer's requirement is urgent.
- The supplier is indifferent about accepting the business.
- The supplier is in a monopoly (or near monopoly) market.
- The supplier has a high reputation for quality and reliability, so that the buyer has little choice but to deal with him.
- The supplier owns the essential tools or machinery.
- The supplier is well briefed about the buyer's position.

3 Managing the meeting

Parameters for negotiation terms and conditions

3.1 The above caption appears in your syllabus at this point. It is not clear what it means, and the CIPS guidance for lecturers does not even mention the topic. A best guess is that there should be a colon (:) between 'negotiation' and 'terms', indicating that the terms and conditions of a supply contract define the range of possible negotiation for the buyer. This is discussed in Section 4 of Chapter 8 below.

Personnel attending the meeting

3.2 Lewicki uses the image of a football stadium to analyse the personnel who may be involved in a negotiation meeting: see Figure 6.5.

Figure 6.5 *A field analysis of negotiation*

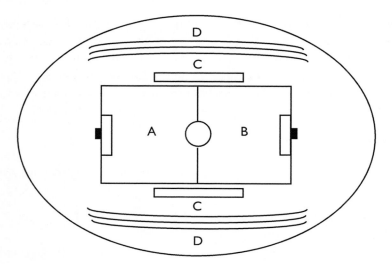

3.3   In the diagram, the personnel represented are as follows.

- A: the negotiators, appearing for our team – this could include support personnel, such as our legal representative, our accountants etc
- B: the opposition negotiators, appearing for the other team
- C: indirect actors, on the sidelines (people who influence our negotiators, and people who influence their negotiators, eg senior managers)
- D: interested observers – this could include shareholders, competitors, the media etc

3.4   The personnel on both sides will have been selected for their knowledge of the issues, their skills as negotiators, their past record of success in negotiations of the kind contemplated etc. In relation to the personnel appearing for the other side, our preparation should have covered the following points.

- Their likely objectives
- Their reputation, negotiating style and likely tactics (perhaps known from previous experience, or from contact with another party who has negotiated with them)
- Their BATNA and resistance points
- The level of their authority

3.5   The actions of both sets of personnel will be influenced by various context issues identified by Lewicki.

- The history of the relationship between the two parties
- The kind of relationship desired for the future
- Expectations as to whether negotiations with this party are likely to recur in future
- The deadlines surrounding the negotiation process
- The 'rules of the game', including common and generally accepted practices that govern negotiations in a particular cultural setting

Positions and interests

3.6 Refer back again to the point made by Gavin Kennedy about the distinction between our objectives (or our positions) and our interests (earlier in this chapter). Essentially, our position may be that we want X from the negotiation. Our interest is the reason we want X. The other party may not be able to accept our position, but may be able to see constructive ways of meeting our interests. That is the point of separating positions from interests: it opens up the possibility of alternative, creative ways of approaching the area of debate.

3.7 Lewicki points out (following the work of Lax and Sebenius) that there may be many different interests at work in a negotiation. He identifies substantive interests, process interests, relationship interests and interests in principle.

3.8 **Substantive interests**. These concern the main points at issue in the negotiation, such as price or the division of resources between buyer and supplier.

3.9 **Process interests**. These concern the way in which disputes are settled. Different negotiators may have a preference for distributive approaches or for integrative approaches, for example.

3.10 **Relationship interests**. These reflect the fact that each party may value the relationship with the other party. This could influence their approach to the negotiation: they may be unwilling to take actions that could damage the relationship.

3.11 **Interests in principle**. Both parties may hold deep convictions about what is fair and ethical.

3.12 It is common to find that in distributive negotiation the parties focus on their positions. Each attempts to impose his own position on the other, or at least to get an outcome as close as possible to his own position. By contrast, in integrative negotiation the parties will attempt to identify the underlying interests. This may lead to unexpected ways of satisfying both parties' needs.

Power base

3.13 Lewicki refers to a comparison (due to Ury, Brett and Goldberg) between three different strategic approaches to negotiation: focus on interests (as discussed above); focus on rights (based on a contract, or on general ethics and fair play); and focus on power. It is the use of power to coerce the other party that is of interest to us in this area of the syllabus.

3.14 Clearly if one party to the negotiation has greater power than the other there is an opportunity for coercion. This may occur in situations of distributive negotiation, but is not characteristic of integrative negotiation. In an integrative negotiation the more powerful party is interested in the long-term advantages that may accrue from an outcome satisfactory to both sides. He will realise that the exercise of coercion, while potentially giving him an immediate 'win', may hinder his long-term objectives by alienating the opposite party.

3.15 Between a buyer and a supplier negotiations are often distributive, simply from the nature of the situation. This can mean that power relationships are very important. In a negotiation between a large supplier organisation and a small buyer organisation, the buyer will inevitably feel pessimistic about the outcome because it may not be possible to resist the power of the supplier. In this context, power may derive simply from the **size of the organisation** or the **commercial strength of purchaser or supplier**.

3.16 Lewicki identifies the main sources of power: see Table 6.3.

Table 6.3 *Major sources of power*

Sources of power	Description
Informational	• Information: the accumulation and presentation of data intended to change the other person's point of view or position on an issue. • Expertise: an acknowledged accumulation of information, or mastery of a body of information, on a particular problem or issue.
Personality and individual differences	Power derived from differences in • Psychological orientation (broad orientations to power use). • Cognitive orientation (ideologies about power). • Motivational orientation (specific motives to use power). • Dispositions and skills (orientations to cooperation/competition). • Moral orientation (philosophical orientations to power use).
Position-based power	Power derived from being located in a particular position in an organisational or communication structure; leads to several different kinds of leverage: • Legitimate power, or formal authority, derived from occupying a key position in a hierarchical organisation. • Resource control, or the accumulation of money, raw material, labour, time, and equipment that can be used as incentives to encourage compliance or as punishments for non-compliance.
Relationship-based power	• Goal interdependence – how the parties view their goals • Access to or control over information, resources supply flows, or access, derived from location within flows in a network.
Contextual power	Power derived from the context in which negotiations take place. Common sources of contextual power include: • Availability of BATNAs. • Organisational and national culture. • Availability of agents, constituencies, and audiences who can directly or indirectly affect the outcomes of the negotiation.

3.17 The possession of power can make a party to a negotiation particularly persuasive. This leads us on nicely to the topic of the next chapter.

Chapter summary

- The dual concerns model suggests different approaches to negotiation depending on our concern for the substantive outcome and our concern for the relational outcome.

- Negotiation is only possible where the range of outcomes acceptable to one party overlaps with the range of outcomes acceptable to the other.

- A BATNA is a 'best alternative to a negotiated agreement'. Buyers should always consider their best alternative before entering a negotiation.

- Various authorities have tried to identify separate stages in a negotiation meeting. Lewicki in particular distinguishes between the stages in an integrative negotiation and those in a distributive negotiation.

- The resources needed to support a negotiation are personnel, money and time.

- The participants in a negotiation, apart from the negotiators themselves, include indirect actors (eg senior managers to whom the negotiators report) and interested observers (eg shareholders).

- Lewicki identifies the main sources of power in a negotiation: informational; personality and individual differences; position-based power; relationship-based power; and contextual power.

Self-test questions

Numbers in brackets refer to the paragraphs where you can check your answers.

1   What type of negotiation will occur if our concern for the substantive outcome is high, but our concern for the relational outcome is low? (Figure 6.1)

2   In what circumstances should we avoid negotiation altogether? (1.7)

3   Distinguish between interests and positions. (1.9)

4   What is a walkaway position? (1.22)

5   List Lewicki's stages of an integrative meeting. (Figure 6.4)

6   In an integrative negotiation, Lewicki describes five elements involved in identifying and defining the problem. List them. (2.5)

7   What types of behaviour does Kennedy describe for 'conditioning' the other party to a negotiation? (2.24, 2.25)

8   What context issues, according to Lewicki, will influence the actions of both sides to a negotiation? (3.5)

9   What are the four different types of 'interest' that may be at work in a negotiation? (3.7ff)

10   What are the five main sources of negotiating power identified by Lewicki? (3.16)

CHAPTER 7

Techniques and Tactics of Persuasion

Learning objectives and indicative content

3.4   Evaluate a range of persuasion methods and tactics used in negotiation.

- Threat, emotion, logic, compromise and bargaining
- Tactics
- Creating negotiation leverage
- The psychology of concessions

Chapter headings

1   Tactics for negotiations

2   Techniques of persuasion

3   Creating negotiation leverage

Introduction

In this chapter we look in more detail at the various techniques that can be used by buyer and seller in order to persuade the other party of the merits of his case. We begin by reminding you of the crucial differences between distributive and integrative approaches. We then move on to the tactics and ploys that can be used to persuade and to 'turn no into yes'.

1   Tactics for negotiations

Distributive approaches

1.1   In Chapter 1 we outlined two contrasting approaches to negotiating: distributive and integrative. The distributive approach is based on the idea that there is a fixed 'pie' and our only objective is to maximise our share of it. We do so by obtaining concessions which reduce the supplier's share of the pie. By contrast, in an integrative negotiation we focus on joint problem solving in order to increase the size of the 'pie'. You should refer back to Chapter 1 to revise the characteristics of these two styles.

1.2   In this chapter our focus is on tactical moves by buyer and supplier. Once again the distinction between distributive and integrative approaches is a useful one. We begin by discussing tactics associated with distributive bargaining. These are helpfully set out by Lewicki, on whose analysis the following paragraphs are based.

1.3   A first step is to assess the other party's target (ie his hoped for outcome), his resistance point (ie his minimum acceptable outcome), and his costs of terminating the negotiation. The buyer may simply ask these questions directly, if he thinks this will elicit reliable answers. Or he may proceed by indirect means.

1.4   As an example of this, a buyer may check out his supplier's published financial accounts, or may take out a credit check via a company such as Dun & Bradstreet. The objective would be to analyse the financial strength of the supplier and possibly to obtain information about his normal profit margins.

1.5   Another tactical task for the buyer is to manage the other party's impressions. As we have seen, the buyer wants information about the supplier's target, resistance points etc. But he is equally keen to withhold the equivalent information about his own position. And it may go further than this: he may actively foster a misleading impression in the supplier's mind. For example, he may seek to convey an impression that any price above £X per unit is totally unacceptable, whereas in truth it might not be.

1.6   Of course there is an ethical dimension in this. A straight lie (eg about the volume of business the buyer wishes to place with the supplier, in order to induce a more favourable price) is simply unacceptable. But selective presentation (putting forward information that strengthens the buyer's case, while suppressing information that weakens it) is not regarded as unethical, at least by most buyers.

1.7   Another tactical task is to change the supplier's perceptions. This means putting the supplier's own objectives in a different light – making them seem less attractive or more costly than the supplier had originally thought. If the supplier can be made to think in this way, he will be more ready to move his position, hopefully in a direction favourable to the buyer.

1.8   Lewicki suggests that this can be achieved by, for example, pointing out a consequence that the supplier has overlooked. Or, more controversially, it may be achieved by withholding information that the buyer is aware of but the supplier is not. Again, this is dubious ethically, and each case has to be judged on its individual merits.

1.9   Finally, Lewicki suggests that negotiators may be able to manipulate the costs of delaying or terminating a negotiation. For example, a supplier may be under pressure to achieve a deal by a certain deadline in order to meet sales targets. If the buyer is free of time pressures, he can exploit the supplier's anxiety.

1.10   Notice that all of these tactics assume that buyer and supplier are on opposite sides. If we were collaborating, we might be more prepared to share information and the element of deviousness in the above tactics would be out of place. This leads us on to consider tactics in integrative negotiations.

Integrative approaches

1.11   In discussing the integrative approach in Chapter 1, we noted that one stage in the process (according to Lewicki) is to generate alternative solutions. (You should refer back to Chapter 1 to remind yourself of how this fits in with the integrative approach generally.) Lewicki goes on to suggest tactical means by which such alternatives may be developed. These are explained in the paragraphs that follow.

1.12 One approach is simply to brainstorm the problem with a view to generating as many solutions as possible. Small groups of people throw out possible solutions without detailed examination of their pros and cons: that will come later. The objective is to think about the issue in a creative, freewheeling way, rather than being confined within the narrow limits in which the problem may originally have been framed.

1.13 Other techniques rely on redefining the problem. Lewicki mentions five possibilities: expanding the pie; logrolling; non-specific compensation; cutting the costs for compliance; and finding a bridge solution.

1.14 **Expanding the pie**. Instead of haggling over limited resources, the parties aim to find ways of increasing the resources available. For example, a buyer who can not obtain a satisfactory price from his supplier, but still wishes to do business with the supplier (eg because of his high quality), may consider ways in which he can increase the proposed volume of business. This may make the supplier more inclined to offer a keen price.

1.15 **Logrolling**. This means identifying different issues on which the parties have different priorities. A buyer who is not too concerned about Issue X may offer concessions on this point, in return for concessions from the Supplier on Issue Y (Issue Y being a low priority for the supplier).

1.16 **Non-specific compensation**. This means that a buyer may seek a concession from a supplier by offering some unrelated concession in return. For example, a supplier may be promoted to a 'preferred' list, increasing his chances of gaining future business.

1.17 **Cutting the costs for compliance**. For example, in return for a supplier's concession on price, the buyer may offer to bear all the legal costs of drawing up and agreeing the supply contract, both his own and the supplier's.

1.18 **Finding a bridge solution**. This implies a fundamental reformulation of the issues so that entirely new solutions may be devised. This is only likely to happen if buyer and supplier are strongly committed to working together.

1.19 With all these approaches, Lewicki emphasises the need for information sharing so that each party truly understands the other's needs and interests. This is characteristic of the integrative approach to negotiation, but not of the distributive approach.

1.20 Table 7.1 shows Lewicki's summary of the above tactical moves.

Table 7.1 *Refocusing questions to reveal win-win options*

Expanding the pie	1.	How can both parties get what they want?
	2.	Is there a resource shortage?
	3.	How can resources be expanded to meet the demands of both sides?
Logrollling	1.	What issues are of higher and lower priority to me?
	2.	What issues are of higher and lower priority to the other negotiator?
	3.	Are there any issues of high priority to me that are of low priority for the other negotiator, and *vice versa*?
	4.	Can I 'unbundle' an issue – that is, make one larger issue into two or more smaller ones that can then be logrolled?
	5.	What are things that would be inexpensive for me to give and valuable for the other negotiator to get that might be used in logrolling?
Non-specific compensation	1.	What are the other negotiator's goals and values?
	2.	What could I do that would make the other negotiator happy and simultaneously allow me to get my way on the key issue?
	3.	What are things that would be inexpensive for me to give and valuable for the other negotiator to get that might be used as non-specific compensation?
Cost cutting	1.	What risks and costs does my proposal create for the other negotiator?
	2.	What can I do to minimise the other negotiator's risks and costs so that he or she would be more willing to agree?
Bridging	1.	What are the other negotiator's real underlying interests and needs?
	2.	What are my own real underlying interests and needs?
	3.	What are the higher and lower priorities for each of us in our underlying interests and needs?
	4.	Can we invent a solution that meets the relative priorities, underlying interests, and needs of both negotiators?

2   *Techniques of persuasion*

How to apply influence on the other party

2.1   Lewicki argues that the effectiveness of our persuasion depends on the effectiveness of our communication methods. In this context it is worth looking at a model of the communication process: see Figure 7.1.

Figure 7.1 *The communication cycle*

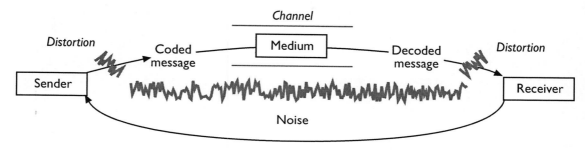

Feedback ('Message understood?')

2.2   In the model, the coding of the message refers to the language in which it is expressed, which must be comprehensible to the receiver. Distortion refers to the way that meaning may be 'lost in translation' as the message is received by the target. Noise refers to interference in the environment which prevents the message from getting through clearly. We return to this model in Chapter 9.

2.3   According to Lewicki, the key question is whether the target of our persuasion (usually, the supplier) is motivated and able to carefully process the message. If he is, we enjoy a **central route to influence**: this can lead to enduring commitment by the supplier. If he is not, we enjoy only a **peripheral route to influence**: this may secure short-term compliance, but not commitment, and the supplier will be open to counter-influences.

2.4   Lewicki also explains how we can secure the central influence rather than merely the peripheral influence: see Table 7.2.

Table 7.2 *Making messages central to influence*

Content	• How can the offer be made attractive to the other party?
	• How can the message be expressed in such a way that they say 'yes'?
	• Is the message in accordance with the other party's values?
	• Suggest 'agreement in principle'.
Structure	• Present the argument from both sides.
	• Present complex arguments in small components.
	• Repeat the message.
	• Conclude the argument.
Style	• Involve the other party by encouraging participation in the discussion.
	• Use metaphors to draw attention.
	• Provoke emotional response.
	• Say the unexpected.

Threat, emotion, logic, compromise and bargaining

2.5 One of the recommended texts for this module is *Business Negotiation: A Practical Workbook* by Steele and Beasor. The authors identify the above approaches to influencing suppliers, which explains where the syllabus caption comes from. They also mention a sixth option: acceptance (ie we don't influence our supplier, but instead accept his position – not necessarily recommended!)

2.6 Steele and Beasor explain each of these techniques as follows: Table 7.3.

Table 7.3 *Techniques of persuasion*

Technique	Explanation
Threat	An antagonistic method, which should be used carefully. May be veiled or explicit.
Emotion	This is the ability to make the supplier move by means of goodwill or similar feelings.
Logic	This is naturally a central tool in most negotiations. It depends on carefully marshalling facts and figures in support of our case. If logic is on our side, it is very difficult for a supplier to resist.
Compromise	This means finding the middle ground between buyer and supplier. Steele and Beasor describe this as an easy option and suggest that it should only be adopted if the buyer has given up on getting the whole of what he wants.
Bargaining	This is a method of extracting value from a deal by the exchange of various items that each party values.

2.7 The effectiveness of any of these approaches will, of course, depend on the context of the negotiation: the relationship between the buyer and seller, the buyer's orientation to negotiation, and the balance of power between buyer and seller.

2.8 Where the supplier is in a strong bargaining position, for example:

- Threat may be difficult (because there is little to genuinely threaten the supplier with) and counter-productive (because the supplier can simply walk away from the negotiating table).

- Emotion may be useful, if goodwill or similar feelings can be used to overcome the weakness of the buyer's objective position. Goodwill, for example, may be applied to make the supplier want to give generous concessions. More manipulatively, the buyer may attempt to make the supplier feel unreasonable in his position, or guilty for creating hardship for the buyer.

- Logic is generally an effective and ethical approach. It may be effective if it can be logically shown that the buyer's case also benefits the supplier. If this is not the case, however, logic may fail in face of the supplier's exerting his power.

- Compromise is generally a weak option. With the balance of power favouring the supplier, there is little incentive for him to seek middle ground – however desirable this may be for the buyer – unless emotion and logic can also be brought to bear to support some form of mutual concession.

- Bargaining may be effective, depending on the 'currencies' on the table. The buyer may have a number of 'straw issues' (see Chapter 6) which cost little to give, but which can be talked up, using emotion, to seem valuable to the supplier, and exchanged for items which are important to the buyer. Similarly, the supplier may be able to offer terms which cost little, but which meet the objectives of the buyer.

2.9 For any persuasive technique, ploy or strategy you read about (in this text and elsewhere), get used to thinking in contingency terms. In what negotiating contexts might it work best? In what contexts might it work least well, or not at all? How might its effectiveness be altered by relationships, currencies, personalities, ethics, power balances? What might be its effect on the relationship between the negotiating parties (and is this desirable or undesirable)? What might be its effect on the outcome of the negotiation (and is this desirable or undesirable)?

Tactics and ploys

2.10 There is much material in the purchasing literature on the subject of tactics and ploys. Often these are characterised by an element of deviousness, amounting in some cases almost to sharp practice. They are therefore more likely to be met with in distributive negotiations rather than integrative negotiations.

2.11 A representative selection of such ploys is contained in a short booklet by Gavin Kennedy, *The Perfect Negotiation*: see Table 7.4 (which also includes some examples from Lewicki).

The role of ethics

2.12 Over centuries of trading, from ancient times, the main guarantee of honest dealing was the personal integrity of the trader himself. Before the rise of the modern corporation most business deals were initiated and performed by individuals. Although there has never been a golden age of sea-green incorruptibles, it is still true that the consequences of dishonourable behaviour in business would be immediately attributable to an individual and his future would be at risk if his standards were dubious.

2.13 In those early days it must have been hard to separate the notions of personal integrity and business integrity. However, as economic activity passed mainly into the hands of large organisations there arose a distinction: individuals who were gentle and honourable in their private lives found themselves pressured by a business philosophy that all efforts must be expended to promote the organisation one worked for. In some cases, this was taken to extremes and an idea emerged that any kind of behaviour was acceptable if the good of the organisation was the goal.

2.14 Of course, there were always individuals who challenged this view, but at times they were in a minority. That situation has changed significantly in recent decades. Increased pressure from consumer groups, an increased hostility in society generally towards a perceived 'bullying' attitude in large corporations, and the advance in standards laid down by professional bodies, have all led to a higher level of ethical behaviour.

Table 7.4 *Persuasive ploys*

Name of ploy	How it works	How to counter it
Tough guy/soft guy (or good cop/bad cop)	The supplier explains how much he sympathises with your view, but 'unfortunately' he has a much tougher boss who won't allow him much leeway.	Reply in kind.
Salami tactics	The supplier can't get you to move on a large issue, so he slices it into a collection of smaller issues and tries for movement on each.	Salami back by attaching a cost to every concession demanded.
Add-on	The supplier makes out that the agreed price, which you thought was all-inclusive, in fact did not include various extras, all of which have to be paid for separately.	Insist on a clear statement of what is included.
Mother Hubbard	The supplier loves doing business with you, but 'the cupboard is bare' – they just have no further leeway on the issues under debate.	Refuse the deal if the supplier can't meet your objectives.
Russian front	The supplier presents two alternatives, one of them so awful (the Russian front) that you may be forced into accepting the other.	Generate other options.
Split the difference	The supplier knows that the midpoint between your two positions is favourable to himself, and uses this tactic to persuade you it is a fair solution.	The split need not be even – you can split a price difference of £10 in the ratio £9: £1.
Now or never	The supplier hustles you to accept quickly – 'we can't hold this price beyond today'.	Find out why – is it really credible?
Lowball/highball	The supplier begins with a ridiculously low (or high) offer, hoping you will re-evaluate your own opening offer.	Request a more reasonable opening offer.
Bogey	The supplier pretends that a trivial issue is very important, intending to trade this issue later for major concessions.	Prepare in advance so that you know which issues the supplier really values.
The nibble	When the deal is almost concluded, the supplier asks for one more (small) concession, not previously discussed.	Have your own nibble prepared in advance.
Chicken	The supplier makes an extravagant demand and bluffs that it must be accepted 'or else'.	Use external experts to evaluate the threat.
Snow job	The supplier overwhelms the buyer with confusing information.	Keep asking questions until you get an answer you can understand.

2.15 Supporting these developments has been a realisation among top management that unethical behaviour is in any case not productive. Although a short-term advantage may result, in the long term the firm benefits more from being, and being seen to be, strictly ethical. The old yardstick of (short-term) profit has been exposed as not the most valuable criterion of effectiveness, and attention has shifted to a measurement system in which multiple criteria are adopted.

2.16 Nowadays, policies on ethical behaviour are considered an essential element in strategic management. This, and the importance rightly accorded to these issues by professional bodies, makes it vital that you study this area closely. Notice as you do so that the appearance of inappropriate behaviour is often as damaging as actual abuse: even untrue rumours of unethical behaviour can damage your firm and your profession.

Professional codes of practice

2.17 Buyers are more exposed to temptation than most professionals. They control large sums of organisational funds. They are engaged in decisions between one supplier and another, all such suppliers having an interest in influencing the buyer's decision. It is difficult to determine wholly objective criteria for deciding between rival suppliers, and non-objective criteria may enter by the back door. This places great responsibility on the buyer's shoulders.

2.18 National and international bodies representing purchasing professionals have published codes of practice setting out (usually in fairly broad terms) what activities are considered unethical and giving general guidance on the ethical performance expected of members. A starting point in studying this area is a consideration of the ethical code published by the Chartered Institute of Purchasing and Supply.

2.19 The code makes it clear that seeking membership of the Institute is in itself an undertaking to abide by ethical standards. Failure to do so may be punishable by disciplinary process.

2.20 Not surprisingly, the guidance emphasises the overriding principle that members should not use a position of authority for personal gain. Equally, members have a responsibility to uphold the standing of the Institute by their behaviour both inside and outside their employing organisations.

2.21 Specific guidance is also offered in the following areas.

- Members must declare any personal interest which might impinge on their work activities, or which might appear to do so in the eyes of others.
- Members must respect confidentiality of information and must not use information received for personal gain. The information they provide should be true and fair.
- Members should avoid any arrangements which might prevent fair competition.
- Except for small-value items, business gifts should not be accepted.
- Only modest hospitality should be accepted. Members should not accept hospitality which might influence a business decision, or which might appear to do so.
- Any doubt on these last two points should be discussed with the individual's superior.

2.22 The source of our ethical concerns is an area of debate raised by Lewicki. He identifies four sources of moral standards.

- **End-results ethics** are based on the consequences of our actions. An action is good if its consequences, on the whole, are good.

- **Rule ethics** are based on compliance with laws and standards. In the context of buyers and suppliers this would include both general legislation (eg in relation to health and safety) and the specific terms of a supply contract. An action is good if it is within the laid-down rules.

- **Social contract ethics** are based on compliance with prevailing customs and norms. In the context of buyers, this would include current 'best practice' as specified by codes of professional practice. An action is good if it meets these requirements, bad otherwise.

- **Personalistic ethics** are based on one's own innate sense of right and wrong. This of course is extremely subjective, and it would be difficult to lay down rules of commercial behaviour based on this source of ethics.

2.23 Also relevant to the topic of ethics is the question of how to uncover any unethical practices effected by the other party. Once again Lewicki is helpful: see Table 7.5, which is Lewicki's adaptation of earlier research.

Table 7.5 *Detecting deception*

Tactic	Explanation and examples
Intimidation	Force the other to admit he is using deception by intimidating him into telling the truth. Make a no-nonsense accusation of the other. Criticise the other. Hammer the other with challenging questions. Feign indifference to what he has to say ('I'm not interested in anything you have to say on the matter').
Futility portrayal	Emphasise the futility and impending danger associated with continued deceit: 'The truth will come out someday,' 'Don't dig the hole deeper by trying to cover it up', 'If you try to cover it up, it will only be worse in the future', 'You are all alone in your deception.'
Discomfort and relief	State the maxim, 'Confession is good for the soul'. Help the other reduce the tension and stress associated with being a known deceiver.
Bluffing	Lie to the other to make him believe you have uncovered his deception: 'Your sins are about to be uncovered'. Indicate that you know what he knows but will not discuss it.
Gentle prods	Encourage the other to keep talking so that he gives you information that may help you separate true facts from deceptions. Ask him to elaborate on the topic being discussed. Ask questions but indicate that you are asking because 'other people want to know'. Play devil's advocate and ask playful questions. Praise the other so as to give him confidence and support that may lead to information sharing.
Minimisation	Play down the significance of any deceptive act. Help the other find excuses for why he was deceptive; minimise the consequences of the action; indicate that others have done worse; shift the blame to someone else.

Tactic	Explanation and examples
Contradiction	Get the other to tell his story fully in order to discover more information that will allow you to discover inconsistencies and contradictions in his comments or reports. Point out and ask for explanations about apparent contradictions. Ask the speaker the same question several times and look for inconsistencies in his response. Present contradictions back and ask the speaker to explain. Put pressure on the speaker and get him to slip up or say things he doesn't want to say.
Altered information	Alter information and hopefully trick the other into revealing deception. Exaggerate what you believe is the deception, hoping that the other will jump in to 'correct' the statement. Ask the suspected deceiver a question containing incorrect information and hope he corrects you.
A chink in the defence	Try to get the other to admit a small or partial lie about some information, and use this to push for admission of a larger lie: 'If you lied about this one little thing, how do I know you have not lied about other things?'
Self-disclosure	Reveal a number of things about yourself, including, perhaps, dishonesty on your own part, hoping the other will begin to trust you and reciprocate with disclosures of dishonesty.
Point out deception cues	Point out behaviours you detect in the other that might be an indication he is lying: sweating, nervousness, change of voice, inability to make eye contact, and so on.
Concern	Indicate your true concern for the other's welfare: 'You are important to me', 'I care deeply about you', 'I feel your pain'.
Keeping the *status quo*	Admonish the other to be truthful in order to maintain his good name. 'What will people think?' Appeal to his pride and desire to maintain a good reputation.
Direct approach	'Simply tell me the truth'. 'Let's be honest here'. 'Surely you have no objection to telling me everything you know.'
Silence	Create a 'verbal vacuum' that makes the other uncomfortable and gets him to talk and disclose information. When he tells a lie, simply maintain direct eye contact but remain silent.

3 Creating negotiation leverage

Managing conflict

3.1 The nature and effects of conflict have been frequently studied, mostly in the context of single organisations. However, the academic analysis of intra-organisational conflict can easily be adapted to provide insights into conflict between buyers and suppliers in different organisations.

3.2   Conflict can be highly desirable. It can energise relationships and clarify issues. John Hunt suggests that conflict is constructive, when its effect is to:

- Introduce different solutions to problems
- Define power relationships more clearly
- Encourage creativity and the testing of ideas
- Focus attention on individual contributions
- Bring emotions out into the open
- Provide opportunity for catharsis: the release of hostile feelings that might otherwise be repressed

3.3   Conflict can also be destructive, negative and damaging. Hunt suggests that conflict of this kind may act to:

- Distract attention from the task
- Polarise views and 'dislocate' the parties concerned
- Subvert objectives in favour of secondary goals
- Encourage defensive or 'spoiling' behaviour
- Result in disintegration of the relationship
- Stimulate emotional, win-lose conflicts, or hostility

3.4   There are many approaches to the management of conflict and the suitability of any given approach must be judged according to its relevance to a particular situation. There is no 'right way'. In some situations, the best outcome may be achieved by compromise; in others, imposition of a win-lose solution may be required; in others, the process of seeking a win-win solution, whatever the eventual outcome, may be helpful.

3.5   Robbins provides the following classification of possible strategies for resolving conflict.

Table 7.6 *Robbins's strategies for resolving conflict*

Problem-solving	The parties are brought together to find a solution to the particular issue
Superordinate goals	The parties are encouraged to see the bigger picture and identify shared goals that override their differences
Expansion of resources	Resources are freed and mobilised to meet both parties' needs, eliminating the need for competition
Avoidance	One or both parties withdraws from the conflict or denies/conceals the incompatibility
Smoothing	One or both parties plays down the differences and 'papers over the cracks'
Compromise	Bargaining, negotiating and conciliating, so that each party makes some concessions in order to obtain some gains
Altering the human variable	Effort is made to change the attitudes, beliefs and perceptions underlying the conflict

3.6 Another useful model for conflict resolution is the win-win model. Cornelius and Faire (*Everyone Can Win*) suggest that there are three basic ways in which a conflict or disagreement can be worked out.

- **Win-lose**: one party gets what he wants at the expense of the other party. However well justified such a solution is, there is often lingering resentment on the part of the 'losing' party, which may begin to damage working relationships.

- **Lose-lose**: neither party gets what he really wants. Compromise comes into this category. However logical such a solution is, there is often resentment and dissatisfaction on both sides: even positive compromises only result in half-satisfied needs.

- **Win-win**: both parties get as close as possible to what they really want. Whether or not the outcome is possible, the approach generates more options, more creative problem-solving, more open communication, enhanced cooperation and preserved working relationships.

3.7 Cornelius and Faire outline a win-win approach as follows.

- **Step 1: find out why each party needs what they say they want**. Getting to the other party's fears and needs in the situation facilitates meaningful problem-solving. It also encourages communication, supports other people's values, and separates the problem from the personalities involved.

- **Step 2: find out where the differences dovetail**. Diverging needs may seem like the cause of conflict – but they also offer potential for problem-solving, since the different needs may not be mutually exclusive, but may dovetail at some point.

- **Step 3: design new options**, where everyone gets more of what they need. Techniques include: brainstorming; chunking (breaking a big problem down into manageable chunks and seeking solutions to those); and devising usable 'currencies' (suggestions and concessions which are easy or low-cost for both parties, and can be traded). The aim is mutual gain.

- **Step 4: cooperate**. Treat the other person as a partner, not an opponent.

3.8 The example given is of two men fighting over an orange. The win-win approach would ask each man why he needs the orange. One may want to make orange juice, while the other wants the skin of the orange to make candied peel: the conflict disappears. If they both want the juice, other options will be explored: sharing the juice; getting more oranges; diluting the juice; buying one man some bottled orange juice and so on. Even if compromise is settled on, the outcome will be a win-win, because both parties will have been fully assertive and willingly cooperative, enhancing the relationship between them (which adds to the 'win' outcome).

The psychology of concessions

3.9 Lewicki discusses the way in which a buyer can analyse the pattern of concessions made by a supplier. His main point is that a series of concessions at the same monetary value suggest that the supplier still has room for manoeuvre; the buyer should therefore continue to seek further concessions. By contrast, a pattern of reducing concessions may suggest that the supplier is approaching his resistance point; the buyer cannot (if he believes the supplier) expect to gain much more ground in the negotiation.

3.10   This can be illustrated graphically: see Figure 7.2.

Figure 7.2 *Patterns of concessions*

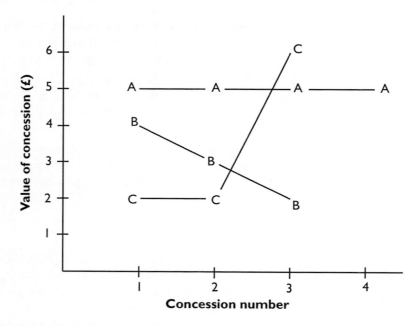

3.11   Supplier A has made four concessions, each with a value of £5. On the above analysis, it looks as though there is still plenty to be gained by seeking further concessions.

3.12   Supplier B has made three concessions valued at £4, £3 and £2 respectively. Applying Lewicki's analysis again, it is likely that this supplier is reaching his resistance point.

3.13   Finally, there is Supplier C. After two small concessions (each valued at £2), he is suddenly offering a large concession (valued at £6). This suggests either that he is engaged in some kind of tactical ploy, or that he has made a bad mistake and is now rectifying it.

Gaining commitment

3.14   Once all the persuasion and ploys have been exhausted, how do we gain commitment to a final deal? Once again, Lewicki provides the answer. In relation to distributive negotiations, he suggests the following five possibilities: provide alternatives; assume the close; split the difference; exploding offers; and sweeteners.

3.15   **Provide alternatives**. Suppliers like to have choices. A buyer can offer two or more variations of the intended final deal, each more or less equivalent in value in his own eyes, and ask the supplier to choose whichever suits him best.

3.16   **Assume the close**. This is a technique much used by suppliers: buyers beware! Before the buyer has even agreed the deal, the sales person starts completing the paperwork, as though agreement had already been reached.

3.17   **Split the difference**. This may be a sensible compromise, but on the other hand it may favour one party more than the other. We discussed this point in Chapter 1.

3.18 **Exploding offers**. This is an offer stated to be open for only a very limited time. The aim is to encourage acceptance by the other party before he has any opportunity to shop around for alternatives.

3.19 **Sweeteners**. When agreement has almost been reached, one party makes a final attractive concession that he has held 'up his sleeve' from the beginning.

3.20 As we mentioned earlier, these techniques are unlikely to be found in integrative negotiation. Apart from the first one, they all involve more or less 'hustling' the other party, which is not in the spirit of the integrative approach.

Chapter summary

- Lewicki identifies a number of tactical tasks to be undertaken by a buyer in a distributive negotiation: assess the supplier's target and resistance point; manage the supplier's impressions; change the supplier's perceptions; manipulate the costs of delay or termination.

- And similarly in an integrative negotiation: brainstorming alternative solutions; expanding the pie; logrolling; non-specific compensation; cutting the costs for compliance; finding a bridge solution.

- The effectiveness of a buyer's persuasion depends on whether the supplier is motivated and able to carefully process the message.

- Steele and Beasor identify five techniques of persuasion: threat, emotion, logic, compromise and bargaining.

- Buyers are exposed to financial temptation more than most professionals. The CIPS ethical code gives guidance on how buyers must behave in this area.

- Lewicki identifies four sources of moral standards: end-results ethics; rule ethics; social contract ethics; personalistic ethics.

- In some circumstances conflict can be desirable. For example, it can help to encourage creativity. In other circumstances it may be destructive. Either way, conflict must be managed effectively.

- Robbins identifies strategies for resolving conflict: problem solving; superordinate goals; expansion of resources; avoidance; smoothing; compromise; and altering the human variable.

- Cornelius and Faire outline a win-win approach to conflict resolution: find out what each party wants; find out where the differences dovetail; design new options; cooperate.

- To gain commitment at the end of a distributive negotiation, Lewicki suggests five possibilities: provide alternatives; assume the close; split the difference; exploding offers; and sweeteners.

Self-test questions

Numbers in brackets refer to the paragraphs where you can check your answers.

1   How might a buyer determine a supplier's target and resistance point? (1.3)

2   How might a buyer alter a supplier's perceptions? (1.7, 1.8)

3   What is meant by 'logrolling'? (1.15)

4   Sketch a model of the communication process, identifying the key elements in the process. (Figure 8.1)

5   How can a buyer secure central influence rather than merely peripheral influence in negotiating with a supplier? (2.4)

6   Explain the following tactical ploys and how to counter them: salami tactics; split the difference; bogey. (Table 8.4)

7   Why are buyers more exposed to financial temptation than most professionals? (2.17)

8   List examples of specific guidance given to buyers by the CIPS ethical code. (2.22)

9   What effects may arise from constructive conflict? (3.2)

10   List and briefly describe the conflict resolution strategies suggested by Robbins. (3.5)

11   What is meant by an exploding offer? (3.18)

CHAPTER 8

Closing the Deal

Learning objectives and indicative content

3.5   Explain how to follow up negotiations and finalise the deal.

- Informal and formal ratification
- How to evaluate the negotiation process and recommend improvements
- The importance of reviewing the ongoing relationship, including requirements and necessities to re-negotiate at appropriate intervals

Chapter headings

1   Ratifying the agreement

2   Evaluating the negotiation

3   The ongoing relationship

4   Legal requirements

Introduction

Arriving at an agreement is not the end of the negotiation process. The agreement must be ratified, and there is then the issue of managing the ongoing relationship. We must also consider what lessons have been learned during the negotiation process: this can help us to do better in future negotiations. Finally, we must ensure that we comply with any legal obligations arising from the agreement.

1   Ratifying the agreement

What is meant by ratification?

1.1   The word 'ratify' is defined as 'to give formal consent to [an agreement], especially by signature' (Chambers Concise Dictionary). Ratification in our present context is the process by which the negotiated agreement is formally adopted and endorsed by relevant authorities.

1.2   If negotiators are not invested with sufficient authority to conclude an agreement, the negotiation process is likely to be frustrating. There will be too many issues on which the negotiator has to refer back to his superiors, causing interruptions and delays. On the other hand, there must be some limits on any individual's authority to commit his organisation. Otherwise, the organisation might be obliged to carry out unduly burdensome obligations.

1.3   In practice, there is normally a compromise. Negotiators are given sufficient authority to discuss and agree on all points likely to arise in a planned negotiation, but with the proviso that the final agreement once concluded must be ratified by a designated authority. In a buying organisation, it might be that an agreement must be ratified by the Head of Purchasing or the Director of Purchasing.

1.4   This should normally be a straightforward process. If it often happens that an agreement is not ratified it suggests poor planning on the part of the organisation, and poor delegation of authority to the negotiators. The objective should be to ensure that the negotiators have sufficient authority to conclude a binding agreement, perhaps working within parameters laid down beforehand (eg 'In no circumstances are you to accept a price higher than £X per unit').

1.5   Lewicki discusses these issues in terms of a negotiator's **audiences**. For our purpose, the most important audience is the organisational authorities to whom the negotiator must report back. For simplicity, let us assume that this is the Head of Purchasing.

1.6   The Head of Purchasing will maintain control over the negotiators by holding them accountable for their performance and by giving rewards or punishments based on that performance. This will induce negotiators to favour approaches that accord with the Head of Purchasing's objectives. Often, this will lead to a tough, firm and unyielding style of negotiation, which in most organisations would be regarded as the most appropriate behaviour.

1.7   Lewicki also identifies that the role of the audience (in our example, the Head of Purchasing) can include control over the negotiators in terms of preventing them from making extreme or outrageous commitments.

1.8   To meet the needs of the audience, negotiators must be individuals who are capable of understanding and bargaining on all the relevant issues, and who are also capable of selling the eventual agreement to their audience.

Formal and informal ratification

1.9   CIPS guidance issued to lecturers distinguishes between formal and informal ratification.

1.10   A formal ratification is what we have been discussing so far. Negotiators take the agreement back to their 'audience' and sell it to them. If they are successful, the relevant authorities will be prepared to sign off the deal. This will only be possible if all relevant information is available. If information is incomplete, it will be impossible to ratify the deal.

1.11   Informal negotiation is more often found in internal negotiations and is therefore less immediately relevant to our interest in negotiating with suppliers. However, it is not completely irrelevant either: in many cases the internal negotiation will involve the parameters within which the negotiators are to act when the external negotiation begins. We say more about internal negotiations in Chapter 11.

1.12 Buyers will typically seek to win support from influential internal groups (finance, production etc) in order to get the best possible results from such internal negotiations.

1.13 According to the CIPS guidance, it may be appropriate to include in the eventual agreement a 'post-settlement settlement' (PSS) option. This means that the parties are enabled to return to issues they have agreed on with a view to subsequent refinement. In the case of an integrative negotiation, this may involve identifying the **Pareto efficient frontier**: see Figure 8.1.

Figure 8.1 *Creating and claiming value and the Pareto efficient frontier*

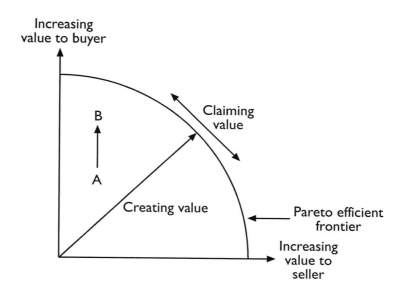

Based on Lewicki et al

1.14 The key features of the diagram are as follows.

- The radius of the circle indicates how much value we have created. In an integrative negotiation, we aim to push the radius outwards as far as possible, ie to create as much joint value as possible.

- Movement around the circumference indicates how the total value is shared among the negotiating parties. In our example, clockwise movement indicates an increased share for the seller; anticlockwise movement means an increased share for the buyer.

- All solutions – ie all negotiated agreements – lying on the circumference are Pareto efficient (or **Pareto optimal**). This refers to an allocation of resources such that no rearrangement can be made that improves the position of one party without damaging the position of the other party.

1.15 In case this final point is not quite clear (we are involved in subtleties of economic theory) imagine that our negotiated agreement is represented by the Point A on the diagram. This is not Pareto optimal, because it is not on the circumference. Maybe we were not clever enough to see how the deal could be improved for both parties, or maybe there were obstacles to an improved agreement (eg intransigence by one or other of the parties).

1.16   Because our original agreement is not Pareto optimal, we can envisage improving it. For example, we might suggest an improvement which moves the agreement from Point A to Point B. In doing so, we have increased value to the buyer without damaging the position of the seller. This would not be possible if the original agreement had been sited on the circumference, and this is what is meant by the final bullet point in our description of the diagram above.

2   *Evaluating the negotiation*

Recommending improvements

2.1   Hindsight is a wonderful thing, and we could all do better if only we could turn the clock back and start again. Of course, that's impossible – but we can gain some of the benefits of hindsight by evaluating our performance at each stage of the negotiation process.

2.2   In Chapter 1 we listed the various phases identified by Lewicki as parts of the planning process. For convenience, here is a brief reminder.

- Defining the issues
- Assembling issues and defining the bargaining mix
- Defining interests
- Defining limits
- Defining objectives and opening bids
- Defining one's constituencies
- Understanding the other party
- Selecting a strategy
- Planning the presentation and defence
- Defining protocol

2.3   In evaluating the progress of a negotiation the above list provides a useful framework. If things did not go exactly as planned, presumably we failed in one or other of the areas listed. Identifying where the failure occurred can lead to improvements next time round. (We pursue this analysis further in Chapter 11.)

2.4   However, buyers should not be blinded to other possibilities. It is not necessarily a failure of preparation if a negotiation goes wrong. Circumstances can change, both during the course of the negotiation and after it has finished. An outcome that looked satisfactory at the time may appear unsatisfactory in the light of later technological or market changes.

Planning for the next stage

2.5   Evaluating a negotiation need not wait until the end of the process. On the contrary, by evaluating progress continuously we can if necessary re-shape our approach to forthcoming stages in the process.

2.6   As an example, if we conclude during the 'bidding' phase that our approach has been too aggressive – perhaps indicated by an attitude of resentment evident in the other party's negotiators – we may want to soften our approach. Perhaps our target for certain issues in the negotiation were too ambitious or unreasonable. If this is the conclusion, we can modify our behaviour in the remainder of the bidding phase, and in the phase of closing the deal.

2.7   Of course, this does not mean that we should forget our original planning. If the supplier is showing resentment towards a target that we genuinely need to achieve, then we cannot afford to back down just to retain his goodwill.

2.8   The outcome of the final evaluation should be a written record covering the following points.

- A comparison of actual outcomes achieved with the objectives originally set
- A review of the agreement achieved, with analysis of goals achieved and concessions granted in order to achieve them
- An evaluation of the performance of both individuals and the team as a whole, identifying areas requiring improvement and/or training
- A checklist of points learned for use in future negotiations

3   *The ongoing relationship*

Benefits of good supplier relations

3.1   Once suppliers are on stream, it is important to manage the relationship carefully. It is not correct to assume that the legal agreement detailing the supply arrangement is sufficient to ensure the required standard of performance. Instead, buyers have a responsibility to motivate suppliers so that maximum value is obtained from the relationship.

3.2   One vital step in the process is to convince the supplier that the benefits are two-way. As a supplier becomes more familiar with the buyer's operations there is less scope for misunderstanding and mistake. There is also less need for direct selling effort on the part of the supplier. This frees up resources to concentrate on areas where cost savings can be achieved to the benefit of both parties.

3.3   From the buyer's point of view the benefits of good supplier relations are very tangible. The need to identify, appraise and train new vendors is avoided if a core group of trusted suppliers can provide most of the firm's materials requirements. Quality problems are ironed out over a period of mutual cooperation. In case of emergency, such as materials shortages or incorrect usage forecasts, suppliers will make every effort to help out if their goodwill has been secured by a systematic policy of maintaining good relations.

3.4   These benefits are most apparent when relationships reflect long-term agreements based on partnership between buyer and supplier. These give suppliers a strong motivation to perform to the best of their ability, because they know that the result will be a reliable stream of work. They also give needed encouragement if the buyer depends on the supplier to invest in research and development in order to provide state-of-the-art solutions to manufacturing problems.

3.5   In purely financial terms there are significant advantages to be derived from good relations with suppliers.

- As mentioned above, motivated suppliers are encouraged to invest in research and development. This frequently leads to lower-cost solutions.

- Use of multiple sourcing and competitive bidding involves the buyer in elaborate and lengthy communications and training with a wide variety of suppliers. The process is much streamlined, and waste is avoided, if just a few reliable suppliers are used instead.

- Long-term agreements mean that the supplier's production costs will fall as a result of the learning effect. This gives scope for price reductions that will benefit the buyer.

Managing supplier relations

3.6   Buyers have often given high priority to identifying and evaluating potential suppliers, while paying less attention to the management of supplier relations once contracts have been awarded. Partly this arose from a climate in which large stockholdings were accepted as an indispensable safety mechanism: if a supplier let you down, it need not be a disaster.

3.7   The discussion above has outlined why such neglect is to be regretted. An active approach to supplier management can bring benefits to both sides. In an era where stockholding is seen as an evil to be avoided, this is even more important because supplier failings have a proportionately greater impact. This section sets out some of the measures that purchasing specialists should take to ensure that such failings do not occur.

3.8   To minimise the possibility of misunderstandings buyers should adopt a comprehensive approach to the issues for discussion. These should not be confined to the terms and conditions of the agreement. It helps to look behind the agreed terms so that each party knows how the other is operating in order to achieve the requirements. This could involve discussion and clarification of any or all of the following matters.

- Timetable of stages in the operation
- Staff planning: grades of staff, estimated number of hours, arrangements for supervision etc
- Rules and procedures relating to site conditions, operations and safety issues
- Invoicing and payment procedures
- Buyer's responsibilities to provide tools, facilities etc
- Supplier's responsibilities for reporting on progress
- Procedures and timetable for review of progress

3.9   Once these initial procedures have been completed, it remains the buyer's responsibility to motivate the supplier. Of course the supplier should in any case be motivated by the thought of not gaining repeat business if performance is poor, but this is a somewhat negative factor. On a more positive note, many buyers have introduced systems of recognition for suppliers who achieve consistently high performance. This may take the form of private communication with the supplier concerned, or may be a more high-profile exercise involving publishing the names of selected suppliers.

3.10 Another method of smoothing supplier relations involves the provision of training. Many companies train their suppliers in techniques of statistical process control, just in time manufacturing and total quality management.

3.11 Another area of cooperation is in problem solving when suppliers run into difficulties. Instead of walking away with a shrug of the shoulders, buyers should be ready to accept that their own firm's success depends on the supplier's ability to perform. This should encourage a joint approach to dealing with the difficulties that inevitably arise during complex supply agreements.

3.12 This last issue leads on to another question: how closely should buyers monitor the progress of suppliers to ensure that all is going according to plan? Clearly, it is the supplier's responsibility to ensure that contractual agreements are fulfilled to the desired standard. However, this does not mean that the buyer can simply sit back and hope for the best. Particularly on large-scale one-off projects buyers should take an active interest in the supplier's operations.

Stages in relationship growth

3.13 If the supplier performs well, it may be that a gradual deepening in the relationship will take place. A helpful model for understanding this development is referred to as **key account management** (KAM). This model, as the name suggests, was developed from the perspective of marketers, but it can be turned on its head to reflect the perspective of buyers.

3.14 Table 8.1 outlines the stages in the KAM model.

Table 8.1 *Stages in the KAM model*

Stage	Explanation
Pre-KAM	Relationship is distant. Transactions are market based. Negotiations focus on product exchange and price.
Early-KAM	Exploration of potential for development. Buyer and supplier build trust and begin to communicate more freely.
Mid-KAM	Stronger social ties develop between buyer and supplier organisations. Joint systems are developed and negotiating focus moves to refinement of processes.
Partnership-KAM	Evolution of joint working teams. Integration of buyer's systems with supplier's systems. Joint problem solving.
Synergistic-KAM	Buyer and supplier organisations 'fuse' together in alliance. Buyer and supplier begin to align their respective strategies. Negotiation focus is on joint value creation.
Uncoupling-KAM	This can occur at any stage. It represents the dissolution of the relationship or a return to a former stage of the relationship.

4   *Legal requirements*

Are contracts necessary?

4.1   Most commercial relationships are formalised with a written contract, setting out the undertakings and the rights of both parties, the buyer and the supplier.

4.2   It has been suggested that a written contract should not be necessary, and is a sign of a lack of trust between the parties. If there is a dispute about the performance of the contract, the written contract will be used to establish which party is at fault, and what should be done to put things right. It can be argued that the need for a written contract means that the parties have some expectation that there will be a dispute about the contract. If the buyer and the supplier have a close relationship, surely a written contract will be unnecessary?

4.3   Further arguments against written contracts are that long and complex legal documents are costly to draw up, and adversarial in nature.

4.4   It is certainly true that where there is a written contract, and there is a dispute about performance, the contract will be used as a point of reference to establish what the rights and obligations of the buyer and the supplier are. However, written contracts have other benefits, particularly where:

- the purchase is a one-off transaction
- the buyer is using a supplier for the first time, or
- the supplier is relatively new, and the relationship has not yet had time to develop.

4.5   In these circumstances, written contracts can have a number of other advantages, as well as helping with the resolution of disputes.

- Either party can refer to the contract, in case it is in doubt about what it has undertaken to do.
- The product specifications might be included in the contract, in which case the contract will be an essential point of reference.
- A written contract can be a short document, and need not be long, complex, legalistic and adversarial.

The terms of a contract

4.6   For a transactional supply contract, or a supply arrangement with a new supplier, a written contract can be used to identify potential problems that might arise, and to determine in advance how these problems should be dealt with. Table 8.2 lists just a few such problems and how a contract can provide for dealing with them.

Table 8.2 *Contract provisions*

Potential problem	Contract provision
The supplier delivers the wrong quantity.	The quantity to be supplied, how the quantity delivered should be established, and who in the supplier's organisation should deal with any query.
The product is not made to the correct specification.	The contract provides the product specification, and sets out how rectification should be made in the event of the product not being supplied to specification.
The buyer fails to pay a supplier invoice.	The contract specifies when payments should be due, and perhaps provides for an 'interest payment' if the buyer pays after the due date.
The supplier is late with delivery.	How potentially late deliveries should be dealt with, and by whom.
There is disagreement about who should pay for transportation charges.	The contract will specify how the goods should be delivered and who is responsible for the cost.
The service might be performed or installation carried out by individuals who are insufficiently qualified.	The contract will specify the qualifications or experience of anyone carrying out a service or making an installation, and will state how the qualifications or experience of the individuals will be established.
Employees of the buyer organisation will be unfamiliar with how to use the item delivered.	The contract could provide for training of a number of the buyer's employees by staff of the supplier.
The product might be dangerous to handle.	The contract will specify how the product should be delivered and packaged, or what type of containers it should be delivered in, so as to avoid health and safety risk.
Changes may be required to the contract, relating to the specification, the provision of new services, design or performance measurement.	A variation clause, detailing the procedures that should be followed if changes are needed which still ensure value for money.
The parties may wish to vary the prices charged.	A price variation or contract price adjustment (CPA) clause, possibly based on a mutually agreed cost index.
A dispute arises	A dispute resolution clause, detailing the procedures that should be followed, such as mediation or arbitration.

Buyer's and supplier's terms of contract

4.7   After the contract has been made it is too late for either party to alter its terms unilaterally – such a variation is effective only if it is made by mutual agreement.

4.8   It is useful to consider some of the areas where the buyer and seller have opposite interests and therefore use conflicting clauses.

- Is it a fixed price contract or has a price escalation clause been inserted?

- If the supplier delivers late, will the buyer be entitled to terminate the agreement?

- Who pays the costs of carriage?

- Who bears the risk of accidental loss or damage in transit?

- When is ownership in the goods to pass to the buyer? Does the contract contain a reservation of title clause?

- If the supplier delivers goods which do not match the specification or which are not of satisfactory quality or fit for their purpose, will the buyer be able to reject them and claim damages, or has the supplier tried to exclude or limit their liability for such breaches of contract?

4.9   There are two ways of drafting terms and conditions of contract. The first is to deal only with those points where the buyer and supplier are changing the ground rules set out in the Sale of Goods Act 1979 (as amended). If this approach is adopted there will be few conditions of purchase since many of the obligations are imposed on the supplier by statute, eg the requirement to supply goods of satisfactory quality.

4.10   The second, more common, approach is where the conditions may re-iterate obligations, rights and remedies which would apply in any case. Thus, conditions of purchase frequently deal with compliance with the specification, fitness for purpose, rights of rejection, damages and remedies for non-delivery.

4.11   There are two good reasons for using the second approach discussed above. The first is that many small suppliers are not aware of their responsibilities and an express reference to their most important duties will put them on the alert. Secondly, in the event of a dispute it is often easier for the buyer to succeed if he or she can point to an express term of the contract rather than having to rely on an implied term.

4.12   Business contracts must not be viewed alone and the supplier or buyer must bear in mind that the other party may have some responsibility or right which is not specifically dealt with in the terms of contract. The printed terms and conditions must be viewed as part, and only part, of the general legal framework, both statutory and common law.

The buyer's responsibility

4.13   Naturally, the buyer must ensure that his organisation fulfils any contractual obligations it enters into. This may require liaison with other departments outside the purchasing function. For example, the buyer must ensure that the Finance department are aware of any terms agreed in relation to the due dates for payment; failure to observe such dates is a frequent cause of friction between buyers and suppliers.

4.14   The terms, once agreed and included in a contract, must obviously be ratified by both buyer and supplier: see Section 1 of this chapter.

Chapter summary

- Ratification is the process of giving formal consent to an agreement. Often, a deal agreed between negotiators may need to be ratified by senior managers.

- The Pareto efficient frontier indicates an agreement of maximum combined value to the parties. No rearrangement of resources can be made that improves the position of one party without damaging the position of the other party.

- It is good discipline to evaluate the outcome of a negotiation, looking separately at each stage of the process.

- The outcome of a final evaluation should be a detailed written record, including lessons learned for negotiations in the future.

- Buyers sometimes great efforts to identifying suitable suppliers, but then neglect to attend to the ongoing relationship once a deal is done.

- The KAM model provides a way of understanding the stages in a deepening relationship between buyers and suppliers.

- A contract between buyer and supplier includes both express and implied terms. The terms typically cover areas such as price, quality, delivery times, methods of dispute resolution etc.

Self-test questions

Numbers in brackets refer to the paragraphs where you can check your answers.

1   Define 'ratification'. (1.1)

2   What is meant by a negotiator's audiences? (1.5)

3   What is meant by a Pareto optimal outcome? (1.14)

4   Indicate how our evaluation of performance during one phase of a negotiation may influence our behaviour at a later stage. (2.6)

5   What are the advantages to a buyer of good relations with suppliers? (3.3–3.5)

6   List and briefly describe the stages in the KAM model. (3.14)

7   What are the advantages of a written contract? (4.5)

8   Describe two approaches to drafting the terms of a supply contract. (4.9)

CHAPTER 9

Skills and Attributes of a Negotiator

Learning objectives and indicative content

4.1   Evaluate the relative importance of verbal and non-verbal communications in negotiation situations.

- Reducing the potential for conflict
- Sales influencing tools
- The other person's perspective
- Body language
- Behavioural technologies

4.2   Identify and explain how to apply the attributes of a good negotiator to effective negotiations.

- Interpersonal sensitivity
- Characteristics of a skilled negotiator
- The emotionally intelligent negotiator
- How to improve negotiation capabilities

4.3   Evaluate the effect of effective listening and questioning skills in the negotiation process.

- Different types of questions
- Effective listening
- Timing of questions

Chapter headings

1   Communication in negotiation

2   Behavioural technologies

3   Attributes of a good negotiator

4   Effective questioning skills

Introduction

Section 4 of your syllabus concerns effective behaviour for negotiation. In this chapter we look at the main behavioural aspects, including communication techniques, personal attributes of good negotiators and the art of effective questioning (and listening). In the following chapters we look more closely at specialised negotiation situations and attempt to identify behaviours appropriate for each.

1 Communication in negotiation

Verbal and non-verbal communication

1.1 It is common to begin discussion of communication by presenting a model of the communication process. We have already done this in Chapter 7 (refer back to Figure 7.1).

1.2 The model depicts a sender (someone with a message that he wants to communicate), a receiver (the person the sender wants to send his message to), and a medium (a means by which the message is conveyed). The model also indicates how transmission of the message may be distorted by 'noise'. We will discuss this further below, under the heading 'Barriers to communication'.

1.3 In terms of the medium, your syllabus refers specifically to verbal and non-verbal communication. Verbal communication means communication by means of words (whether in writing, or face to face – oral communication). Non-verbal communication includes such cues as the following.

- Facial expression
- Eye contact
- Gestures (eg using the hands and head)
- Posture
- Proximity (how near you stand or sit to others)
- Personal appearance (including grooming and dress)
- Noises and silences

1.4 Lewicki asks the question 'What is communicated during negotiation?' In reply, he identifies five different categories: offers, counter-offers and motives; information about alternatives; information about outcomes; social accounts; and communications about process.

1.5 **Offers and counter-offers** lead to a narrowing of the differences between the positions of the parties. Eventually, if all goes well, this will result in an agreement.

1.6 **Information about alternatives**: research suggests that telling the other party that we have a good BATNA can strengthen our position and lead to a superior eventual outcome. It is important to do this in a polite, possibly subtle manner, rather than flaunting it in the supplier's face.

1.7 **Information about outcomes**. Lewicki recommends that we do not share our evaluation of the negotiation's outcome with the other party. They may be downcast if we are pleased with our performance, and this could affect our future negotiations with them.

1.8 **Social accounts**. Lewicki reports research indicating that negotiators are best advised to give explanations when their positions appear to be negative or to justify bad news. For example, they might cite mitigating circumstances.

1.9 **Communications about process.** If the other party is acting negatively, it pays to point this out explicitly, but it does not pay to retaliate in kind.

1.10 Lewicki makes the further point that communication exchanges take place at three different stages of the negotiation, which he labels initiation, problem solving and resolution. In an integrative negotiation the exchange of information is a much greater part of the overall process than in a distributive negotiation. In a distributive negotiation, the largest part of the process is the bargaining; this is a much smaller part of the process in an integrative negotiation.

Barriers to communication

1.11 Lewicki identifies four factors that can cause faulty perceptions in the communication process: stereotyping; halo effects; selective perception; and projection.

1.12 **Stereotyping** occurs when one party assigns attributes to the other party on the basis of the other's social or demographic category. For example, a buyer might decide that a supplier is disrespectful just because he is young. It is hard to break free from stereotypes once they have formed.

1.13 **Halo effects** are similar. On the basis of some slight factor (eg a smiling disposition) a supplier is regarded as a trustworthy, honest, open and accommodating negotiator.

1.14 **Selective perception** occurs when a buyer notices information that accords with a pre-formed impression, while filtering out information that tends to contradict it.

1.15 **Projection** occurs when a buyer assigns to the supplier characteristics that he himself possesses. For example, if the buyer believes that he would be frustrated in the supplier's position, he is likely to believe that the supplier is frustrated.

1.16 Lewicki also dwells on the issue of **framing**. This refers to the way in which we focus, shape and organise the world about us. Researchers now recognise that a buyer and a supplier may view the issues under negotiation in completely different ways, which can lead to unnecessary conflict. The way in which a party to the negotiation 'frames' the issues is a clear reflection of what they see as the main negotiating objectives.

1.17 For these reasons, negotiators should be alert to the possibility of altering the other party's frame of reference. For example, a buyer may be able to show a supplier that a proposed supply agreement is much less risky than the supplier supposes.

1.18 However, this process is bedevilled by problems of **cognitive bias**. This refers to errors we make when processing information. Lewicki identifies 12 categories of cognitive bias relevant to negotiations: these are discussed in the paragraphs that follow.

1.19 **Irrational escalation of commitment.** A negotiator may stick to a point of view through thick and thin, even though new information should convince him that the view is untenable. This may be caused by a fear of admitting error.

1.20 **Mythical fixed-pie beliefs.** A negotiator may view everything in win-lose terms. He may overlook the opportunity for an integrative negotiation, in which the size of the 'pie' may be increased to everyone's benefit.

1.21 **Anchoring and adjustment**. A negotiator may set an 'anchor' – ie a fixed point of reference – and may then be reluctant to retreat from it. For example, if a buyer is convinced that his opening bid on price is a sound one, he may be reluctant to move at all if he hears a much higher price quoted by the supplier.

1.22 **Issue framing and risk**. The way an issue is framed (see earlier) affects a negotiator's perception of risk. If the frame is unreliable, the risk may be wrongly evaluated.

1.23 **Availability of information**. Information presented in a vivid or compelling manner is more easily remembered, and evaluated more highly, than information presented in confusing detail. This occurs even when both sources of information are equally true.

1.24 **The winner's curse**. Negotiators often feel uneasy when agreement is reached quickly: 'Could I have done better?' The cure lies in good preparation – negotiators should come to the table with a reliable view of what is a good outcome.

1.25 **Overconfidence**. This causes negotiators to stick to their own views and ignore conflicting views expressed by others.

1.26 The **law of small numbers**. Negotiators may extrapolate from their own experience; for example, they may conclude that all negotiations are win-lose. If their experience is limited, this can lead to major errors.

1.27 **Self-serving biases**. A buyer tends to believe that a supplier's insistence on a high price arises from characteristics of the supplier ('he's tough on price') rather than from the situation (the supplier's cost structure makes a lower price difficult or impossible).

1.28 The **endowment effect**. This is the tendency to overvalue something you believe or possess. A supplier may believe that his product has quality features unmatched elsewhere; this will lead him to adopt a tough bargaining position that is not in fact justified.

1.29 **Ignoring others' cognitions**. A buyer may be uninterested in the supplier's perceptions about an issue under debate, focusing instead only on the expressed arguments. This tends to increase the likelihood of a distributive rather than integrative approach.

1.30 **Reactive devaluation**. A buyer may devalue a supplier's concessions for unreliable reasons (eg because he has found the supplier untrustworthy in the past).

Sales influencing tools: the use of language

1.31 Lewicki reports research by Gibbons, Bradac and Busch indicating that negotiation 'represents the exchange of information through language that coordinates and manages meaning'. By way of illustration, the researchers identify five uses of language in the making of threats. These are discussed below.

1.32 **The use of polarised language**. A buyer may use words such as 'generous' or 'reasonable' when referring to his own position, but 'heavy-handed' or 'unreasonable' when referring to the supplier's position.

1.33 **The conveyance of verbal immediacy.** The language chosen may be urgent and compelling, or distant and aloof.

1.34 **The degree of language intensity.** High intensity, possibly involving profanity, conveys strong feelings. Low intensity conveys the opposite.

1.35 **The degree of lexical diversity.** A wide vocabulary denotes comfort and competence in using language; a limited vocabulary suggests discomfort or inexperience.

1.36 **The extent of high-power language style.** Hesitation and exaggerated politeness denote low power. Clarity and firmness of expression suggest high power.

Other sales influencing tools and approaches

1.37 The topic of sales influencing techniques occupies whole volumes all on its own. However, the following are some additional approaches and tools which might be used by a supplier in influencing a supplier during negotiations. You might start by reviewing the earlier material on persuasion, considering how it might be applied from the 'selling' – as well as from the 'buying' – side of a negotiation.

- Persuasive approaches and ploys (see Tables 7.3 and 7.4)
- Use of concessions (see 'the psychology of concessions', Chapter 7)
- Pushing for 'closure' (see 'gaining commitment', Chapter 7, and 'pressure ploys, Chapter 1).

1.38 Other mainstream selling approaches (Kotler) include the following.

- **Conditioning buyer responses**: eg through image management, rapport-building, positive enthusiasm for the product/service, stated intent to benefit the buyer and offer value, 'tough guy/soft guy' team selling approaches and so on.

- **Need-satisfaction approach**: investigating the customer's needs by getting the buyer to do most of the talking initially – and then focusing the subsequent sales/offer presentation specifically to demonstrate how the product/service will meet or match the buyer's requirements.

- **Handling objections**: reading verbal and non-verbal signals and deliberately seeking out hidden objections, blockages or resistance; asking the buyer to specify and clarify objections; using objections as opportunities to provide information; and gaining agreement that the objection has been met (leaving the buyer with no logical ground from which not to proceed to close the deal). See also Table 9.3 later in this chapter.

- **Closing**: recognising readiness-to-close signals from the buyer (physical actions, comments, final objections and questions) and initiating closure by reviewing points of agreement, offering to help write up the order, injecting urgency (eg the buyer will lose out if the order is not placed now), adding final incentives (eg discount for immediate order) or assuming closure (eg requesting a suitable delivery date).

1.39 More sophisticated sales 'technologies' have also been developed, such as psycho-linguistics (discussed above) and Neuro-Linguistic Programming. NLP is based on understanding how sensory perception and language influence behaviour, enabling sales people (and other influencers) to act more intentionally to produce the results they want. Some key NLP sales/influencing techniques are listed below.

- **Pacing and leading**: 'walking alongside' by establishing rapport and empathy (reflecting back the other party's statements, summarising, mirroring their body language and so on) and then changing tone, pace and body language, or reframing the issue – taking the other person with you.

- **Utilising information processing channels**: determining how the other party prefers to process information (visual, hearing, touch/feeling). This can be used to establish rapport, by mirroring the other person's dominant channel expressions ('I see what you mean', 'I hear what you're saying'). It can also be used in convincing/influencing: visual people need to see evidence; hearing people need to be told; readers need it in writing; doers need to sample/trial.

- **Anchoring and mental rehearsal**: using conditioning and visualisation techniques to evoke resourceful states (confidence, calm, power) when required.

- **Re-framing**: putting things in different contexts (eg initiating 'imagine if'/creative problem-solving, or rephrasing or reinterpreting positions) to shift assumptions and generate options

- **Positioning**: shifting the issue upward (to higher outcomes/criteria), downwards (to details), sideways (to alternative options) or outwards (to other viewpoints), to shift assumptions and objections

1.40 It is worth noting that, like buyers, sellers are subject to professional ethics and regulation. Sales people must follow rules of 'fair competition' and 'fair trading': they may not, for example, mislead buyers about the advantages of a product or service, and their statements must match any advertising claims made. (In relation to consumers, there are additional protections in law against high-pressure selling techniques, such as 'cooling off' periods to reconsider purchase.)

Body language

1.41 We have already referred to aspects of non-verbal communication. Lewicki emphasises three particular aspects of body language.

1.42 **Eye contact**. Failure to make consistent eye contact suggests dishonesty. But it would be inappropriate to make too much eye contact: this comes across as staring, and may be perceived as threatening. As a technique of persuasion, it is important to make eye contact when delivering the most important part of a message.

1.43 **Adjusting body position**. To show attention, it is important to adopt an appropriate body position. Slouching suggests lack of attention or interest. Turning away may suggest rudeness.

1.44 **Non-verbal encouragement or discouragement**. Nodding the head slightly, murmurs of approval or interest, hand gestures encouraging the speaker to continue can all convey agreement or at least engagement with the other party.

2 *Behavioural technologies*

Negotiation behaviour

2.1   The behavioural style adopted by a negotiator can have an important effect on eventual outcomes. There has been extensive research into the styles of behaviour adopted by successful negotiators. For example, Lewicki cites the research of Neil Rackham: see Table 9.1.

Table 9.1 *Behaviours of superior negotiators identified by Rackham*

During pre-negotiation planning
Considered more outcome options for the issues being discussed
Spent more time looking for areas of common ground
Thought more about the long-term consequences of different issues
Prepared their goals around ranges rather than fixed points
Did not form their plans into strict sequential order

During face-to-face bargaining
Made fewer immediate counterproposals
Were less likely to describe their offers in glowingly positive terms
Avoided defend-attack cycles
Used behavioural labelling, except when disagreeing
Asked more questions, especially to test understanding
Summarised compactly the progress made in the negotiation
Did not dilute their arguments by including weak reasons when they were trying to persuade the other party

During post-negotiation review
Reserved time to review what they learned from the negotiation

2.2   Tracy Harwood (an influential researcher into negotiation behaviour) distinguishes between behaviours in integrative and distributive negotiations. Her analysis is adapted in Table 9.2.

Conflict behaviour

2.3   Conflict is a natural part of the negotiation process. Buyer and supplier come to the table with different objectives, and unless care is exercised these differences can break out into conflict. We have already seen that conflict can have beneficial effects (refer back to Chapter 7). But where conflict is preventing a satisfactory outcome to negotiations it is important to manage it constructively.

2.4   KW Thomas suggested that individuals' conflict-handling styles could be mapped on two dimensions, according to the intentions of the parties involved: their assertiveness (the extent to which they try to satisfy their own concerns) and their co-operativeness (the extent to which they try to satisfy the other party's concerns). The five key points on this map are shown in Figure 9.1. (We referred to this model briefly in Chapter 1 but repeat the diagram here for convenience.)

Table 9.2 *Behaviours in integrative and distributive negotiations*

Behaviour category	Integrative approach	Distributive approach
Scene setting behaviours	Establishing a climate of openness; generating information for problem solving; developing understanding on underlying interests.	Establishing or confirming power; generating information for later use distributively.
Specifying behaviours	Developing further detail on interests and positions; identifying difficulties and problems as part of problem solving and information exchange.	Buying time (by asking questions to get the other party talking) before moving to the bargaining phase.
Social behaviours	Developing the relationship between the individuals in the negotiation.	As for integrative approach.
Initiating behaviours	Procedural proposals are used more than other bargaining behaviours because there is greater openness about the process of the negotiation itself.	Bargaining behaviours are used extensively in distributive situations; counter proposals indicate that you have not listened to the other party's offer before making one of your own.
Reacting behaviours	Showing openness: seeking better understanding of the other party's response; supporting behaviour is used to draw the other party into further disclosure.	Communicating dissatisfaction with a comment or offer. Tactical supporting can be used to generate information for subsequent use. Defend/attack is aggressive adversarial behaviour.
Clarifying behaviours	Testing understanding of discussion; communicating active listening.	Testing (incredulous, rational) can both be used tactically to cast doubt on the other party's comments.

Figure 9.1 *Model of conflict-handling styles*

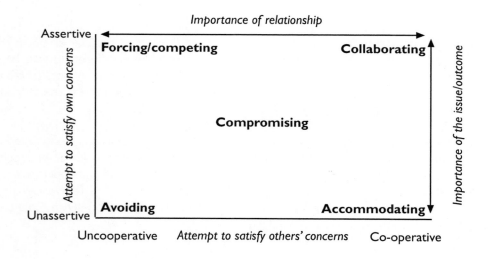

2.5   In **avoiding**, you withdraw from the conflict or attempt to sweep it under the carpet. This allows you to avoid dealing with conflict, and avoids immediate tensions: it may be appropriate if the issue is genuinely trivial, or you need a 'cooling off' period, or someone else is better placed to deal with the conflict. However, underlying problems don't get resolved: long-term frustrations and resentments may emerge in other ways.

2.6   In **forcing/competing**, you impose your solution on the problem. This allows you to get your way, and may be appropriate for issues that need winning: breaking down the inflexibility of others or implementing unpopular measures quickly in a crisis, say. However, the other party is likely to feel defeated and demeaned, and this can damage ongoing collaboration and trust.

2.7   In **accommodating**, you concede the issue without a fight, to preserve harmony. This avoids upsetting people, and may be appropriate where maintaining the relationship is more important than the issue (or you realise you are wrong!). However, you are giving permission for the other person to take advantage of the situation, and your authority may be undermined.

2.8   In **compromising**, you use bargaining or negotiation, so that each party trades some concessions for some gains. This reaches an agreement that both parties can live with, and enables you to get on with work: it may be necessary where power is evenly balanced and there is genuine conflict of interest. However, the solution is often more expedient than effective, and may leave both parties unsatisfied.

2.9   In **collaborating**, you work together to try and find an outcome which meets the clearly stated needs of all parties as far as possible: a problem-solving or 'win-win' approach. This assumes that both positions are important, even if they are not necessarily equally valid. It takes time, but at the end of the process, both parties should be committed to the solution and satisfied that they have been treated fairly. This facilitates learning, generates more creative options and encourages trust.

2.10   Note that there is no one best style: managers need behavioural flexibility! Thomas suggests that research backs collaboration as the best way to settle conflict. Derr, however, disagrees, suggesting that:

  •   Compromise can be a bridge between collaborative approaches and power-plays.
  •   Competition is a valid response to a different set of assumptions than those underlying collaboration. It may be necessary for solving ideological disputes, obtaining flexibility, avoiding vulnerability and establishing autonomy: in other words, sometimes you just have to 'stick to your guns'.
  •   Collaboration is a useful way to resolve conflict when there is at least a moderate amount of interdependence among the parties (so that a win-lose situation would damage both); a perceived equality of power exists between the two parties (so that both can afford to be as open as collaboration requires); there are mutual advantages to collaboration that can be seen by both parties; and the collaborative process is supported by the organisation.

2.11   Lewicki mentions another approach to conflict resolution, which he attributes to Ury. This is the **breakthrough approach**, used when the other party is being difficult. Ury proposes a five-stage approach: see Table 9.3.

Table 9.3 *Ury's strategies for managing difficult negotiations*

Barriers to cooperation	Challenges	Strategies
Your natural reaction to the other side's competitive behaviour	Don't react	Go to the balcony, ie mentally distance yourself from their tactics
Other's negative emotions	Disarm them	Step to the side, ie respond positively to their negative approach
Other's positional behaviour	Change the game	Don't reject, reframe the issue, to search for new solutions
Other's scepticism about benefits of agreement	Make it easy for them to say yes	Build them a golden bridge, ie make them an offer they can assent to
Other's perceived power	Make it hard to say no	Bring them to their senses, making sure they understand our BATNA

2.12 Lewicki also suggests that third parties (eg mediators) might be brought in to help the parties find a way out of their conflict. However, he emphasises that the use of third parties can increase the likelihood of win-lose decisions. He illustrates this by means of a continuum devised by C Moore: Figure 9.2.

Figure 9.2 *Continuum of conflict management and resolution approaches*

Decisions made by negotiators				Decisions made by private third parties		Decisions made by legal (authoritative) third parties		Extralegal decisions	
Conflict avoidance	Discussion and problem solving	Informal negotiation	Mediation	Administrative decision	Arbitration	Judicial decision	Legislative decision	Nonviolent direct action	Violence

——— Increased coercion and greater likelihood of win-lose decisions ⟶

3 Attributes of a good negotiator

Characteristics of a skilled negotiator

3.1 The individuals engaged in a negotiation will have different backgrounds, knowledge bases and skill sets. Their technical knowledge may cover different areas. But they have all presumably been chosen as negotiators because they exhibit characteristics which are thought to contribute to the likelihood of a successful outcome.

3.2 So what are the personal attributes that make a successful negotiator? We have touched on this subject earlier in the chapter: refer back to Table 9.1. Researchers have attempted to go further than this, and the list of characteristics identified by various different authors is a very long one indeed. The list includes such attributes as skill in preparation and planning, technical knowledge of the issue to be negotiated, clarity of thought under pressure, verbal expression, listening skills and numerous others.

3.3 In guidance published by CIPS for this unit there are two long lists of such characteristics identified by different researchers. The main conclusion to be drawn from such research is the lack of agreement on key characteristics. As an example, one of the lists cites 'preparation and planning skill' as the number one priority, ranked as 'very important'. In the second list, ranked only as 'important', this same attribute is number 11 in the list.

3.4 One topic in this general area has received especial attention in the literature: this is the difference between men and women as negotiators. Lewicki summarises six different ways in which researchers have purported to find stable differences between men and women negotiators. ('Stable differences' means that we are looking for differences that can be detected in all or most men and women in the negotiating arena. Obviously there will be individual differences that characterise particular men and women, but these offer no general insight into gender-based differences.)

3.5 The first difference concerns the **relational view of others**. Women are more likely to recognise the complete relationship among the parties negotiating. They are more likely to be driven by interpersonal aspects of the negotiation, whereas men are more likely to focus on task-specific goals.

3.6 The second point is the **embedded view of agency**. Women are less likely to differentiate negotiation from other behaviours that flow into and out of it. Men are more likely to see negotiation as having a beginning and end within a larger relationship.

3.7 The third point concerns **beliefs about ability and worth**. Women may have a lower estimation of their own abilities, which may make them less ambitious in the negotiation outcomes they hope to achieve.

3.8 The fourth point concerns **control through empowerment**. Men are seen as using power to achieve their own ends. Women are said to seek empowerment of all parties. This may make women more comfortable than men with the idea of integrative approaches.

3.9 The fifth point concerns **problem solving through dialogue**. Women are more likely to listen and contribute alternately, and to seek a joint exploration of ideas. Men are more likely to use dialogue to enforce their own position.

3.10 The final point concerns **perceptions and stereotypes**. Negative perceptions of women as negotiators may limit the outcomes that women can hope for.

3.11 Please don't berate us for listing these research findings! We don't necessarily agree with any of them – we just have to report them in case you are asked about them in the exam!

The role of personality

3.12 When we talk about 'attributes' or 'characteristics' that negotiators (or people in general) have, we are partly talking about personality: a concept used by psychologists to identify, explain and describe the ways in which people differ.

Personality may be defined as 'the psychological qualities that influence an individual's characteristic behaviour patterns, in a distinctive and consistent manner, across different situations and over time' (Huczynski and Buchanan).

3.13   Attempts to describe personality focus on two broad concepts.

- Personality **traits** are relatively stable attributes or qualities of an individual's personality which cause a tendency for them to behave in certain ways. If we say that someone is 'impulsive', for example, this trait will make them respond to situations in predictable ways: making rapid decisions, say, or saying what they think without pausing for reflection. We discuss the 'Big Five' trait model of personality a bit later.

- Personality **types** are descriptive labels for distinct patterns or clusters of traits which reflect their underlying psychological preferences. Type classifications include 'extrovert' (sociable, expressive, impulsive, practical and active: generally 'outward focused') versus 'introvert' (unsociable, inhibited, controlled, reflective, inactive: generally 'inward focused'). Lewicki highlights other categories such as 'pro-social' and 'pro-self', and 'high trusters' and 'low trusters', as significant to negotiation: again, these are discussed further below.

3.14   Identified personality traits and types can be used to compare, explain and predict negotiation behaviour. A person who is extroverted, for example (sociable, assertive and talkative) may make a good sales negotiator, because of his or her natural ability to build rapport and relate to people. On the other hand, it should be remembered that:

- No one personality trait or type is 'better' than another: all have strengths and weaknesses that must be managed for desired outcomes. The extrovert might have to train himself to avoid impulsive decisions, for example, while an introvert may make a valuable contribution to the negotiating team by focusing on problem-solving and analysing the opposing position.

- Personality only reflects preferences or tendencies: skilled behaviours can still be learned and adopted, even if they are not 'natural' to us. Hence, when we talk about 'attributes of effective negotiators' we are talking both about personality (what they are 'like') and learned/skilled behaviours (what they actually 'do').

Interpersonal sensitivity

3.15   Researchers distinguish between two main social value orientations (the terminology comes from Lewicki). Some individuals are **proself**; others are **prosocial**. The former are interested in personal outcomes and have little regard for outcomes obtained by the other party; the latter prefer outcomes that benefit both self and others with whom they are interdependent.

3.16   These two categories should remind you of the distinction between distributive and integrative approaches to negotiation. Proself individuals are likely to favour distributive negotiations; prosocial individuals are more likely to embrace an integrative approach.

3.17   A key issue in negotiation is the extent of interpersonal trust between the parties. Individuals differ in the amount of trust that they extend to others. 'High trusters' (again, the terminology comes from Lewicki) are disposed to expect others to be trustworthy and feel obliged to behave in the same way themselves. 'Low trusters' believe that the other party is likely to cheat, and may themselves be less ethical in their behaviour as a result.

3.18 There is a self-fulfilling aspect to this. If you approach your supplier with an attitude and style that communicates trust you are more likely to excite similar behaviour in the supplier. If instead you communicate suspicion and distrust, the result may be a less cooperative relationship.

3.19 A final point under this heading concerns what Lewicki calls the 'Big Five' personality factors. This is an attempt to focus on just a few key personal characteristics instead of examining numerous unrelated factors in the make-up of negotiators. The idea is that most of a negotiator's personality can be captured by examining how he scores on each of these five measures.

- Extroversion – being sociable, assertive, talkative
- Agreeableness – being flexible, cooperative, trusting
- Conscientiousness – being responsible, organised, achievement oriented
- Emotional stability – being secure, confident, not anxious
- Openness – being imaginative, broad-minded, curious

3.20 Research by Barry and Friedman suggests that extroversion and agreeableness are not necessarily a good thing in distributive negotiations. Individuals of this kind are most susceptible to the trap of 'anchoring' behaviour (refer back to Section 1 above). This is apparently because they value social relations too highly, and are less likely to resist when the opposite party makes a bid far from their own position.

The emotionally intelligent negotiator

3.21 Emotional intelligence is a current buzzword in the social sciences. It refers to an ability to perceive, assess and manage one's own emotions and those of others (eg the other party in a negotiation). It is often referred to as EI, and measured in terms of EQ (an emotional intelligence quotient – the term is modelled on the IQ score measuring general intelligence).

3.22 Investigations into the behaviour of negotiators have often assumed that they can be regarded as always acting rationally. The implication is that logical reasoning is the key driver of a negotiation.

3.23 This view has been challenged by researchers who emphasise the role of emotion in negotiations. A negotiator is a human being, not an automaton, and is affected more or less by non-rational, emotional considerations. A skilled negotiator must be able to exploit this in others, while being aware that he himself may be acted upon by non-rational factors. If he can achieve this, he can be described as an emotionally intelligent negotiator.

3.24 Lewicki analyses the effects that emotions can have on negotiations. His conclusions are summarised in the paragraphs that follow.

3.25 Negotiations create both positive and negative emotions. Positive emotions can arise from liking the other party and feeling good about progress in the negotiation. Negative emotions can arise from disliking the other party and from frustration at lack of progress.

3.26 Positive emotions generally have positive consequences for negotiations, while negative emotions have negative consequences. In particular, positive emotions are more likely to lead to integrative approaches, whereas negative emotions can lead to distributive approaches.

3.27 A final conclusion is that emotions can be used strategically as negotiation gambits. Manipulating emotions is generally regarded as more acceptable than manipulating information; in other words, it is regarded as more acceptable to feign exasperation at a supplier's price offer than to mislead the supplier about intended purchase volumes.

Improving negotiation capabilities

3.28 According to Lewicki, negotiators should develop their capabilities in three areas: cognitive ability, emotional intelligence, and perspective-taking ability. We have discussed emotional intelligence above. We now move on to discuss the other two topics.

3.29 **Cognitive ability** is defined as 'a very general mental capability that, among other things, involves the ability to reason, plan, solve problems, think abstractly, comprehend complex ideas, learn quickly and learn from experience'. It seems likely that such a capability would very much benefit a negotiator.

3.30 Research appears to indicate a strong link between cognitive ability and the achievement of integrative solutions in negotiations. In distributive situations, no clear advantage has been demonstrated for negotiators with good cognitive ability.

3.31 **Perspective-taking ability** is defined as 'a negotiator's capacity to understand the other party's point of view during a negotiation and thereby to predict the other party's strategy and tactics'. Again, it seems highly likely that such a capacity would benefit a negotiator.

3.32 Once again, research appears to support this initial reaction. As reported by Lewicki, a study by Neale and Bazerman indicates that negotiators with perspective-taking ability are able to extract more valuable concessions from the other party.

3.33 So how can negotiators improve their skills in this area? Two points to emphasise are experience and learning.

3.34 In relation to experience, David Kolb's **experiential learning cycle** shows how everyday work experiences can be used for learning, personal development and performance improvement, through the process of 'learning by doing': Figure 9.3.

3.35 Figure 9.3 illustrates the following stages.

- The learner has a concrete experience of the technique or concept to be learned. (For example, the buyer engages in a negotiation.)
- He thinks back over the negotiation later, perhaps using a personal development journal.

- Using theory and experience, he develops some abstract concepts of what might have been going on, and sets up a hypothesis for future negotiations.

- He applies and tests the hypothesis in a new negotiation.

3.36 The learner is thus supplied with a new or adjusted concrete experience, from which to begin the cycle again.

Figure 9.3 *The experiential learning cycle*

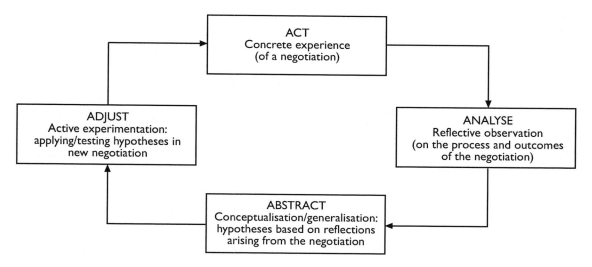

3.37 In relation to **learning**, Honey and Mumford drew up a popular classification of four learning styles for which people may have a natural preference.

- **Theorists** need to understand underlying concepts prior to any hands-on attempt: their preferred approach is intellectual and rational. They prefer training programmes which are structured and theory-based, and which allow time for analysis. They do not thrive on training which is experimental, skims over principles or appears intellectually disorganised.

- **Reflectors** need to observe or research things and think deeply about them before acting or coming to carefully thought-out conclusions. They prefer training programmes which allow them to work at their own pace and with plenty of information. They do not thrive on fast-moving, highly participative training.

- **Activists** want to 'get stuck in': they need to work on practical tasks or problems. They prefer training based on hands-on experience, and thrive on participation and challenges. They do not have much patience with theory, being easily bored and inclined to take risks.

- **Pragmatists** need to see a direct link between the subject being studied and a real task or problem for which they are, or may be, responsible: they see no point in learning for its own sake. They are particularly good at learning new techniques in on-the-job training: their preferred outcome from learning is to be able to implement an action plan or do a job better.

3.38 Once again, it is important to note that no style is 'better' than another – and that individuals can develop good skills in areas that are not their natural preference. All four styles are used in the learning cycle, for example: the pragmatist is strong in the 'act' stage, the reflector in the 'analyse' stage, the theorist in the 'abstract' stage and the activist in the 'adjust' stage.

Negotiating in teams

3.39 There is an extensive literature on the dynamics of working in teams, not just in negotiation, but generally in the approach to organisation of work tasks. We begin by summarising some of the general conclusions that researchers have arrived at. We then move on to apply these conclusions to the specific context of negotiations.

3.40 Certain advantages of working in teams are identified in the literature: see Table 9.4.

Table 9.4 *Advantages of working in teams*

	Advantage	Explanation
1	Teams improve performance	Teams facilitate the performance of tasks which require the collective skills, experience or knowledge of more than one person or discipline. Groups have been shown to produce better evaluated (though fewer) decisions than individuals working separately.
2	Teams facilitate coordination	Teams facilitate the coordination of the work of different individuals or groups, because they bring them together across organisational boundaries (eg disciplines or departments) with shared goals and structured communication
3	Teams facilitate communication	Teams facilitate interactive communication and interpersonal relationships
4	Teams motivate individuals	Teams can motivate individuals to devote more energy and effort to achieving the organisation's goals, since: • They offer rewards in the form of satisfying relationships • Group influences may reinforce performance, as long as the group's aims are harmonised with those of the organisation.

3.41 Improved communication and interpersonal relationships means that teams are particularly well adapted for:

- Testing and ratifying decisions, because they offer multi-source feedback and may make the decision more acceptable (by taking account of a cross-section of stakeholder views).

- Consulting, negotiating and conflict resolution, because they allow an interactive exchange of views and influence

- Generating ideas, because of their potential for 'bouncing' ideas off each other and getting multiple input

- Collecting and disseminating information, because of the multiple networks in which the members are involved.

3.42 R Meredith Belbin researched business-game teams at Henley Management College in the UK and developed a model of the mix of roles in a team. Belbin suggests that an effective team is made up of people who, between them, fill nine roles (Table 9.5).

He notes that 'strength of contribution in any one of the roles is commonly associated with particular weaknesses. These are called allowable weaknesses. Executives are seldom strong in all nine team roles'.

3.43 These team roles are not fixed within any given individual: team members can occupy more than one role, or switch roles according to need. The important thing is to have a healthy mix and balance of roles in the team.

Table 9.5 *Belbin's team roles*

Role and description	Team role contribution	Allowable weaknesses
Plant Creative, imaginative, unorthodox	Solves difficult problems	Ignores details. Too preoccupied to communicate effectively
Resource investigator Extrovert, enthusiastic, communicative	Explores opportunities. Develops contacts.	Overoptimistic. Loses interest once initial enthusiasm has passed
Coordinator Mature, confident, a good chairperson	Clarifies goals, promotes decision-making, delegates well	Can be seen as manipulative. Delegates personal work
Shaper Challenging, dynamic, thrives on pressure	Has the drive and courage to overcome obstacles	Can provoke others. Hurts people's feelings
Monitor evaluator Sober, strategic, discerning	Sees all options. Judges accurately	Lacks drive and ability to inspire others. Overly critical
Team worker Cooperative, mild, perceptive and diplomatic	Listens, builds, averts friction, calms the waters	Indecisive in crunch situations. Can be easily influenced
Implementer Disciplined, reliable, conservative and efficient	Turns ideas into practical actions	Somewhat inflexible. Slow to respond to new possibilities
Completer Painstaking, conscientious, anxious	Searches out errors and omissions. Delivers on time	Inclined to worry unduly. Reluctant to delegate. Can be a 'nitpicker'
Specialist Single-minded, self-starting, dedicated	Provides knowledge and skills in rare supply	Contributes only on a narrow front. Dwells on technicalities. Overlooks the 'big picture'

Source: Team Roles at Work, R Meredith Belbin (Butterworth-Heinemann)

3.44 It is interesting to focus on the middle column here. It should be fairly clear how these separate contributions can assist in a negotiation.

3.45 There are many different techniques of **team building** (creating cohesive groups), but team cohesion is often based on fostering the following elements.

- Team identity: the sense of being a team (sometimes called '*esprit de corps*' or 'team spirit').

- Team solidarity: loyalty to the group, so that team members put in extra effort for the group and in support of its norms and values.

- Commitment to shared goals: cooperation in the interests of team objectives.

- Competition, crisis or emergency: members of a group will act in unison if the group's existence or patterns of behaviour are threatened from outside. Competition within groups erodes cohesion – but competition with other groups enhances it.

3.46 There are a number of factors, both quantitative and qualitative, that might be assessed in order to decide whether or how far a team is operating effectively.

Quantifiable factors

- High quality output (eg successful negotiation outcomes)
- Achievement of specific individual and team targets and standards
- Infrequent disruption through problems, conflicts and so on

Qualitative factors

- High commitment to the achievement of targets and goals
- Clear understanding of team goals
- Clear understanding of the role of each member within the team
- Trust between members, reflected in free and open communication and the willingness to share tasks (trusting others to 'do their part')
- New ideas generation, sharing of ideas and welcoming of divergent views
- Mutual support and facilitation by members of each other's work
- Active interest and involvement in decisions

3.47 Moving on to the specific context of team negotiations, research reported by Lewicki indicates that integrative agreements are more likely to be achieved by teams than by individuals. This applies even when only one of the parties is represented by a team.

3.48 Lewicki also indicates that teams may be more competitive than individuals and may claim more value. Teams tend to be highly competitive in their dealings with other groups.

3.49 Good relations between team members foster success in negotiations. Research by Peterson and Thompson indicates that groups of friends do well when negotiating with groups of strangers, because they are more cohesive and more focused.

4 Effective questioning skills

Types of question

4.1   Skilful questioning is a key technique for negotiators. Various authorities have attempted to classify the types of question that may be asked. As an example, consider the research of Gerard Nierenberg, reported in Lewicki: Table 9.6.

Table 9.6 *Questions in negotiation*

Manageable questions	Examples
Open-ended questions – ones that cannot be answered with a simple yes or no. *Who, what, when, where,* and *why* questions.	'Why do you take that position in these deliberations?'
Open questions – invite the other's thinking.	'What do you think of our proposal?'
Leading questions – point toward an answer.	'Don't you think our proposal is a fair and reasonable offer?'
Cool questions – low emotionally.	'What is the additional rate that we will have to pay if you make the improvements on the property?'
Planned questions – part of an overall logical sequence of questions developed in advance.	'After you make the improvements to the property, when can we expect to take occupancy?'
Treat questions – flatter the opponent at the same time as you ask for information.	'Can you provide us with some of your excellent insight on this problem?'
Window questions – aid in looking into the other person's mind.	'Can you tell us how you came to that conclusion?'
Directive questions – focus on a specific point.	'How much is the rental rate per square foot with these improvements?'
Gauging questions – ascertain how the other person feels.	'How do you feel about our proposal?'

Unmanageable questions	Examples
Close-out questions – force the other party into seeing things your way.	'You wouldn't try to take advantage of us here, would you?'
Loaded questions – put the other party on the spot regardless of the answer.	'Do you mean to tell me that these are the only terms that you will accept?'
Heated questions – high emotionally, trigger emotional responses.	'Don't you think we've spent enough time discussing this ridiculous proposal of yours?'
Impulse questions – occur 'on the spur of the moment,' without planning, and tend to get conversation off the track.	'As long as we're discussing this, what do you think we ought to tell other groups who have made similar demands on us?'
Trick questions – appear to require a frank answer, but really are 'loaded' in their meaning.	'What are you going to do – give in to our demands, or take this to arbitration?'
Reflective trick questions – reflects the other into agreeing with your point of view.	'Here's how I see the situation – don't you agree?'

Source: From Gerard Nierenberg, Fundamentals of Negotiation.

4.2   In a similar vein, Steele, Murphy and Russill (in *It's a Deal*) classify questions as follows. (We discussed these categories of question in more detail when citing the work of Steele and Beasor in Chapter 1.)

- Open questions – when can you deliver?
- Closed questions – can you deliver by 20 October?
- Probing questions – what tests do you use to ensure consistent quality?
- Multiple questions – how can you ensure fixed prices, quality and delivery?
- Leading questions – these prices are fixed for a year, aren't they?
- Reflective questions – you seem a little unhappy about our proposal?
- Hypothetical questions – what if we extended the contract to two years?

4.3   With enough time on one's hands one could extend these analyses almost without limit, but this is probably enough to indicate that buyers use a wide range of questioning techniques throughout the negotiation process. Short of refusing to answer, the supplier is bound to contribute at least a limited amount of information in his reply, which means that the buyer has gained something.

Information seeking questions

4.4   A prime objective of asking questions is obviously to fill in the gaps in our information. This needs no further explanation. But it is worthwhile to consider the incidental effects of the information seeking process.

4.5   One aspect highlighted by Lewicki is that such questions may lead us to uncover deception on the part of the supplier. We displayed Lewicki's full analysis in Chapter 7; a reminder of the main points is presented for convenience in Table 9.7.

4.6   Lewicki also emphasises the use of questions in refocusing an integrative negotiation and generating win-win options. In Section 1 of Chapter 7 we discussed the five broad methods he suggests in this context: expanding the pie; logrolling; non-specific compensation; cutting the costs for compliance; finding a bridge solution.

4.7   Each of these can be facilitated by asking appropriate questions. For example, in terms of logrolling, we can ask 'What issues are of higher and lower priority to each party?' In terms of non-specific compensation, we can ask 'What could I do that would make the supplier happy and simultaneously allow me to get my way on the key issue?'

4.8   Another incidental effect of questioning is that by promoting an exchange of information we may also be building trust. The literature emphasises the importance of a full exchange of information. This is characteristic of integrative negotiations and may lead to more profitable outcomes for both sides.

Table 9.7 *Detecting deception*

Tactic	Explanation and examples
Intimidation	Force the other to admit he is using deception by intimidating him into telling the truth. Make a no-nonsense accusation of the other. Criticise the other. Hammer the other with challenging questions. Feign indifference to what he has to say ('I'm not interested in anything you have to say on the matter').
Futility portrayal	Emphasise the futility and impending danger associated with continued deceit: 'The truth will come out someday,' 'Don't dig the hole deeper by trying to cover it up,' 'If you try to cover it up, it will only be worse in the future,' 'You are all alone in your deception.'
Bluffing	Lie to the other to make him believe you have uncovered his deception: 'Your sins are about to be uncovered.' Indicate that you know what he knows but will not discuss it.
Gentle prods	Encourage the other to keep talking so that he gives you information that may help you separate true facts from deceptions. Ask him to elaborate on the topic being discussed. Ask questions but indicate that you are asking because 'other people want to know.' Play devil's advocate and ask playful questions. Praise the other so as to give him confidence and support that may lead to information sharing.
Minimisation	Play down the significance of any deceptive act. Help the other find excuses for why he was deceptive; minimise the consequences of the action; indicate that others have done worse; shift the blame to someone else.
Self-disclosure	Reveal a number of things about yourself, including, perhaps, dishonesty on your own part, hoping the other will begin to trust you and reciprocate with disclosures of dishonesty.
Direct approach	'Simply tell me the truth.' 'Let's be honest here.' 'Surely you have no objection to telling me everything you know.'
Silence	Create a 'verbal vacuum' that makes the other uncomfortable and gets him to talk and disclose information. When he tells a lie, simply maintain direct eye contact but remain silent.

Source: Adapted from Pamela J Kalbfleisch, 'The language of detecting deceit,' Journal of language and social psychology

Questions for tough situations

4.9   Finally in this chapter we refer to Lewicki's analysis of questions for tough situations: see Table 9.8.

Table 9.8 *Questions for tough situations*

The situation	Possible questions
'Take it or leave it' ultimatums	If we can come up with a more attractive alternative than that, would you still want me to 'take or leave' your offer? Do I have to decide now, or do I have some time to think about it? Are you feeling pressure to bring the negotiation to a close?
Pressure to respond to an unreasonable deadline	Why can't we negotiate about this deadline? If you're under pressure to meet this deadline, what can I do to help remove some of that pressure? What's magical about this afternoon? What about first thing in the morning?
Highball or lowball tactics	What's your reasoning behind this position? What would *you* think I see as a fair offer? What standards do you think the final resolution should meet?
An impasse	What else can either of us do to close the gap between our positions? Specifically what concession do you need from me to bring this to a close right now? If it were already six weeks from now and we were looking back at this negotiation, what might we wish we had brought to the table?
Indecision between accepting and rejecting a proposal	What's your best alternative to accepting my offer right now? If you reject this offer, what will take its place that's better than what you know you'll receive from me? How can you be sure that you will get a better deal elsewhere?
A question about whether the offer you just made is the same as that offered to others	What do you see as a fair offer, and given that, what do you think of my current offer to you? Do you believe that I think it's in my best interest to be unfair to you? Do you believe that people can be treated differently, but still all be treated fairly?
Attempts to pressure, control, or manipulate	Shouldn't we both walk away from this negotiation feeling satisfied? How would you feel if our roles were reversed, and you were feeling the pressure I'm feeling right now? Are you experiencing outside pressures to conclude these negotiations?

Chapter summary

- Negotiators communicate: offers and counter-offers; information about alternatives; information about outcomes; social accounts; and information about process.

- Faulty perceptions may arise in the communication process as a result of: stereotyping; halo effects; selective perception; and projection.

- The term 'framing' refers to the way in which we focus, shape and organise the world about us. If a buyer and supplier frame issues in different ways it can lead to unnecessary conflict.

- Problems of cognitive bias may lead to errors in processing information. Examples of cognitive bias include irrational escalation of commitment, mythical fixed-pie beliefs and many others.

- Body language includes eye contact, adjustment of body position, and non-verbal encouragement or discouragement.

- Researchers have attempted to identify behaviour patterns associated with successful negotiators. The conclusions may differ depending on whether the negotiation is integrative or distributive.

- KW Thomas identifies five main techniques for dealing with conflict: avoiding, forcing/competing, collaborating, accommodating, and compromising. Which we choose depends on two factors: the importance of the relationship, and the importance of the negotiation's immediate outcome.

- Attempts to identify attributes of successful negotiators are inconclusive. Many researchers have attempted to do this, and their conclusions differ in many important factors.

- Differences have been identified in the behaviour of male and female negotiators: relational view of others; embedded view of agency; beliefs about ability and worth; control through empowerment; problem solving through dialogue; perceptions and stereotypes.

- Emotional intelligence refers to an ability to perceive, assess and manage one's own emotions and those of others. This is a valuable attribute in a negotiator.

- According to Lewicki, negotiators should develop their capabilities in three areas: cognitive ability, emotional intelligence, and perspective-taking ability.

- David Kolb's experiential learning cycle shows how everyday work experiences can be used for learning, personal development and performance improvement.

- Honey and Mumford devised a popular classification of learning styles: theorists; reflectors; activists; and pragmatists.

- Negotiation is often carried out by teams rather than individuals. This makes it useful to study the dynamics of team interaction.

- Negotiators should develop effective questioning skills. It helps to be able to identify different types of question. Various authorities have tried to categorise questions and you should be familiar with the results of Gerard Nierenberg; Steele, Murphy and Russill; and Lewicki's 'questions for tough situations'.

Self-test questions

Numbers in brackets refer to the paragraphs where you can check your answers.

1   List cues of non-verbal communication. (1.3)

2   Describe what is meant by 'framing' and its importance in negotiations. (1.16)

3   What is meant by irrational escalation of commitment? (1.19)

4   Describe the style of successful negotiators, according to the research of Neil Rackham. (Table 9.1)

5   Sketch KW Thomas's model of conflict-handling styles. (Figure 9.1)

6   Outline the differences identified by researchers in the approaches to negotiation in women as compared with men. (3.4ff)

7   Explain what is meant by emotional intelligence. Why is this an important attribute of negotiators? (3.21ff)

8   What is 'cognitive ability'? (3.29)

9   Explain the four stages in Kolb's experiential learning cycle. (3.35)

10 List the team roles identified by R Meredith Belbin. (3.43)

11 List examples of manageable questions and unmanageable questions, as identified by Nierenberg. (4.1)

12 Give examples of tactics for detecting deception. (Table 9.7)

CHAPTER 10

The International Dimension

Learning objectives and indicative content

4.4 Analyse and explain different negotiation practices in international cultures.

- • Culture and negotiation
- • Body language
- • Barriers to international negotiation

Chapter headings

1 Barriers to international negotiation

2 Culture and negotiation

3 Preparing for cross-cultural negotiations

Introduction

So far we have assumed that both parties to the negotiation are from the same cultural background. International negotiations give rise to additional considerations, and these are the subject of the present chapter.

1 Barriers to international negotiation

The language problem

1.1 One of the more obvious problems in dealing with overseas suppliers is that they are not British! This remark is not intended in any racist or xenophobic sense. It is merely intended to make the obvious point that the residents of a particular country, such as the United Kingdom, share a common culture and a common language, both of which influence their business dealings with each other. When dealing with overseas suppliers it is necessary to adjust to a different culture and language.

1.2 The difficulties here are both technical and behavioural. Technical difficulties concern the simple issue of understanding what is being offered and accepted, and what has eventually been agreed. Behavioural difficulties are related to how people interact with each other and form pleasant and rewarding business relations.

1.3 To deal first with the technical difficulty of communication, it is clearly vital that agreements once concluded are expressed in language that both parties understand. But before that stage is reached oral discussions will take place during which offers and commitments will be expressed that have a great influence on the course of negotiations. Buyers must make every effort to ensure that such discussions are unambiguous.

1.4 It is an essential element in a binding contract that the parties reach agreement. That element is absent if there is misunderstanding: one party believes he understands what the other has said, but in fact has not done so. Even leaving aside the legal niceties, it is clear that successful business relations are endangered if the two parties have different ideas as to what has been agreed.

1.5 Native speakers of English are in a fortunate position in that their first language is widely recognised as the standard language of international trade. However, that should not lead buyers to think that they can ignore communication difficulties. Even if negotiations are conducted in English, it is important to ensure that the supplier understands technical terms and idioms in the same way as the buyer.

1.6 An effort to acquire some understanding of the relevant foreign language can be a great help in this respect. It is also a major step in improving business relations. It is a positive sign that the buyer has made efforts to adapt to the supplier's position and will usually be welcomed even if the level of proficiency is not great.

Body language

1.7 Frank Acuff (*How to Negotiate Anything with Anyone Anywhere in the World*) emphasises the importance of body language in international negotiations. He states that facial behaviours, hand gestures, eye contact, touching and other non-verbal communication patterns are culturally driven. For an American, a firm handshake is expected and a limp handshake may suggest lack of assertiveness. In other cultures, the perception may be quite different: the US approach may appear unduly aggressive.

1.8 In many parts of Latin America and the Middle East it is common for business associates to embrace each other, or even to kiss lightly on the cheek. US and British negotiators are accustomed to greater physical distance between themselves and others.

1.9 Hand gestures are open to misinterpretation. While a US or British negotiator may use a 'thumbs up' sign to indicate that everything is OK, in many Mediterranean countries this gesture conveys a very rude message.

1.10 Acuff presents an interesting comparison of behaviours in Japanese, American and Brazilian negotiators: Table 10.1.

Table 10.1 *A multicultural comparison of negotiating communication patterns*

Behaviour	Japanese	Americans	Brazilians
Verbal communication			
Conversational overlaps (number per 10 minutes)	12.6	10.3	28.6
Non-verbal communication			
Silent periods (number of periods greater than 10 seconds, per 30 minutes)	5.5	3.5	0
Facial gazing/direct eye contact (minutes per 10-minute period)	1.3	3.3	5.3
Touching (not including hand-shaking, per 30 minutes)	0	0	4.7

Behavioural problems

1.11   This leads on naturally to the less technical and more behavioural problems of dealing with overseas suppliers. As in all negotiations, it is important to make a positive impression on one's business partners. This is more difficult in the case of overseas partners because of cultural differences.

1.12   Many of these differences have been described in the purchasing literature. For example, it is common to refer to Japanese patterns of business behaviour which can cause confusion to British and American buyers.

1.13   One instance of this is the much greater link between social and business relations in Japan; social communication forms a larger part of the negotiation process than is common in Britain or America. Buyers doing business in Japan should not assume that extensive entertaining by their hosts is an unimportant prelude to the main talks.

1.14   Another instance sometimes cited is the Japanese practice of avoiding a direct 'no', so as not to cause embarrassment to their guests. This can sometimes leave a British or American buyer believing that something is still up for debate, when the truth is that the supplier regards it as unacceptable.

1.15   Instances such as this could be multiplied by reference to other countries where business practices differ from those of Britain and America. However, the best practical measure is to benefit from the experience of others. Buyers doing business with overseas suppliers should brief themselves by discussing such points with colleagues who have previous experience.

Table 10.2 *Suggestions for negotiating with overseas suppliers*

1.	Speak slowly and ask questions to check understanding.
2.	Print business cards in both English and the foreign language.
3.	Study the culture in advance.
4.	Be prepared for negotiations to be drawn out over a longer period than usual.
5.	Become familiar with local regulations, tax laws etc.
6.	Prepare in advance on technical issues, financing arrangements, cost and price analyses etc.
7.	If possible, ensure that the person recording the discussions is drawn from your team.
8.	Arrange discussions so that the other team can 'win' their share of the issues.

2 Culture and negotiation

The macro-environment and the immediate context

2.1 Lewicki describes research by Phatak and Habib suggesting that two overall contexts have an influence on international negotiations: the environmental context and the immediate context.

2.2 The **environmental context** includes factors that influence the negotiation but are outside the control of the negotiators. Seven such factors are mentioned: see Table 10.3.

Table 10.3 *The environmental context of international negotiations*

Political and legal pluralism	Different political and legal systems prevail in different countries, and even in the same countries at different eras (eg the much more open political system in modern Russia compared with the old Soviet Union).
International economics	Fluctuations in foreign exchange rates and the existence of currency controls pose additional problems.
Foreign governments and bureaucracies	While US and British firms are relatively free from government interference, the governments of many developing countries supervise imports and joint ventures very closely.
Instability	This includes political instability, as well as shortage of basic resources in many developing countries (eg shortages of paper, electric power, computers).
Ideology	US and British negotiators are wedded to the benefits of capitalism, but in other countries there is greater emphasis on state control of the economy.
Culture	This affects negotiating style, behavioural habits etc, as discussed elsewhere in this chapter.
External stakeholders	Examples include Chambers of Commerce (who can provide assistance to exporters) and trade unions (who may resist imports because of threats to local labour).

2.3 The **immediate context** of international negotiations is said to include five main factors: see Table 10.4.

Table 10.4 *The immediate context of international negotiations*

Relative bargaining power	This may be influenced by factors such as special access to markets, eg in former communist countries
Levels of conflict	This can be strongly influenced by how the parties 'frame' the negotiating issues (refer back to Chapter 10), and this in turn may differ widely from one culture to another.
Relationship between negotiators	The history of relations between the parties will affect the current round of negotiations.
Desired outcomes	Lewicki points out that in trade negotiations between Japan and the USA both sides often settle for less than they would wish because of the importance of the long-term relationship.
Immediate stakeholders	This can include the skills of the negotiators themselves, as well as the influence of their managers 'back home'.

Hofstede's dimensions of culture

2.4 Geert Hofstede carried out a cross-cultural study to identify the similarities and differences among a large number of employees working for the same multinational company but located in 40 different countries. He identified five dimensions along which the various cultures differed from each other.

- Power distance: the extent to which the unequal distribution of power is accepted by members of a society. Cultures with greater power distance will concentrate decision making at the top level; all decisions will have to be finalised by the leader. This tends to lead to a slower negotiation process.
- Uncertainty avoidance: how much members of a society are threatened by uncertain and ambiguous situations. If a negotiator comes from a country with high uncertainty avoidance, he is likely to seek stable rules and procedures for the negotiation.
- Individualism-collectivism: the tendency to take care of oneself and one's family versus the tendency to work together for the collective good. In a collectivist society, negotiations with the same party can continue for years, and a change of negotiator means a change in the relationship. In individualistic societies negotiators are considered interchangeable.
- Masculinity-femininity: the extent to which highly assertive masculine values predominate (eg acquisition of money at the expense of others), as opposed to sensitivity and concern for others' welfare. Negotiators from 'masculine' societies are more likely to favour distributive negotiations over integrative negotiations.
- Long-term orientation: the extent to which thrift and perseverance are valued (long-term orientation) over respect for tradition, fulfilling solid obligations and protecting one's 'face' (short-term orientation).

2.5 It is instructive to visit www.geert-hofstede.com for a list of the countries in the world and how they score on each of the five dimensions above.

2.6   There are many aspects of negotiation that are likely to be affected by the position of a particular society within these four dimensions. Here are some examples.

- The selection of negotiators. For example, if we are visiting a strongly 'masculine' culture, we had better choose people who can handle a distributive negotiating style.

- The agenda for the negotiation process. If we are visiting a country with a high avoidance of uncertainty, we had better lay down detailed procedures and process in advance.

- The timetable for the negotiation process. If we are visiting a country with a high power distance, we must prepare for a lengthy process with frequent recourse back to higher authorities.

2.7   In a similar vein, Lewicki lists the following issues that may be affected by our assessment of the 'other' culture.

- Definition of what is negotiable and what the process consists of
- Distributive or integrative approach
- Selection of negotiators
- Protocol (use of first name vs use of formal titles etc)
- Communication, including body language
- Time sensitivity (some cultures are used to more leisurely approaches than we favour in Britain and the US)
- Risk propensity
- Team negotiation versus individual negotiators
- Nature of agreements (eg whether or not a written memorandum is binding)
- Extent to which emotion is used in the negotiation

Culturally responsive negotiation strategies

2.8   What are the effects of different cultures on the actual behaviour of negotiators? Lewicki points out that many commentators suggest a policy of 'When in Rome, do as the Romans do'. In other words, the advice is to modify our negotiation behaviour so as to take account of cultural differences.

2.9   However, as Lewicki argues, this may not be the most sensible course of action. There are several reasons why negotiators might be better advised to stick to their normal style of doing business.

- They may not be able to modify their style effectively – after all, it is difficult enough to master even one style of negotiation, never mind two or more.

- Even if they can, it may not lead to a better outcome – particularly if the other party is also modifying his behaviour to suit his notion of his opposite number's likely preferences!

- Research suggests that moderate adaptation of behaviour may be more effective than wholesale adoption of the other party's presumed style.

2.10   Lewicki also reports research by Stephen Weiss suggesting that the approach to take will depend on the level of our familiarity with the other culture.

- If we have little familiarity with the other culture it may be appropriate to use an agent who can help remedy this shortcoming. Alternatively, we might bring in a mediator, or we could induce the other party to use our own approach.

- If we have moderate familiarity with the other culture we could either adapt to the other party's behaviour, or suggest coordinate adjustment (ie each party modifies behaviour to a limited extent so as to conform with each other).

- If we are very familiar with the other culture we can embrace the other negotiator's approach. Alternatively, we may try to fashion a 'third culture' that both negotiators are happy with.

3 Preparing for cross-cultural negotiations

Communications technology

3.1 One vital factor in the growth of global sourcing has been the development of communications technology. This has made it possible for buyers and suppliers to communicate more rapidly and effectively than ever before and has encouraged the idea of a 'global market place'.

3.2 Here are some examples of the technological advances in this area.

- Electronic mail (email). This enables immediate communication of complex documents by way of attachments to text messages. A buyer can be confident that his supplier has received the message, and can ask for instantaneous response if necessary.

- Online visual conferencing aided by web cameras. This enables buyer and supplier to converse almost as easily as if they were in the same room.

- Increasingly sophisticated mobile phone technology. This allows buyer and supplier to communicate even when one or both of them are away from the office.

Advance planning

3.3 As in so many areas, the key to successful negotiation is advance planning. The buyer must take account of numerous factors that impact particularly on international negotiations.

- The local language of the supplier
- The culture (both social and business) in the supplier's country
- The political system in the supplier's country
- The infrastructure (transportation modes, manufacturing facilities, distribution networks etc) in the supplier's country
- Any local restrictions on trading with overseas partners
- Export regulations

3.4 All of these must be carefully researched as initial background before the detailed planning can begin. The buyer must also investigate his supplier.

- The structure and organisation of the firm
- The identity of key decision-makers
- The published financial accounts
- The manufacturing facilities
- The research and development programme
- Projects currently in hand

3.5 The buyer is then in a position to prepare a negotiating plan incorporating a carefully defined objective: what are we trying to achieve in the negotiation? He should consider such matters as the following.

- Product specification
- International quality standards
- Delivery mode and lead time
- Payment method and how to fund it
- The currency in which the agreement will be framed
- The use of Incoterms 2000 (standard terms of international trade)
- Any risk areas and how they can be managed
- The applicable law and any provisions for dispute resolution

3.6 The lead member of the buying team must then draw up an agenda for the negotiation and must communicate it fully to the members of his team. Despite the technological advances already mentioned the international dimension is still likely to mean that this kind of negotiation will extend over a longer time frame than a purely domestic negotiation. The agenda must reflect the likelihood of several meetings rather than just one.

During the negotiation

3.7 Alan Branch (in *International Purchasing and Management*) has a helpful list of hints for conducting an international negotiation.

- Provide each team member with a written brief summarising the objectives and agenda of the negotiation. (This goes back to the point mentioned in the preceding paragraph.)
- Ensure that each team member has a business card, preferably printed front and back, in the two relevant languages.
- Ensure that initial greetings respect the traditions of the host country. It is not safe to assume that a handshake is the normal greeting in every country.
- Establish a personal relationship with the members of the supplier's team.
- Avoid discussing contentious points in the early stages of the relationship – they will be easier to deal with once the relationship is stronger.
- Ensure that all members of the team are professional in appearance and demeanour. Beware of using first names from the beginning – in some cultures this is not acceptable.
- In some cultures it is customary to evade difficult questions or to respond with silence. In such cases, it is preferable not to pursue the point immediately, but to reflect on why the point caused such a response.
- Start each session with a review of the main points agreed in previous sessions.

- Communicate in clear language, avoiding slang or idiomatic phrases.
- Avoid discussing business matters in social meetings.

The work of Frank Acuff

3.8   We have already mentioned Acuff's book *How to Negotiate Anything with Anyone Anywhere in the World*. This contains a wealth of advice on preparing for cross-cultural negotiations. We end this chapter by describing some of Acuff's ideas.

3.9   Acuff highlights the six most difficult problems faced by international negotiators: culture shock; negotiating with one's own boss; dealing with one's own negotiating team; resolving ethical issues; establishing an international joint venture; and deciding the 'home or away?' question.

3.10   To deal with **culture shock**, Acuff advises us to find a cultural mentor. This can be combined with other steps, such as maintaining patience and flexibility with oneself and those in the host culture.

3.11   **Negotiating with one's own boss** can be difficult if he does not appreciate that things may be developing differently from what he would expect in a home negotiation. For example, it is well known that protracted social interchanges are a feature of negotiating with Japanese business people; our boss may not understand why we are spending so long over this!

3.12   **Dealing with one's own negotiating team** can be expensive, as well as difficult in terms of man management. Acuff's advice is to limit the size of the team, clarify the roles of team members, and ensure that all are briefed thoroughly.

3.13   **Resolving ethical issues** may be difficult in countries where bribery (or at least generous 'gifts') is an accepted part of the culture. Acuff's advice is to check first with your boss and your legal department.

3.14   **Establishing an international joint venture** means setting up a jointly owned trading vehicle in order to carry out mutually beneficial activities. It is important to ensure that both parties have similar goals, and to maintain control of the critical management responsibilities.

3.15   Deciding whether to meet **home or away** involves a number of considerations. We have already mentioned this in Chapters 1 and 6. Acuff suggests that if possible we should meet on our own home ground. This avoids the costs and culture shock of negotiating abroad.

3.16   Acuff also highlights a number of ways in which negotiations differ from one culture to another.

- The **pace of negotiation** is more rapid in North America than in most other cultures.
- **Negotiation strategies** differ too. In some countries (Acuff suggests Russia, Egypt and China) extensive haggling is the norm, which means that the opening bid may be far removed from the final settlement. In other countries, such as Australia and Sweden, the opening bid and the final settlement will tend to be very close. Equally, there are differences in the use of tactical ploys and concessions.

- The emphasis on **personal relationships** is more pronounced in some cultures than others. British and German negotiators have a reputation for wishing to keep an interpersonal distance, whereas in some cultures a close personal relationship must be built up prior to negotiating an agreement.

- The use of **emotion** is regarded as normal in some cultures (eg Latin America), but tends to arouse distrust in other cultures (eg in Switzerland or Germany).

- There are important differences in methods of **decision making**. Acuff illustrates this in an interesting table: see Table 10.5.

- Finally, there are differences in **contractual and administrative factors**, such as the need for an agent (or not), the degree of bureaucracy, and the need for an agenda at meetings (or not).

Table 10.5 *Cultural differences in decision making*

Five steps in decision making	Cultural variations	
	A	**B**
1. Problem recognition	*Problem solving* Situation should be changed	*Situation accepting* Some situations should be accepted, not changed
2. Information search	*Gather facts*	*Gather ideas and possibilities*
3. Construction of alternatives	*New, future-oriented alternatives*	*Focus includes past, present, and future alternatives*
4. Choice	*Individuals make decisions* Decisions made quickly Decision rule: Is it true or false?	*Groups make decisions* Decisions made slowly Decision rule: Is it good or bad?
5. Implementation	*Slow* Managed from the top Responsibility of one person	*Fast* Involves participation at all levels Responsibility of the group

Chapter summary

- Language differences present an obvious problem in dealing with overseas suppliers. It is essential that buyer and supplier understand each other thoroughly, both during the course of the negotiation and in the terms of the final agreement.

- The difficulty applies as much to body language as to verbal communication, because the use of body language differs from one country to another.

- Behavioural and cultural differences may also present difficulties in dealing with overseas suppliers.

- Phatak and Habib identify two contexts that have an influence on international negotiations: the environmental context and the immediate context.

- Geert Hofstede identified four dimensions along which various cultures differ from each other: power distance; uncertainty avoidance; individualism-collectivism; and masculinity-femininity.

- Some authorities recommend 'When in Rome, do as the Romans do'. Others suggest that it may be difficult and perhaps undesirable to modify one's negotiation style when dealing with different cultures.

- Developments in communication technology have given a major boost to growth in international sourcing.

- Acuff highlights six problems faced by international negotiators: culture shock; negotiating with one's own boss; dealing with one's own negotiating team; resolving ethical issues; establishing an international joint venture; and deciding the 'home or away?' question.

Self-test questions

Numbers in brackets refer to the paragraphs where you can check your answers.

1 Why is it helpful to a negotiator to acquire some understanding of foreign languages? (1.6)

2 What kinds of behavioural problems may complicate negotiations with overseas suppliers? (1.11ff)

3 List the seven factors involved (according to Phatak and Habib) in the environmental context of international negotiations. (2.2)

4 Briefly describe each of the four 'dimensions of culture' identified by Hofstede. (2.4)

5 Why may it not be advisable to 'do as the Romans do'? (2.9)

6 What areas should a buyer consider when planning an international negotiation? (3.5)

7 What does Acuff recommend in order to deal with culture shock? (3.10)

8 List the ways in which Acuff believes that negotiations differ from one culture to another. (3.16)

CHAPTER 11

Specialised Situations

Learning objectives and indicative content

4.5   Analyse and explain the features of effective negotiation by telephone and email.

- Factors affecting telephone negotiation
- Factors affecting email negotiation
- Good practice when negotiating by telephone/email

4.6   Identify and evaluate the key features of effective negotiation with internal customers across the organisation.

- Listening to the internal customer's perspective
- Rapport building techniques
- Dealing with difficult customers
- Concessions, and the impact on purchasing

4.7   Evaluate personal effectiveness in negotiations in different contexts.

- Reflecting on performance
- Feedback mechanisms
- Looking ahead to improvement and development

Chapter headings

1   Negotiating on the telephone

2   E-negotiations

3   Negotiating with internal customers

4   Evaluating personal effectiveness

Introduction

In this chapter we round up some specialised techniques that are applicable when the negotiation is not face-to-face with an external supplier. Negotiating by telephone or by electronic means (especially email and electronic auctions) removes the visual element from our dealings. Negotiating with internal colleagues gives rise to considerations that are absent from negotiations with external suppliers. All of these topics are covered in this chapter. Finally, we end the textbook by looking at how we evaluate our effectiveness as a negotiator.

1   *Negotiating on the telephone*

Factors affecting telephone negotiations

1.1   A good deal of a buyer's time is spent on the telephone, so it makes sense to recognise the importance of this medium in negotiating. Although an important and complex negotiation is likely to be concluded face-to-face there is a place for the telephone, especially in the preliminary stages of the process. There are a number of factors that distinguish telephone negotiation from face-to-face contact.

1.2   To begin with, it is worth pointing out that much of the information we obtain comes to us via our sense of sight. (Steele et al in *It's a Deal* estimate that about 75% of our information comes to us this way.) Without the benefit of seeing the other party it is likely that there will be some loss of information. Steele's chapter on the subject of telephone communication is a very useful summary, and many of the points we make below originate with him.

1.3   Steele cites research suggesting that on the telephone the stronger case tends to prevail to a greater extent than in face-to-face meetings. This is apparently because when negotiators meet personally they work harder to reach an agreement acceptable to both sides.

1.4   On the telephone we are not able to check for consistency between verbal and non-verbal clues because the latter are denied to us. This may prevent us from challenging the impression of insincerity that sometimes arises in face-to-face discussions. It is easier for someone to lie, or at least to withhold the full truth, when he is not present in person.

1.5   In a face-to-face negotiation we are devoting all or most of our attention to the other party. On the telephone we may be subject to distractions that prevent us from devoting our full attention to the negotiation.

1.6   On the telephone it is difficult or impossible to use back-up data such as spreadsheets, charts, or sample products. This can mean that we are unable to express our case as forcefully as we could do in a personal meeting. We may also be reluctant on the telephone to make very forceful points, because we are unable to soften their impact by means of appropriate body language (such as a smile).

1.7   On the telephone there tends to be an advantage with the person who made the call. He knows what he is calling about and has prepared in advance. The recipient of the call may be less prepared, and should be careful not to concede any important point without having the chance to go away and consider it carefully.

1.8   A telephone call has a definite end, and this puts pressure on the parties to reach some kind of conclusion before they hang up. This should be resisted: don't give hasty agreement. On the other hand, if you are looking for a concession from the other party, this same consideration may suggest that a telephone call is appropriate.

1.9 Steele emphasises that the phone can be a useful means of conditioning expectations. For example, a supplier proposing a price rise may make a preliminary telephone call, so that the buyer may be more in the mood to accept (at least partially) when the face-to-face meeting takes place. More generally, it is often said that it is easier to impart bad news over the telephone than face-to face.

1.10 Steele also suggests that people are prepared to talk for longer on the telephone, which can make it a good means of obtaining information in advance of a meeting.

1.11 There are also some purely physical difficulties peculiar to telephone calls. For example, it is sometimes difficult to hear the other party clearly because of interference on the line, or because one party or the other may be working in an open-plan office with noise in the background.

1.12 As we have seen in earlier chapters, a part of negotiation is concerned with building relationships. This is less easy to do over the telephone because the visual dimension is lacking. However, this may be an advantage in cases where we are not seeking a relationship.

1.13 In the case of doubt or ambiguity, it is probably easier to seek clarification in a personal meeting than on the telephone. Use of a slang phrase or technical jargon may go past only partly understood. This makes it all the more necessary to seek clarification when necessary.

Good practice when negotiating by telephone

1.14 What are the implications of all this for our own practice in using the telephone for negotiation? Steele is again helpful in listing ten key points that should be observed: see Table 11.1.

Table 11.1 *Good practice when negotiating by telephone*

1   Use a receptionist or secretary as a 'buffer', someone who takes the call initially and gives you time either to prepare or to make yourself unavailable.

2   If you are likely to be phoning an individual frequently, find out when best to contact him and try to ensure you have his direct line number or his extension.

3   Have a clear idea of what you want from the phone call, and ring off as soon as you have got it.

4   Establish facts clearly by using simple 'Yes or no' questions for clarity.

5   Where assumptions are made, you should write them down carefully. Don't ring back later to clarify – this could re-open the whole negotiation!

6   Listen carefully to what is said, and observe what is not said. The absence of non-verbal signals makes it doubly important to pick up every scrap of information possible from the conversation.

7   Listen for what Steele calls 'moving signals', eg questions such as 'What if we were to …?'

8   Close the conversation positively with a succinct summary of what has been agreed and what action needs to follow.

9   Aim high – this is as important on the phone as face-to-face.

10   Confirm the conversation in writing as soon as possible.

1.15 Steele also points out the usefulness of having a proforma document designed for recording telephone conversations. Even if your organisation does not use such a document, you should certainly jot down in advance your 'agenda' for the phone conversation, ie the points you intend to make and the information you need. Keep this to hand during the conversation as a memorandum.

1.16 When planning a call, it may be appropriate to arrange a suitable time when both you and the other party can devote sufficient attention to the issues.

1.17 Equally, it may be appropriate to prepare an agenda for the telephone conversation by means of some other medium. For example, you might send an email to the other party listing the points that you need to discuss with him.

1.18 During the conversation, make every effort to understand what the other person is saying. If necessary, ask for information to be repeated or explained more clearly. It is often helpful to summarise as you go along what has been dealt with and what remains to be discussed.

1.19 It can be difficult for the speakers to take their turns appropriately. When speaking face-to-face it may often be clear from a person's demeanour that he has finished speaking and is now awaiting your response. This may be less clear over the telephone. Appropriate signalling can help in this area: for example, you may want to signal that you have more than one point to make, so as to avoid interruption. This can be done by sentences such as 'There are two comments I'd like to make in response to that ...'

Listening for language cues

1.20 We have already emphasised the importance of careful listening during telephone conversations. Lewicki emphasises the importance of **active listening** (not only in the context of telephone conversations).

1.21 By active listening Lewicki means the practice of re-stating or paraphrasing what the other speaker has said. He gives several examples, of which this is one:

SPEAKER: Please, don't talk to me about that now

LISTENER: Sounds like you're awfully busy right now

1.22 This technique is particularly important on the telephone where the chance of misunderstanding may be high. According to Lewicki, citing research by Athos and Gabarro, reflective responding is an essential part of active listening. Reflective responding is characterised by the following five factors.

- A greater emphasis on listening than speaking
- Responding to personal rather than abstract points (ie responding to feelings, beliefs and positions)
- Allowing the speaker to frame the direction of the conversation, rather than dictating to him
- Clarifying what he has said, rather than suggesting what he should have been thinking and saying
- Responding to the feelings he has expressed

2   E-negotiations

Distinguishing features

2.1   Email is generally regarded as a less formal communication medium than other written forms. People are more prepared to dash off an unpolished message, with minimum attention to grammar and spelling, than they would be if communicating by letter. However, email is not just a substitute for other written media: it often embodies communication that would otherwise be carried out face-to-face or on the telephone.

2.2   Research reported by Lewicki suggests that email negotiations sometimes end in impasse. Attempts to identify why this is so are inconclusive, though there is some evidence indicating that impasse is less likely if the email exchanges are more 'personal', ie they include self-disclosure of personal information and are conducted with parties with whom we already have some kind of relationship.

2.3   Lewicki's analysis leads him to develop 'ten rules for virtual negotiation': see Table 11.2.

Table 11.2 *Ten rules for virtual negotiation*

1   Take steps to create a face-to-face relationship before negotiation, or at least early in the negotiations.

2   Be explicit about the process to be followed during the negotiation.

3   Make sure everyone understands who is present in the virtual negotiation and why.

4   Select the channel (email, e-auction or whatever) that is most appropriate at getting all the information and detail in the open.

5   Avoid 'flaming', which is undue emotion in the expression of your messages.

6   Synchronise offers and counter-offers; speak up if it is not clear whose turn it is.

7   Check out assumptions you are making about the other's interests, offers, proposals and conduct.

8   Email is a written medium, so be sure not to make unwise commitments that can be used against you. Equally, do not try to take advantage of careless slips made by the other party.

9   Resist the temptation to use unethical tactics, even though these may be easier to implement in a virtual environment where facts are harder to establish.

10   Work to develop a personal negotiation style that is a good fit with the communication channel you are using.

Problems with e-negotiations

2.4   Lewicki suggests that a main problem with e-negotiations is the lack of what he calls 'schmoozing'. His point is that in face-to-face negotiations there is an element of 'off-task' interaction, helpful in building up relationships. This is usually absent in e-negotiations. Lewicki reports research indicating that a telephone call prior to beginning the e-negotiation can help to remedy this.

2.5   Lewicki also reports research by Thompson and Nadler, who identify four biases that can threaten e-negotiations.

- **Temporal synchrony bias**: unlike in a face-to-face negotiation, there may be time delays separating one party's contributions from the other's. This can lead to annoyance, which in turn can have a bad effect on the negotiations.

- **Burned bridge bias**: use of email leads to a social distance that would not apply in face-to-face negotiations. This can lead to some individuals adopting riskier behaviour than they would otherwise do. For example, they may set deadlines or ultimatums that prejudice a successful outcome.

- **Squeaky wheel bias**: negotiators are apparently more inclined to use intimidation, and to be guilty of rudeness or poor etiquette, when using email. As with 'burned bridge bias' this may be because the social norms applying in face-to-face contact are absent.

- **Sinister attribution bias**: a lack of trust may lead negotiators to attribute sinister motives and/or bad behaviour to the other party.

Online auctions

2.6   In recent years, purchasing techniques have been greatly affected by technological developments. These have come to a head in the arrival of complete e-sourcing or e-procurement systems. This essentially means the purchase of items using the internet. One possible application is a method of inviting suppliers to bid for supply contracts electronically. This is what is meant by **online auctions**. The basic idea is that a buyer advertises contracts on the internet and solicits bids. The contract is then (usually) awarded to the lowest bidder.

2.7   According to some commentators (especially those with an interest in promoting e-commerce, such as e-auction providers) there are significant benefits in online auctions.

- They save time for buyers, enabling them to concentrate on more strategic areas. Time used up in conventional negotiation is reduced or eliminated.

- Established suppliers can be benchmarked to find out whether they still represent best value.

- Although savings achievable are proportionate to the size of the purchasing budget, even small companies can participate via consortia auctions.

- By making the true market price for a product or service transparent auctions enable buyers to analyse price differentials properly.

2.8 The technique is not necessarily ideal for all possible purchases. For example, the danger of selecting an unsuitable supplier for a critical component may well outweigh any potential cost saving. On the other hand, the risk involved in putting a stationery contract up for auction is minimal. Risks can in any case be minimised by pre-selecting suppliers.

2.9 A serious danger that buyers must be aware of and must manage is the risk of alienating existing suppliers. A supplier who has invested time and money in servicing a customer is likely to be unhappy if he hears that his efforts are to be undermined by a buyer intent on offering the business by auction. Indeed, in some cases existing suppliers have refused to participate when a buyer decides to take this route.

2.10 An online auction is prepared in advance by the buyer, who advertises contracts and solicits interest from possible suppliers. When the advertised time arrives the participants join each other online, effectively simulating the physical reality of an auction room. In line with this, each participant can see the offers made by others.

2.11 The buyer is hoping to attract as low a price as possible, which means that bidders (ie potential suppliers) must continually come down in price. (For this reason, such auctions are sometimes referred to as **reverse auctions**, because of course in a regular auction it is buyers who are competing upwards rather than suppliers competing downwards.)

2.12 It has been said by a CIPS examiner that this kind of process is used primarily to reduce prices for inputs such as cement, steel, tyres, packaging and other leverage items. To judge from articles in the professional press the process is much more widely adopted than this, and virtually any commodity appears to have a potential market online.

Benefits of online auctions for suppliers

2.13 Our discussion of online auctions has highlighted many potential advantages for buyers. However, we must also consider the subject from the perspective of suppliers. What advantages and disadvantages may suppliers perceive in the use of e-purchasing techniques?

2.14 The most immediate advantage for suppliers is the general benefit provided by increased automation. In all areas of business, this has led to increased efficiency and accuracy of processing transactions, as well as reduced costs.

2.15 Many examples of this could be cited. There is no longer a need for producing and mailing paper invoices. Payment is received more quickly and with less processing. Electronic communications, eg automatic updates on delivery schedules, remove the need for expensive man hours spent on phone calls. The list could go on.

2.16 Suppliers also enjoy the many benefits that technology has created in terms of generating sales. Every supplier organisation now uses a website to attract potential customers. This not only opens up a much wider potential market, but also reduces the need for expensive selling staff. In addition, when orders are accepted by electronic means, the effort and cost of processing them is much reduced.

2.17 Suppliers can benefit from being invited to tender in an online auction. If the auction is transparent, they get to see the prices quoted by their competitors, which is useful information not normally available. They can use such information when bidding for business in future.

2.18 Finally, the greater ability of buyers to identify potential suppliers has a 'mirror image' benefit for suppliers: any particular supplier has a greater chance than before of being invited to tender.

Disadvantages of online auctions for suppliers

2.19 As usual, the situation is not entirely clear cut. Balancing the above benefits are a number of disadvantages.

2.20 Firstly, the benefits of reduced transaction costs come at a price. In particular, supplier organisations must spend significant sums of money on information and communication technology. Most suppliers would admit instantly that this is justified, and indeed essential to survival, but it is wise to recognise the costs involved.

2.21 Not all of these costs are entirely under the control of the supplier. For example, the supplier can choose to spend as much or as little as he likes on website development. But he may not be able to choose how much he spends on ensuring system compatibility with a buyer. In a case like this, if he wishes to acquire or retain the business, the cost of systems development may be unavoidable.

2.22 Another issue concerns online auctions. On the one hand, this technique should open up the potential for doing business with a wider class of buyers. But many suppliers complain that buyers are over-using the technique. In particular, a supplier who already has the business may argue that the buyer is wrong to seek a better deal by means of an online auction. Often their argument will be based on a claim that the nature of a supply is more strategic than a reverse auction implies.

2.23 It is natural for an incumbent supplier to feel this way, because it may lead to loss of business. In particular, they may feel that it encourages an undue concentration on price. If a supplier believes that his offering is differentiated by quality, delivery, service etc, he may feel disadvantaged by a focus on price. However, a supplier not currently having the buyer's business can only regard the online auction as a welcome opportunity to tender.

3 Negotiating with internal customers

Introduction

3.1 Most of what has been said in this book concerns negotiations between buyers and external suppliers. However, a buyer is usually representing other groups within his own organisation: user departments. In other words, he is not usually buying things because he personally needs them for his own work; he is buying them because some other department (production, IT or whatever) has a requirement.

3.2   Because of this, it is important that the buyer should do a good job on behalf of his internal 'customer'. This in itself may require a negotiation process. For example, it is common to find that a manufacturing or engineering department will want to buy materials of the highest possible specification. This is fine, if that is really what the organisation needs. But it may be possible to achieve important savings if a lower specification is used. Buyers must sensitively negotiate with user departments to ensure that specifications represent the best possible balance between quality and price.

3.3   Richard Morse (in 'Internal Negotiations: Supporting the External Deal', printed in *Negotiator Magazine*) identifies the following five reasons why a failure to achieve negotiated internal agreement will cause serious problems. (Morse writes from the perspective of a seller rather than a buyer, but his conclusions are easily adapted, and remain valid, in the context of a buyer.)

- Resources will not be available. Suppose a buyer agrees a programme of supplier development, involving training the external supplier's staff. He must first agree with the internal staff who will be providing the training; otherwise, they may not have the resources to do it within the agreed timeframe.

- Implementation will falter, because internal staff involved in the process may not have bought into the agreement.

- There is a risk of internal resistance or even sabotage.

- Team members will lack a common voice. It is vital that the members of the negotiating team 'sing from the same hymn sheet'. This may not happen if there is internal dissension as to the objectives of the negotiation with the external supplier.

- There is a risk of alienating internal supporters.

3.4   To avoid all this, the negotiator should apply the same kind of communication techniques that would be relevant in dealing with an external supplier. Keeping the internal groups informed as to plans and progress against plans is vital. This emphasises the essential similarity of internal and external negotiations.

3.5   However, it would not be true to say that there are no differences. For example, while an external negotiation may not have a successful outcome – the parties may simply not be able to reach agreement – this is not an option with internal negotiations. Somehow or other, before approaching the external supplier, the buyer must achieve agreement with the internal stakeholders affected by the negotiation.

3.6   This suggests that internal negotiations will usually be conducted on an integrative, win-win basis, rather than an adversarial, distributive basis.

Listening to the internal customer's perspective

3.7   Morse, in the article already cited, describes a number of steps the negotiator should take by way of understanding the perspective of the internal customer.

3.8   His first piece of advice is to know the interests of internal partners and acknowledge potential political ramifications of your proposed solution. This involves the buyer putting himself into the shoes of his internal customers and considering the problem from their point of view: what are their interests and their concerns?

3.9   From there, the buyer should seek to communicate and build relationships. He should seek feedback on an ongoing basis, developing a reputation for integrity by consistent action and intent. He should be ready to share the information at his disposal and in return he should expect full communication from other stakeholders in the organisation.

3.10   The buyer should co-create options and help quantify the benefits and costs both to the organisation and to the internal customer. He should also be prepared to find that his options are scrutinised thoroughly and adapted in the light of questioning. Perhaps other possible solutions will be added by the other internal stakeholders.

3.11   The buyer should identify criteria that will be used by his internal partners to evaluate the deal: defect rates, on-time delivery, price, or what? This will help him to obtain their support for the deal he eventually negotiates.

3.12   The buyer should close the internal deal before presenting the final agreement to the supplier. This helps present a united front for dealing with the supplier, and ensures that the deal eventually agreed will fall within the parameters laid down by the key stakeholders.

Rapport building techniques

3.13   Rapport may be defined, most simply, as the sense of relationship or connection we have when we relate to another person.

3.14   We have 'positive rapport' with people we find warm, attentive and easy to talk to: we are inclined to feel comfortable and relaxed with them, or attracted to them. We all know from experience that some people are easier to relate to than others. Some individuals seem distant or uninterested in us, or we feel less comfortable around them: we would call this low or negative rapport. (Fortunately for managers, this is not a matter of personality, but of behaviour: establishing positive rapport is a skill which can be learned.)

3.15   Rapport is a core skill for influencing, in simple terms, because: 'influencing is easier if the other person feels comfortable with you; if they feel they trust you; if they feel you understand them' (*Gillen*). In more detail, rapport:

- Helps to establish trust and a belief in the common ground between you and the other person: your viewpoint is then more likely to be received openly, rather than defensively.

- Is the basis of the positive influencing approach, sometimes called '**pacing and leading**'. First you 'pace' the other party (listening to, empathising with and reflecting back their views, feelings and needs). This earns trust and rapport from which you can 'lead' (influence) the other person (eg by reframing the problem or changing the emotional tone of the discussion).

- Creates a reason for people to agree with you, or do what you want them to do, because they like you! (A powerful motivator, even in business contexts...)

- Overcomes some of the barriers created by power imbalances and differences/conflicts of interest, reducing the tendency towards adversarial or defensive attitudes.

3.16 Key **rapport-building techniques** are based on the idea that it is easier to relate to someone who is (or appears to be) *like* us in some way; with whom we share some beliefs, values, interests or characteristics; and who treats us as a valued and interesting person. Some useful techniques therefore include:

• Subtly matching or 'mirroring' the other person's posture, body language and/or volume, speed and tone of voice. (This also reflects their mood and helps them to feel understood.)

• Picking up on the other person's use of technical words, colloquialisms and metaphors – and using them too (if you can do so with understanding and integrity) or incorporating them in comments and discussion summaries.

• Picking up on the other person's dominant way of experiencing and expressing things, which tend to be based on sight, sound or feeling ('I see what you mean', 'I hear what you're saying', 'That just hit me') and using similar modes of expression ('Do you see?', 'How does that sound to you?', 'What's your feeling about that?')

• Listening attentively and actively to what the other person is saying; demonstrating this with encouraging gestures, eye contact (where culturally appropriate) and so on; and asking supportive questions or summarising, in order to show that you are interested and want to understand. (This is the skill of **empathy**.)

• Finding topics of common interest, and emphasising areas of agreement or common ground where possible

• Remembering and using people's names.

3.17 These general techniques can be bolstered by specific strategies for dealing with internal negotiations. Morse (in the article already cited) lists three of these.

• Avoid surprising internal partners with external negotiation outcomes.

• Enlist internal partners in joint problem solving.

• Build internal working relationships to support the external deal.

3.18 Communication is needed so that buyers can cultivate relationships through consistency. To do this, you first need to identify the key internal parties. Morse suggests asking the following questions.

• Who is interested in this deal? Who will be affected?

• Whose support will be necessary for implementation?

• Who can torpedo the deal?

• Who will serve as ally, coach and sponsor?

Dealing with difficult customers

3.19 All of these recommendations can be bedevilled if there is a history of bad relations between the buyer and other internal stakeholders, or if any of the internal parties has an unhelpful attitude to the negotiation process. For example, it may be that one of the parties instinctively prefers a distributive approach to negotiation. As we mentioned earlier, this is rarely or never appropriate in internal negotiations.

3.20 Once again, Richard Morse is a useful source of ideas for dealing with such 'difficult customers'. His article 'Strategies for Negotiating with Difficult People' outlines three approaches that may be helpful.

3.21 First, the buyer should set boundaries outside of which certain behaviour will not be tolerated. For example, the buyer might draw up 'ground rules', including such instructions as 'Before challenging someone else's view, use active listening to be sure you understand it'.

3.22 Second, the buyer should 'de-legitimise' certain behaviour. For example, it can happen that an internal party indulges in 'triangulation'. As Morse explains, this is 'the behaviour that Sam displays as he tries to criticise, undermine or influence Jane by speaking to Phil'. To de-legitimise this, any member of the negotiating group must tell Sam to speak directly to Jane.

3.23 Third, the buyer may confront the behaviour directly. If one of the parties presents their case in a hostile or belligerent manner, the buyer must find the fortitude to speak to them directly, explaining firmly but gently that the case will not be heard unless it is presented in a professional manner. This stance may in extreme cases be supported by internal disciplinary measures.

Concessions, and the impact on purchasing

3.24 In all of this process, the buyer must regard his own attitude to the eventual external negotiation as provisional. In talking with interested internal parties he will adjust his own position by making concessions to accommodate the concerns of his internal partners. If done fairly and firmly, this process should not damage the position that the buyer will eventually present to the external supplier.

4 Evaluating personal effectiveness

Reflecting on performance

4.1 A negotiation is in many respects like a project. It has a defined beginning and end; we work towards achieving predetermined objectives; and at the conclusion we look back to evaluate how successful we have been, and what lessons can be learned for the future. This last point is the subject of the current section.

4.2 To give some structure to our evaluation, it is helpful to look back on the phases of negotiation and to ask ourselves how we performed in relation to each phase. We use the seven phases identified by Greenhalgh and cited in Lewicki: see Table 11.3

4.3 We can also reflect usefully on cases where we failed to achieve our negotiation objectives.

- Were our objectives reasonable and achievable?
- Did we fail to identify the key variables?
- Did we choose an inappropriate supplier to negotiate with?
- Did we fail to align our objectives with theirs?
- Did we fail to deal with their reasonable concerns?
- Did we fail to use appropriate and powerful persuasion?

Table 11.3 *How did we perform?*

Phase of negotiation process	Evaluation checklist
Preparation	Did our evaluation of the market identify all the relevant factors? Did our evaluation of the supplier identify all the relevant factors? Was our analysis of supplier cost structures correct? Did we select an appropriate negotiation strategy?
Relationship building	Did we select an appropriate relationship to aim for? Did we have sufficient information about the supplier to choose a relationship strategy? Did we establish trust and rapport?
Information gathering	Did we gather all the information we needed? Was the information we gathered correct? Did we ask the right questions of the supplier?
Information using	Did we identify common interests? Did we identify appropriate variables that could be traded? Did we identify a range of possible solutions to problems?
Bidding	Did we make enough (not too many) concessions? Did we extract sufficient, valuable concessions in return? Did we use appropriate techniques of persuasion? Did we trade variables appropriately
Closing the deal	Did we summarise the conclusions in writing? Did we write to the supplier formalising the agreement?
Implementing the agreement	Did we conclude with sufficient detail to enable smooth implementation? Did we leave any important issues unresolved? Has the agreement been working well in practice?

Feedback mechanisms

4.4   We have already mentioned that a negotiation is in some respects like a project. It is useful to refer to the literature on project work at this stage. In particular, we cite the work of Harvey Maylor in his text *Project Management* (2005). Maylor has helpful analysis of the criteria on which we should seek feedback at the end of our project/negotiation. This is adapted in Table 11.4.

Table 11.4 *Areas of feedback in negotiation*

Criterion	How to audit outcome	How to assess performance
Financial	Accounting systems	Contract price
Time	Conformance to plan	Customer satisfaction
Quality	Quality standards	Customer perceptions
Human resources	Conformance to policy	Team spirit, motivation
Planning	Conformance to plan	Techniques used
Control	Systems for control	Basis for improvement

4.5   Apart from the tangible outcomes (in terms of agreed price, quality standards, delivery times etc) we should also pay attention to relationship development. We can obtain feedback from suppliers both formally and (by means of their behaviour and performance) informally.

4.6   To evaluate relationship issues, we need to have a clear idea of the type of relationship that is appropriate to the deal we have concluded. If we have been negotiating for supply of an item that is critical to our core business we would have been hoping to develop a close relationship with the supplier. Have we succeeded in doing so, or have we ended with an agreement in which the supplier essentially regards us as just an arm's length customer?

4.7   The relationship issue must also be seen from the supplier's perspective. In other words, we must attempt to build a relationship that suits the objectives of each party.

Improvement and development

4.8   An important outcome of the negotiation process should be to obtain ideas for improvement. Maylor, in the work already cited, points out that we can learn both **by doing** and **before doing**: see Figure 11.1.

Figure 11.1 *Performance improvement*

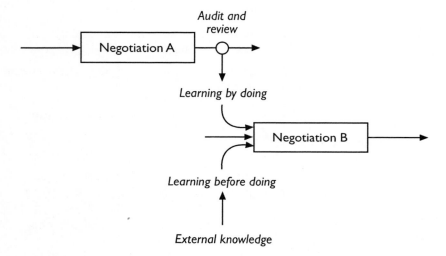

4.9   The diagram indicates that in entering Negotiation B, we can draw on our experience of Negotiation A (learning by doing), and also on our prior preparation (learning before doing).

4.10   Another model that is helpful in this context is the experiential learning cycle devised by David Kolb. Refer back to Figure 9.3 to refresh your memory of this.

Training needs analysis

4.11   A learning or training specification is yet another way of defining the knowledge, skills or competences needed to achieve an acceptable level of performance – but it is used primarily as a basis for devising learning and development programmes. In other words, it focuses on defining training needs – in relation to negotiation or any other area.

4.12 Training needs analysis, very simply, involves:

- Measuring what employees need to be *able* to do in order to perform a job competently and in line with performance standards (eg using job, role or competency analysis and descriptions);

- Measuring what employees actually *can* do (eg using self analysis, competency testing or the appraisal system of the organisation); and

- Identifying any 'gap' between the two, as a potential need for learning, training and development.

4.13 At the individual level, training needs analysis may be fairly informal, utilising self-appraisal, or ongoing feedback from a superior or mentor, say: what areas might benefit from improvement? Formal analysis may also be used: if a person is new in the job, say, or if a staff member is experiencing problems, or as part of ongoing appraisal and development planning for individuals. What does this individual need to be able to do in order to perform better, or be considered for promotion?

Training methods

4.14 A wide variety of training methods and media are available: on-the-job (such as job instruction, coaching or job rotation) and off-the-job (such as taught classes, use of case studies and role plays, open/distance learning, visits and tours, video- or computer-based training and e-learning); formal (such as courses, planned coaching and so on) and informal (such as picking up information from reading, watching how others perform activities, or getting informal advice and feedback from co-workers or managers).

4.15 On-the-job training in the workplace is very common, especially where the work involved is not complex. Various methods may be used.

4.16 **'Sitting with Nellie'** is an approach whereby the trainee is placed beside an experienced worker (Nellie) and learns by observing her work and imitating her operations and methods, under supervision, working with the actual materials and equipment involved in the job.

4.17 **Coaching** is one element of the 'sitting with Nellie' approach, but may be used flexibly in a wide range of training situations and on an ongoing basis. Coaching is on-the-job guidance, advice, correction and teaching with a view to improving performance: it is a process of collaboration between the coach and trainee.

4.18 **Mentoring** by more senior staff includes personal and career development guidance, as well as job training. A mentor may occupy a role as the trainee's teacher/coach, counsellor, role model, supporter/sponsor in the organisation, critic and encourager, as appropriate to the situation as the trainee develops over time. A mentor should help the trainee achieve greater self-awareness; encourage him to formulate and clarify career and personal development goals; and support him in taking responsibility for his self-development.

4.19 **Experiencing different roles** may be accomplished by a number of methods.

- Job rotation or 'work shadowing': the trainee is given different jobs in succession, in order to gain wider experience.

- Temporary promotion: an individual is promoted into a superior's position while the superior is absent.

- 'Assistant to' positions: an individual with management potential may be appointed to assist or shadow a manager.

- Project or committee work: trainees might be co-opted to project teams or committees to gain experience of relevant areas of the organisation's activities, as well as multi-functional team processes and problem-solving.

4.20 The most appropriate method should be selected according to the following criteria.

- The nature of the skills/competencies/knowledge to be developed (requiring theoretical knowledge or hands-on practice, say)

- The benefits of learning outside the job context (less risk; less distraction; standardisation; suits theoretical/reflective learners) or within it (relevance to the job, team and environment; better application/transfer of learning; suits 'hands-on' learners)

- The abilities and learning preferences (or 'styles') of the trainees: Honey and Mumford classify learners as theorists, reflectors, activists and pragmatists, for example

- The availability and cost-effectiveness of alternative methods.

Chapter summary

- There are various difficulties that apply to telephone negotiations: no opportunity to check for consistency between verbal and non-verbal clues; possible distractions; inability to use back-up data such as spreadsheets, etc.

- There are also some advantages in telephoning: we tend to gain an advantage if we initiate the call; we may be able to condition expectations, etc.

- It is useful to have a proforma document designed for recording telephone conversations.

- Active listening is an important tool in negotiation, and not only in telephone communication.

- Email is a less formal method of communication than other written forms. There is limited research evidence to suggest that email negotiations may end in impasse, but that the risk can be reduced by inclusion of a 'personal' note in communication.

- Research identifies four biases that can threaten e-negotiations: temporal synchrony bias; burned bridge bias; squeaky wheel bias; and sinister attribution bias.

- Online auctions provide benefits to buyers, especially savings in time and costs.

- There are also benefits for suppliers: reduction in administration, more speedy payment etc. However, suppliers will identify some disadvantages also: the need to invest in technology, the danger of losing business to alternative suppliers identified by electronic means.

- Negotiators must gain agreement from internal stakeholders, eg user departments, before they approach external suppliers. Detailed communication is important.

- In dealing with internal stakeholders, negotiators should aim to build up a positive rapport. This makes it easier to influence other parties.

- Richard Morse identifies three strategies for dealing with 'difficult' internal customers: setting boundaries; de-legitimising certain behaviour; and direct confrontation.

- In evaluating negotiation performance buyers should address each stage of the negotiation in turn. It is also useful to reflect on cases where the buyer failed to achieve negotiation objectives.

- Harvey Maylor explains how our approach to a new negotiation can be improved by reference both to previous negotiations and to our external knowledge.

- A training needs analysis can identify areas where negotiators need to be developed. There are many methods of providing such training and development.

Self-test questions

Numbers in brackets refer to the paragraphs where you can check your answers.

1   Why does the stronger case tend to prevail in telephone negotiations more than in face-to-face negotiations? (1.3)

2   What are the implications of the fact that a telephone conversation has a definite end (when one party hangs up)? (1.8)

3   List as many as you can of Steele's key points of good practice when negotiating by telephone. (1.14)

4   Explain what is meant by active listening. (1.21)

5   List as many as you can of Lewicki's ten rules for virtual negotiation. (2.3)

6   Thompson and Nadler identify four biases that can threaten e-negotiations. List and briefly explain them. (2.5)

7   What are the benefits to buyers of online auctions? (2.7)

8   What are the benefits to suppliers of online auctions? (2.13ff)

9   What five reasons are identified by Richard Morse why a failure to achieve negotiated internal agreement will cause serious problems? (3.3)

10 What are the benefits of establishing a positive rapport with internal stakeholders? (3.15)

11 What three techniques are suggested by Richard Morse for dealing with difficult internal customers? (3.20ff)

12 In evaluating negotiation performance, what questions might we ask in relation to each stage of the negotiation? Give as many examples as you can recall. (Table 11.3)

CHAPTER 12

Mock Exam

THE EXEMPLAR PAPER

The exam paper below was published by CIPS as an illustration of what might be expected under the new syllabus. If you are able to make a good attempt at this you should be very well prepared for the live examination.

Instructions for Candidates:

This examination is in two sections.

Section A has two compulsory questions, worth 25 marks each.

Section B has four questions: answer two. Each question is worth 25 marks.

SECTION A

You are strongly advised to carefully read and analyse the information in the case study before attempting to answer questions 1 and 2.

Newsready plc

Background history

Newsready plc is the fifth largest regional newspaper group in the UK, and was until recently a privately owned company, with the majority of the shares being held by the descendants of the original owners, The Montgomery family. The first paper they established in the 1930s was The Minchester Daily which served a small town in the South West. Harold Montgomery, the head of the family, could see the potential for growth and one year after the initial paper was established a second paper was born, The Southern Daily Herald.

Newsready remained a regional company for several decades, and then, in the 1990s, consolidation of the newspaper market meant that Newsready had a chance to acquire NewsActive, a similarly sized organisation based in Wales. This consolidation meant double the printing requirements, and the Executive Board took a decision to remove all the local printing machinery and invest in two state of the art printing sites, one based in the South West and one in Wales.

The purchasing team

The purchasing team at Newsready comprises the group purchasing manager, Alison Randall, plus one buyer located at each printing site. The company's total expenditure on goods and services is around £50m, most of which relates to direct materials. The department has only been operating for nine months, and the CEO has charged Alison with some early 'wins' in terms of savings.

Alison decides to look into the ink supply. She is aware that, while outwardly the suppliers agree on a 'notional pricing arrangement', if the prize is big enough, one of the players will break ranks.

Alison has a good relationship with the sales manager from Friendly Inks. However, the sales director always by-passes her office in favour of Peter Montgomery's – the deputy chief executive, whom he has known for 20 years or so.

Market information

There are five main players in the ink market. It is thought that there will be some consolidation over the next few years, leaving the market with around three. At the moment size seems to be of importance to the supplier, as this can prevent a potential takeover from occurring, and thus gaining market share is seen as a key business driver.

The leading national suppliers are:

- Sunset Inks – 40% of the market
- Horizon Inks – 21% of the market
- Power Inks – 12% of the market
- Friendly Inks – 10% of the market
- Frazer and Sons – 5% of the market.

The remainder of the market is spread between 15 regional suppliers.

Supplier information

Friendly Inks has been supplying Newsready with 80% of their ink for the last 10 years. The latest deal was done by the Peter Montgomery.

The deal is for five years (two years have already passed). While a contract exists, it is not as legally binding as one might think on initial inspection, as there is a clause relating to early termination as follows:

> "In the event that the customer can source the same quality ink from alternative suppliers at a more competitive price, then Newsready is released from the contract."

When the deal was initially set up, Friendly Inks agreed to loan Newsready equipment worth £30,000, with the caveat that in the event of early contract termination, then the full cost of the equipment would be paid back to Friendly Inks. The equipment currently resides on Newsready Premises and is in frequent use.

Power Inks supplies the remaining 20%, which is used almost exclusively by the printing centre in Wales. The print centre manager has commented that he actually prefers the ink as it 'seems to go further on the paper'.

Total annual requirements for inks for Newsready (80% Friendly / 20% Power)

Newsready currently takes the following ink volumes:

1st print centre
300 tonnes of black ink
120 tonnes of yellow
120 tonnes of cyan
120 tonnes of magenta.

2nd print centre
120 tonnes of black ink
40 tonnes of yellow
40 tonnes of cyan
40 tonnes of magenta.

Note: There are 1,000 kilos in a tonne.

Costs

Friendly Inks:

Colours	£2.70 per kilo
Black	80p per kilo.

Power Inks:

Colours	£2.76 per kilo
Black	82p per kilo.

The competitive quote

Alison Randall decides to test the market, and faxes a request for quotation to Sunset Inks. The following prices are received based on gaining a 10% share of Newsready's business:

Colours	£2.85 per kilo
Black	76p per kilo.

The quote stated that the prices could be fixed for a 12 month period.

Additional information

Friendly Inks' entertainment budget was £10,000 last year. It is custom and practice throughout Friendly to entertain the Newsready print managers at least once a quarter, either for a meal or a day out at a sporting event. In addition, Friendly has a superb technical team who regularly advise the Newsready printers.

Hot off the press

- There are strong rumours within the industry that Horizon Inks is looking for a takeover target.

- Peter Montgomery has announced his retirement at the end of the month.

The information in this case study is purely fictitious and has been prepared for assessment purposes only.

Any resemblance to any organisation or person is purely coincidental.

QUESTIONS

You are strongly advised to read the questions carefully and it is recommended that you spend approximately 35 minutes answering each question.

Question 1

You are an external consultant working closely with Alison Randall, and have two urgent tasks to complete.

(a)   Prepare an informal report for Alison Randall evaluating the existing supplier arrangements at Newsready plc.   **(15 marks)**

(b)   Recommend a strategy for a forthcoming negotiation with Friendly Inks, identifying key areas of leverage.   **(10 marks)**

Question 2

(a)   Analyse the current supply arrangements from Friendly Inks' perspective.   **(10 marks)**

(b)   Make recommendations as to how Friendly Inks might prepare for the negotiation in order to retain its business with Newsready.   **(15 marks)**

SECTION B

You are strongly advised to spend 10 minutes carefully reading the questions in Section B before selecting **TWO** questions to answer. It is recommended that you spend approximately 35 minutes answering each question from this section.

Question 3

Select **FIVE** persuasion methods available to the buyer, and appraise their use in a negotiation where the balance of power lies with the supplier.   **(25 marks)**

Question 4

(a)   Discuss the merits of open book costing from the perspective of the buyer.
                                                                                   (15 marks)

(b)   Explain how being able to distinguish between fixed and variable costs can benefit the buyer during a negotiation.   **(10 marks)**

Question 5

(a)   Review the characteristics exhibited by a skilled negotiator.   **(20 marks)**

(b)   Outline how personality can have an impact on negotiation style and behaviour.
                                                                                    (5 marks)

Question 6

Write an informal report on how good preparation and planning prior to a negotiation can help the buyer to achieve their objectives.   **(25 marks)**

CHAPTER 13

MOCK EXAM:
SUGGESTED SOLUTIONS

THE EXEMPLAR PAPER

Some general observations

Make sure that you have read the 'Instructions for Candidates' section at the front of the Mock Exam, in order to be quite clear as to what is required.

Please bear in mind that our solutions are lengthier than you would attempt in an exam, in order to cover the wide range of points that might be included – and to reflect the suggestions given in the CIPS Answer Guidance.

SUGGESTED SOLUTIONS

SECTION A

Solution 1

Part (a)

The first comment to make is that the command word here is 'evaluate': this means, in essence, that you need to comment on every possible aspect of the specific area to which the question relates, where possible considering both advantages and disadvantages.

Although the question asks clearly for an informal report, the Answer Guidance provided by CIPS states that candidates were expected to use a standard short report format (with terms of reference, short introduction, findings, conclusions and recommendations). Two marks were awarded for this formatting!

The focus in the Newsready plc case study is on **ink supply**. Given that Newsready, having acquired NewsActive and being the fifth largest UK newspaper group, is intending to set up two major printing sites for all its printing requirements, this would be a major, or even crucial, material. This means that Alison Randall needs to ensure, as much as possible, that she gets it right.

Your report should consider all aspects of ink supply and its arrangements which will be considered below (in no particular order of importance)

- A difficulty that undoubtedly arises is that we are not given information on how valuable Newsready's business is to the suppliers it is using at the moment because we are not given details of the turnover or any other financial figures for Friendly Inks nor Power Inks. However, we know that Newsready is the fifth largest newspaper group in the country which means, in itself, that their demand would be significant for any of the available ink suppliers. We could also calculate that Newsready is buying £240,000 worth of black and £972,000 worth of coloured ink from Friendly Inks annually and £98,400 worth of black ink and £331,200 worth of coloured ink from Power Inks. As mentioned, we have no financial figures for these companies from which we could calculate the percentage of turnover that Newsready's business is worth but given that Friendly Inks have 10% of the ink market and Power Inks 12%, we could assume that this would represent significant business for both but especially for Friendly Inks. The importance of this, of course, is to be able to gain some idea of the negotiating strengths and weaknesses of Newsready when compared to those of the two suppliers.

- The purchase figures above could be used also to give an idea of Newsready's likely strengths and weaknesses when compared with any of the major ink suppliers.

- We can add to these figures when we realise that, according to the existing deal, Newsready are committed to buying a further £720,000 worth of black ink and £2,916,000 worth of coloured ink from Friendly Inks over the next three years.

- Friendly Inks spend a considerable amount on 'entertainment' of Newsready's print managers. There are two comments here: the types of entertainment mentioned in the case study would not normally be 'approved' under the CIPS code of ethics; and the entertainment enjoyed by the print managers means that this particular group of internal stakeholders is going to have great interest in the outcome of any negotiation regarding the supply of ink, particularly if this were to lead to ink supply being re-sourced. Despite the ethical 'question mark' over the entertainment, the print managers are a powerful stakeholder group.

- Friendly Inks provides excellent technical support which is considered valuable by the print managers, reinforcing the view above of their power and interest as a stakeholder group in the outcome of any re-sourcing exercise.

- In the supply market there appears to be a kind of informal arrangement ('notional pricing arrangement') on prices, which cynics might say sounds like a cartel, a view supported by the fact that all prices we are given in the case study seem to be remarkably close to each other. Alison strongly believes, however, that 'if the prize is big enough, one of the payers will break ranks'; in other words she obviously believes (we must assume with good reason, given the spend calculations we have already made) that the kind of spend Newsready has would be large enough to tempt one of the suppliers out of the 'informal arrangement'.

- Friendly Inks has been working with Newsready for some time and clearly relationships exist between the two companies although a slightly worrying note is that Friendly Inks' sales director (as opposed to sales manager) always by-passes Alison in favour of dealing with Peter Montgomery, Newsready's deputy chief executive. There is a suspicion here that collusion might occur between these two individuals that could undermine Alison's attempts to achieve better ink supply. That said, Peter Montgomery is due to retire at the end of the month which should allay any such fears and could mean that Alison's good relationship with Friendly Inks' sales manager would become much more important. One possibility (but too vague and tenuous to worry about) is that Peter Montgomery could be persuaded by Friendly Inks' sales director to tie up one last favourable deal before he retires. The upshot of this could be that Alison needs to assert herself and her position as Group Purchasing Manager rather more.

- The contract with Friendly Inks, although it appears to have a generous 'get-out' clause, is tied to the loan/purchase of frequently used equipment. This would mean that, in the event of early termination of Newsready's contract with Friendly Inks, a situation that could happen quite easily from a legal viewpoint, Newsready would, in essence, have to buy the loaned equipment from Friendly Inks at a presumed price of £30,000 (what we are told the equipment is worth). However, given the financial amounts concerned in the purchase of ink, it is unlikely that the need to buy this equipment to satisfy Friendly Inks' contract term would weigh too heavily in terms of any decision to source ink from an alternative supplier.

- There are five major suppliers in the market but this number is expected to fall to three during the next three years because of 'consolidation' (possible takeovers). This could be important because suppliers appear to be looking for major contracts to increase their size to prevent takeover. This could mean that any supplier chosen by Alison might be keen to win the contract and would therefore have a relatively weak negotiating position.

- There are, in addition 15 'regional' suppliers. It is unlikely that any of these would be large enough to supply Newsready although it is possible that, given Newsready's intention to develop two geographically separate print units, regional suppliers local to the print unit sites could be developed to become at least 'support' suppliers (in the way that Power Inks is currently).

- Power Inks currently supplies almost the entire requirement of the Wales unit. The print manager apparently prefers their ink because it appears, in his opinion, to be of better quality than Friendly Inks' product. Again, we have potential stakeholder influence on supplier selection and negotiation. It is interesting that this preference for Power Inks' product is not shared by print managers elsewhere.

You might find it strange that 'tenuous' points are mentioned above but stating them as part of your answer, provided you did not dwell too long on them, would show that you have thought deeply about the case study and have considered all angles in a 'rounded' way.

In summary

The existing supplier arrangements have many **advantages**.

• A tried, tested and (as far as we can see) trusted supplier of ink (Friendly Inks) that has been supplying Newsready for some time.

• Friendly Inks are supported by Power Inks, which appears to be a good supplier although we have no real information to go on.

• Friendly Inks have not caused any supply problems that we can see and have an impressive technical support record as well as good relationships with important stakeholders at Newsready.

There are no real **disadvantages**, as such: more 'question marks'.

• There is an ethical question mark over the 'entertainment' and to what extent it influences the stakeholders mentioned above – stakeholders who *could* have some influence in any future supply selection and negotiation.

• Alison is not *determined* to change supplier but wants to keep her options open and obtain the best supply of ink possible.

• There is, in the background, the question of the cartel in the ink supply market although, as we have said, Alison believes that this could be overcome if one of the suppliers were sufficiently tempted by potential purchases. This might be reinforced by the strong possibility that suppliers are likely to be looking for large contracts as a possible means of avoiding takeover, as mentioned above.

• To reinforce the above point, Horizon Inks are said to be looking to take over one of the other suppliers in the very near future.

Part (b)

Here you are asked to recommend a strategy for Alison's forthcoming negotiation with Friendly Inks and identify points of leverage.

There is no reason here why you should not use many of the points identified in part (a) because they should provide a platform for this answer.

The CIPS feedback suggests that Alison's Request for Proposal would have the effect of conditioning the market. However, this is doubtful because we are told that Alison sent such a request to Sunset Inks, the main player in the market. Would other suppliers hear about this? Normally such business is not 'advertised' and remains confidential, meaning that the rest of the market would be unlikely to be 'conditioned'.

The CIPS feedback also states that the Request for Proposal will allow Alison to identify what prices the market will bear and which suppliers might be prepared to 'break out'. Again, this appears doubtful given that only Sunset Inks have been asked to quote. The one 'fly in the ointment' here is the extent to which the cartel we have identified operates. However, Sunset's quote would provide Alison with an idea of alternative prices and, if the cartel does exist, we can assume that other suppliers, if asked, would give a similar quotation. The prices quoted by Sunset are £228,000 for black ink and £1,026,000 for coloured ink, meaning that, in total, Sunset Inks would cost £42,000 more than Friendly Inks annually. Three points arise from this.

- This difference is only slightly above £12,000 more than the £30,000 that Newsready would have to pay Friendly Inks if their contract were cancelled.

- This figure *might* easily be outweighed by the fact that Sunset Inks' technical support is an unknown quantity as compared to Friendly Inks' support which we are told is impressive.

- In combination, there would appear to be serious doubt as to whether switching from Friendly Inks to Sunset Inks would provide any benefit and *could* actually be disadvantageous.

Specific points of leverage over Friendly Inks might include the following.

- The possibility that Friendly Inks might be taken over if they lose Newsready's business. Friendly Inks are one of the smaller 'players' and if they were to lose this business, it is likely that they would be weakened significantly. This would make them very keen on retaining the business.

- The current deal could be terminated: see the 'get out' clause we referred to in part (a). As we have said, such an event would be very bad news for Friendly Inks.

- It is possible that a new supplier *could* take on board the capital equipment tie-in meaning that Friendly Inks' equipment could be returned without causing a problem although we have no specific information on this.

- Given that there is a preference in the Wales unit for Power Inks product there *could* be a question mark over Friendly Inks' product quality. This could certainly be used as a bargaining tool in any *distributive* negotiation although, given the relationship that exists, this type of negotiation is perhaps unlikely.

- The CIPS feedback suggests the fact that Peter Montgomery's impending retirement might be a point of leverage but this would only be the case due to the apparent relationship between him and Friendly Inks' sales director. Alison could bypass this by developing her good relationship with its sales manager. The truth is that we don't know how influential Montgomery's relationship is.

In terms of strategy, it would appear that Alison's need to reduce prices in order to make savings would dictate that she use the potentially devastating effect on Friendly Inks (if they were to lose the contract) as her main bargaining tool. She could add to this the fact that the contract can be terminated even with the penalty of the return or purchase of the equipment. However, Sunset Inks is only marginally more expensive, and as said above, switching to them might prove disadvantageous. Whether this all adds up to a bargaining advantage depends on whether Friendly Inks know of the situation, given the apparent cartel. On balance, it could be argued that the prospect of switching to Sunset Inks is not a strong bargaining tool in itself.

A secondary bargaining tool could be the apparent quality difference between Friendly Inks' product and that of Power Inks. If Alison finds that she is able to reduce Friendly Inks' prices for the remainder of the contract period, it might be worth trying to add on to this a clause that means that Newsready would not need to return or purchase the Friendly Inks' equipment if the contract were subsequently cancelled.

Solution 2

Part (a)

Here the question requires you to examine the supply arrangements from Friendly Inks' perspective. In many ways, to answer this question, you should reverse your answer to question 1b although it is not quite as simple as that. Certainly, however, you should be able to use the analysis carried out so far as the basis for an answer here. The main points are listed below.

Friendly Inks would like to keep the contract: with the possibility of being taken over (perhaps by Sunset Inks), losing this contract could prove disastrous.

The current situation should give Friendly Inks confidence because of the following factors.

- Other suppliers appear to be no cheaper: certainly Sunset Inks' quotation to Newsready demonstrates this, the only question mark being to what extent Friendly Inks are aware of this.

- There is a good relationship between Friendly Inks' sales manager and Alison

- There have been no problems (that we are aware of) in terms of the past performance of the contract with Friendly Inks.

- Friendly Inks have developed good relationships with Newsready's print managers who, as we have already said, are important stakeholders in any sourcing decision made by Newsready.

- Friendly Inks have been providing impressive technical support during the running time of the contract, such support clearly being greatly valued by Newsready's print managers.

On the other hand, potential problems for Friendly Inks that might reduce confidence are as follows.

- Scope certainly exists for Newsready to source supplies elsewhere

- There is the *possible* quality problem when compared to Power Inks' product although it is not clear whether Friendly Inks are aware of this.

- The relationship between the sales director and Peter Montgomery, which could be seen as 'key', is about to end due to Montgomery's impending retirement.

Part (b)

Here, again there is to some extent a need to view what we have already identified from a reverse viewpoint. Friendly Inks need to make their position as strong as possible although the comment could be made that their position is not disastrous or irredeemable in any way because they do have some significant advantages. What they need to do, therefore, is maximise the effect of those advantages and prepare to ward off any advantages that Newsready might have.

Recommendations for their negotiation preparation (although we are not actually told in the case study that there will be a negotiation!) would include the following.

- Attempting to develop the relationship that already exists with Alison

- Attempting to use the relationship with Peter Montgomery to persuade him to sanction the continuation of the contract as a 'leaving gift' although how likely this is would be open to question.

- They could attempt to work with Newsready's print managers, using the relationship that has been built due to technical support (already mentioned) and 'entertainment'. You should note that, whilst there may be an ethical question mark over the 'entertainment', we have to live in the real world and recognise that such things take place and can bring influence to bear on the outcome of negotiations. We have already made the point that Newsready's print managers would be important stakeholders to any negotiation outcome.

- They could continue to promote the features and benefits of their product and it would be useful to suggest here that they try to build as much as possible on the impressive technical support which has been a hallmark of their contract performance so far.

- They could emphasise that there have been no problems, that we are aware of, in their contract performance and could make much of the 'better the devil you know.....' idea.

- Given that existing relationships that we have mentioned appear to form a large part of their continuing dealings with Newsready, they could try to cultivate new relationships with other senior board members and try to use such influence in, or prior to, any negotiation.

- The CIPS guide answer suggests that 'do nothing' would be a possibility, which of course, it would although it would be unlikely to gain you any marks unless it were justified by supporting argument. Certainly, doing nothing is a possibility: in the real world, it always is. It could be argued that Friendly Inks' current position is not a bad one given their good performance, good relationships of various kinds with Newsready and the fact that, at the moment, there are no real competitors on the horizon that we are aware of. From all of this it could be argued that for Friendly Inks to try to develop an obvious strategy to retain the contract could be construed as panicking, something which always prompts the question of 'why?', what have they go to be concerned about? Given all of this, 'doing nothing' could be put forward as a reasonable argument.

The CIPS feedback suggests using questioning techniques such as FAB (although it is not clear what this is) and SPIN (a questioning technique developed by Huthwaite International). Such questioning techniques are usually considered in terms of the actual negotiation but of course, questions do need to be prepared prior to negotiation. Following SPIN (Situation, Problem, Implication, Need-payoff) might give us questions such as the following.

- Situation: how are you finding our current supply process?

- Problem: are there any problems with our service or our prices?

- Implication (assuming the answer to the previous question indicates that there are problems): what do you feel we need to do to improve the situation?

- Need-payoff: if we reviewed our price levels and contract terms would this give you the changes you need?

The problem with this type of approach is that, if we are not careful, we end up asking questions that, in effect, might give Newsready all the advantage they need.

Solution 3

This question requires you to select five methods of persuasion and appraise their use in a negotiation where the balance of power lies with the supplier. The command word 'appraise' is similar to 'evaluate' in that it requires you to consider both sides of the coin: advantages and disadvantages and in this case, in effect, consider whether each of the persuasion methods selected would be likely to work in the situation given.

Persuasion techniques

Persuasion is an important part of any negotiation because one of the prime objectives of each party will be to **persuade** the other party to accept their point of view. There are five generally accepted techniques that may be used to persuade someone to your way of thinking.

Logic – trying to use rational argument to persuade the other party and bringing 'evidence' to bear to support the 'logical' position. The problem is that there may not be a common perception of what is logical, although if facts and figures that might support our case are carefully put together and brought into play, it would be difficult for the supplier to resist our argument. Logic is one of the chief tools that might be deployed in negotiation and an example of logical argument in a situation of dispute resolution in purchasing and supply might be to say that what was ordered were black grunging irons, not the green ones that were delivered, because it says so on the order.

Bargaining – the main thing here is that the buyer should have a list of possible concessions that could be traded, bearing in mind the areas of caution about concessions already studied, which might make the supplier look favourably on our position elsewhere. This stage is seen by many people as being the 'crux' of negotiation and care should be taken because **proposals** turn into **bargaining** very quickly and at times, the two can be almost indistinguishable. The basic rules of bargaining are as follows.

- Try not to be the first to make a concession.

- Make sure that your early concessions, where possible, are minor ones. These should come from your 'L' objectives (MIL) and are sometimes known as 'straw issues'.

- If you make a concession try to obtain something of equal or greater value in return or, at least, try to attach conditions to a concession. An example might be: 'if we accept this higher price, will you deliver more frequently in smaller quantities so as to give us something approaching JIT service?'. The essence of bargaining is that it is a method of extracting value from a deal by exchanging ideas that each party values.

- Try to trade variables that are minor for you with ones that are more important for the supplier.

- It is better to make numerous small concessions rather than one major one.

- Try not to allow yourself to get into a 'run' of concessions (ie making one after another with nothing in return).

- Always make a note of concessions made so that areas that have been bargained and agreed can be included in the written deal later.

There are certain things you should not do when bargaining.

- Don't be surprised at how quickly this stage is completed – it often takes very little time (although this depends on how far apart the two parties were at the beginning).

- Don't get caught out by the introduction of new issues – be prepared.

- Don't become greedy and ruin the agreed deal by pushing for more than the other party is prepared to give,.

- Don't make unplanned concessions.

Emotion – you may not be able to convince the supplier using logical argument but appeal to emotion might work. An example might be making the point that refusal of the supplier to co-operate will place you in a difficult position. You might not set too much store by this approach, however, as it smacks of trickery although it could be viewed as the ability to make the supplier change their position by means of goodwill or similar feelings. As you should be able to see, it could be divided into 'negative emotion' and 'positive emotion'.

Threat – this is another approach that may be made if logic fails. Threats should be used with care and, if a threat is made and the supplier calls your bluff, you should carry out your threat because, if you do not, your next threat will not have any effect. It is an antagonistic method, whether veiled or explicit, and should be used with care.

Compromise – this is a word with some negative connotations, such as of 'splitting the difference', which is sometimes defined as 'sub-optimal win/win' but could be seen, in some circumstances, as 'lose/lose'. Thus, compromise should only be used as a persuasion technique if your objectives were high to start with so that 'splitting the difference' will still result in your not losing out and should really be used only when there is a small difference in positions.

As a general rule you should always try using logic first and, if that fails, bargaining. The other persuasion techniques should only be used after the failure of these first two.

To begin with, you should outline each of the persuasion techniques, as above although you might not need quite so much detail. The key to this question, however, is to be able to relate these techniques to the negotiation situation where the balance of power lies with the supplier. In the same order as above, the following would be comments to make.

Logic: this may fail if the supplier decides to use power in response. If a supplier quite clearly refuses to answer questions based on logic, the question should arise as to whether we want to continue dealing with him, although the answer to that question might be that we have no choice, which might be why the supplier holds the power. Much depends here on the supplier's perception of how strong their power is.

Bargaining: this may work. After all it is one of the 'key' aspects of negotiation and nearly all negotiations will contain bargaining at some point. Here, it might work although much would depend on how the supplier responds to bargaining over 'straw issues'. If the supplier is clearly not really interested in bargaining over such things, it might result in the supplier wanting to move to bargaining over greater, more important issues, which you might not want to bargain over.

Emotion: this might work, depending on how skilful you are, bearing in mind that, if not used well, it can become an obvious ploy aimed at 'getting round' the other party. 'Positive' rather than 'negative' emotion would be the way to go here, perhaps making the supplier aware that they are important to you. It might have the effect, however, of making the supplier feel unreasonable, which is something that could work in your favour.

Threat: this is perhaps the weakest of all of the persuasion techniques that could be used in this situation because the supplier could probably just walk away if threatened with, for example, loss of the business. In this situation, you would be faced with no supplies at all. Much depends here on the extent to which the balance of power lies with the supplier: if the balance is not tipped too far the supplier's way, threat might work but almost certainly not if the balance is tipped well in the supplier's favour.

Compromise: this is probably the weakest tool because, as well as 'splitting the difference' it has connotations of indicating that you have a weak position and so 'let's not bother to discuss this', in other words trying to walk away from that part of the negotiation. The problem is that it is unlikely to work when the supplier has the balance of power in its favour. After all, in that situation, why should the supplier compromise?

In this situation, the fact is that none of the persuasion techniques listed represents an ideal answer but logic would be a good place to start, followed by emotion which, if it clearly makes the supplier feel unreasonable, could be followed by bargaining. Threat and compromise would almost certainly have no place in this negotiation.

Solution 4

Part (a)

Here you are asked to discuss the merits (advantages) of open book costing from the buyer's perspective.

A good place to start would be with a brief definition although you should note that this should not turn into your whole answer nor anything approaching it.

Open book costing – this is something that usually only happens if there is an existing collaborative relationship between the purchasing organisation and the supplier. It can also help develop a relationship provided both parties want this to happen. Basically, it involves both organisations sharing cost information fully and its purpose is so that the buyer might see if some elements of the supplier's costs are high and from that position might be able to suggest ways of reducing those costs. Similarly the supplier can see that the purchaser is not making exorbitant profits on the back of any cost saving initiative that the supplier has undertaken. It should lead to a situation that encourages mutual cost saving initiatives with the result that the supplier can reduce costs, which would be a benefit to the buyer, while still making the same profit margin.

The perceived advantages of open book costing are as follows.

- Openness reduces conflict: this is perhaps a fairly obvious statement but if openness exists then a more meaningful negotiation is likely to take place because both parties would want a reasonable outcome (win/win).

- Open book costing places a greater reliance on negotiating skills: rather than trying to 'pull the wool over the eyes' of the other party.

- It should help focus on value for both parties.

- It has the potential to further develop a buyer-supplier relationship because, as we have said, it is based on openness.

- Costs are revealed, meaning that there would be much less emphasis on guesswork and that the buyer would have a good idea of issues such as what quantity the supplier would need to sell in order to break even.

- It would help both parties focus on obvious costs and might allow both parties to focus on areas where costs on both sides could be reduced with the possible effect of mutual cost savings. This would give the 'win/win' outcome of the buyer being able to buy the items at a lower price whilst the supplier continues to make an acceptable profit margin albeit on lower costs.

Part (b)

This question requires you to explain how the ability to distinguish between fixed and variable costs can benefit the buyer in negotiation.

It is useful to define these briefly to start with, although as above, this should not develop into the total answer.

- **Fixed costs** – those which tend to remain unchanged over a range of activity levels, eg rent, heating and lighting costs.

- **Variable costs** – those which tend to vary directly with changes in the level of activity, eg cost of materials used or labour employed in the manufacturing process.

There are also 'semi-variable' costs but we are not asked about those in this question.

Essentially, being able to distinguish between fixed and variable costs helps us focus on costs incurred by the supplier that we may have some chance of being able to reduce either by bargaining or by using logic to help the supplier bring about cost reductions. The simple fact is that it is most unlikely that a supplier is going to be able to reduce fixed costs and, therefore, it is variable costs attributable to the item or service we are purchasing that we need to focus on. Specific ways we could do this, so as to give us benefit, might be as follows.

- We could consider reducing the specification of the item purchased (assuming we have this scope), which should mean that the supplier can reduce material and/or labour costs.

- The ability to distinguish the two types of cost would allow us to look at benchmarking the supplier's production costs against those of similar suppliers so that we could find out if there are any areas where cost reductions could reasonably be made.

- It would mean that we could consider increasing or decreasing purchase volumes. For example, we could consider purchasing larger volumes less frequently than we are doing currently. This might have the effect of allowing the supplier to purchase greater quantities of raw material, resulting in a cost reduction that could be passed on to us.

- It might allow us to work with the supplier to try to drive down costs so that, as with open book costing, there is a win/win outcome. Again, it is usually variable costs that provide this scope although there may be some scope to look at driving down (eg) lighting costs by using low-energy bulbs. One area where we could help the supplier with driving costs down is to suggest alternative raw material (or any other input) suppliers so that the supplier can achieve lower costs which can then be passed on to us.

Solution 5

Part (a)

This is by far the major part of the question and requires you to review the characteristics exhibited by a skilled negotiator. Again, there is a possible query regarding the command word: 'review' essentially means provide a list (of characteristics) and explain how they might appear and/or be used in negotiation. More than this, you should try to demonstrate how the characteristics might be used by a **skilled** negotiator. The question rubric does not provide you with a specific number of characteristics to identify. The CIPS feedback lists eight although it is not clear how marks are divided between them. There might be an issue here with the word 'characteristic': many people would regard this as meaning 'a personality trait' whereas what is required here is essentially a list and brief explanation of skills associated with good negotiators. You could however take the view that these skills emanate from personality traits. The thing to avoid is getting into a deep psychological discussion!

One of the problems in answering this question is that there is no one particular type of person or personality that makes a good negotiator. Indeed, we are not concerned with personality studies here but with a checklist of factors that can make any negotiator better and add to any negotiator's skills. Thus, successful negotiators should do the following.

- Spend as much time as is necessary planning and preparing for the negotiation: preparation is widely viewed as the most important aspect of negotiation.

- Give adequate thought to the range of variables that can be traded against concessions in the negotiation.

- Start any negotiation by establishing areas of common ground between the parties. There is no point discussing or negotiating aspects of the prospective deal that both parties agree on and this can prevent much wasted time.

- Distinguish between positions and interests.

- Develop a set of clearly defined objectives.

- Try to use 'open-ended' questions as much as possible.

- Confirm that both parties understand what has been discussed and agreed at regular intervals and regularly summarise progress.

- Be able to cope with pressure. Some people are innately more able to do this than others but everyone who has to negotiate as part of their job must recognise this and try to cope with pressure as well as they can.

Characteristics of skilled negotiators follow on from this list and might be described as 'having the ability' to do the following.

- Be a good listener; this is fundamental to any skilled negotiator – if you don't listen carefully to what the other party is saying, you cannot hope to respond positively or, perhaps, in any meaningful kind of way.

- Assess relationship dynamics: this might be achieved to some extent by commenting on feelings and by trying to gain a 'picture' of the other party's feelings. This would be an important first step in a negotiation and concerns attempting to judge the kind of relationship that exists already and what scope, if any, there might be for developing it. This is an important first step because it would dictate, to some extent, whether the negotiation is likely to be integrative or distributive, concepts which would influence the whole tone of the subsequent negotiation.

- Develop trust: as much as anything this relates to your ability to answer any questions openly and to ask questions such as 'what issues are important to you?'; 'what could we do to assist you....?' And so on

- Seek information: information on the other party's position is fundamental to any negotiation and it is best gained by asking 'open' questions as much as possible.

- Share knowledge: this establishes that you are looking to be cooperative and to work together to develop a 'win/win' outcome. 'Open book' costing might be an aspect of this.

- Test understanding: again, a suitable choice of question types is relevant here: 'closed' questions could be useful to obtain positive answers giving good guidance as to whether the other party has understood something. 'Do you understand our need to reduce costs in order to make savings?' might be a fairly obvious example of such a question.

- Summarise frequently: this helps reinforce understanding and avoids taking for granted aspects of the negotiation that were thought to have been resolved but in fact, had not. It also enables issues to be re-visited where necessary.

- Clarify issues where necessary: seeking information and testing understanding, as we have already mentioned, might be useful here and if it is obvious that issues have not been fully understood by the other party, then re-capping and possibly alternative explanations would be necessary.

- Keep the discussion focused: care must be taken not to digress from the matter at hand, which can lead to issues that should be resolved being 'lost'. A useful approach here would be to summarise, as already mentioned, after every point of discussion before moving on to the next one.

The question asks about characteristics of a skilled negotiator and therefore expects positive comments, as above. However, it might be worth briefly mentioning the 'other side of the coin' and things we should **not** do include the following.

- Give many reasons for a position as this gives too many opportunities for the other party to spot weaknesses.

- Become defensive or attack unnecessarily.

- Use 'irritators'. Examples might include 'this is unreasonable' or 'I certainly expected more than this': this can quickly develop a negative attitude in the other party.

- Make immediate counter-proposals because these are seen by the other party as a negative response.

Section (b)

This part of the question is only worth five marks and should be answered briefly. As a general rule when sitting exams, you should remember that, in a situation such as this, you could write the best, most detailed answer in the world and it would still only gain five marks!

Any answer here, therefore, must only 'scratch the surface' of what can be a very detailed subject. The best way to answer this question, therefore, would be to give an example of how a personality trait (and you only need select one) might influence negotiation behaviour. Examples would be as follows.

- A 'thinker': such a person would tend to use a logical approach and would tend to evaluate everything given by the other party objectively and would always be seeking information that would help approach a resolution. Problems with this approach might be that the negotiator might appear very rigid in their position, seeking always to control.

- Someone that has an 'intuitive' personality would be seen as being imaginative and creative as well as focusing on concepts rather than minute detail. The downside of this type of personality would be that the person might be unrealistic in terms of the outcomes they seek, might appear dogmatic and could be a poor listener.

- Extroverts and those who are 'agreeable' have been found to be relatively unsuccessful negotiators because they tend to focus too much on their own positions.

You would not need to use all of these points to gain good marks here. One of the points above well-explained or two briefly explained should gain full marks.

Solution 6

This question requires you to give an informal report on how good preparation and planning prior to a negotiation can help the buyer achieve their objectives. The first thing to do is to refer you back to the comment about informal reports made in Solution 1a. Once again, the CIPS feedback tells us that two marks are available for following the CIPS informal report format mentioned in Solution 1a.

Most writers (and there are many!) on the subject of negotiation are in agreement that the single most important aspect of negotiation is the planning and preparation carried out beforehand. However, merely repeating this fact will not gain 25 marks: what you need to do is to provide examples of 'how' such preparation and planning might help achieve the negotiator's objectives by giving examples of planning aspects.

- Being aware of how attractive your purchase is likely to be to the seller

- Being aware of how attractive your company is as a customer to the seller

- Knowing what the product to be purchased is made of and how it is produced. This knowledge means that the seller is not likely to be able to 'pull the wool over your eyes' in terms of aspects/features of the production process

- Knowing how competitive the supply market is

- Being aware of how certain the seller feels of gaining your order, come what may, and of how badly the seller wants it

This type of information is crucial to an assessment of your strengths and weaknesses as opposed to those of the seller. Negotiation is often a question of pitting your strengths and weaknesses against the seller's. Planning, preparation and information-gathering are crucial to the process of gaining as much knowledge as possible of how the seller operates. Ideally, you should have as much knowledge of the kind of issues mentioned above as the seller does.

Before any negotiating process can be entered into, it is vital that the buyer or buying organisation has gathered all the relevant and available data on the materials required and the suppliers of those materials.

Poor preparation and planning means you are less likely to be successful. On the other hand, good planning and preparation will present a professional approach and increase your chances of being successful. Keep all your options open.

Your organisation may have a specific procedure for drawing up plans, or you may need to devise one for yourself. Some elements are critical to any plan; others will be specific to particular organisations or even to particular negotiations. If you have no set procedure to follow, you should make careful notes of your own planning procedure over the next few months until experience tells you that the programme you have devised is a good one. It is vitally important that you assess and monitor the success of your plan afterwards. This will enable you to make any necessary adjustments for next time.

Think carefully about your **objectives** in the negotiation and build your plan around them.

Try to keep in mind the **SMART** theory when defining your objectives. SMART tells us that objectives should be:

Specific
Measurable
Achievable
Realistic
Timely

Another excellent model is the MIL approach. MIL stands for the following.

*   Objectives which represent the **minimum ('must achieve'** in some texts) acceptable – the so-called 'walk away' position.

*   Objectives which the purchaser **intends** to achieve – these represent the most realistically achievable outcomes which the purchaser could expect.

*   Objectives which the purchaser would **like** to achieve – these would represent the ideal package.

Objectives help the buyer focus on what should be achieved through the negotiation. In complex negotiations, establishing objectives will require considerable thought, because they often involve interrelated sets of variables, and defining the right 'mix' for the package will not be easy. Should the supplier be unwilling to make an offer which does not meet the requirements of the *minimum target* under the above approach, the buyer must be prepared to end the negotiation and pursue the best alternative option. This is sometimes referred to as the **'Best Alternative to a Negotiated Agreement' (BATNA)**. This planning of objectives is sometimes referred to as a 'wish list'.

Once your objectives have been identified you could refine them in the following way.

*   **Generate and evaluate the options.** How many different options are available? When each possible course of action has been evaluated, which one will best achieve your objectives?

*   **Identify the activities.** What do you need to do in order to implement the options you have chosen?

*   **Sequence the activities.** Which order or tactics will help you to achieve the goal?

*   **Identify the resources.** What resources do you need in order to carry out your plan?

*   **Review the plan.** Will it work? If not, go back to the earlier stages and re-think them. Consider some contingency plans.

*   **Prepare action plans and schedules.** Decide the order in which you want to discuss the various issues you have identified and (in team negotiations) decide who is going to say or do what, and when, etc.

*   **Monitor and control.** Re-plan if necessary although you should understand that this might be difficult without knowing what the tactics of the supplier will be or their reaction to your approach

Supplier and supply market analysis: one of the most important aspects of preparation is to try to put yourself in a position that is as knowledgeable as that of the supplier about such issues as:

- what the product is made of

- the costs of those materials

- how they are processed to obtain the finished product

- how is the supplier's business performing – is it successful or otherwise?

- is the supplier a market leader or follower?

- how badly does the supplier want your business?

- how certain does the supplier feel of gaining your business?

Knowledge of such matters will enable you to confirm or negate claims made by the supplier relative to the product, its features and its production/supply costs. If you know, from your preparation/research prior to the negotiation, that the supplier is exaggerating aspects of the product or making untrue claims, you will be able to challenge them with a degree of strength and certainty.

The question then is how exactly do you do this? Firstly, you can use your general knowledge of the supplier, if you have dealt with the company before and especially if you have had a long relationship with them, and of the supply market that the supplier is part of. Additionally, you can use tools such as SWOT and PESTLE, which you should be familiar with. These should be used to analyse both your position and that of your supplier.

Briefly, your strengths and opportunities are the aspects to be **exploited**, while your weaknesses and threats should be **reduced** or minimised. Strengths and weaknesses are **internal** to the organisation whereas opportunities and threats arise in the **external** environment. When planning a negotiation process, consider SWOT in your positioning and as part of your strategy. It will help answer questions such as the following.

- How badly does the supplier want our business?

- How certain does he feel of gaining it?

- Are we likely to be able to secure a long-term agreement?

PESTLE: Political, Economic, Social, Technical, Legal and Environmental ('Green' as opposed to the organisation's general business environment) is essentially a development of the **PEST** model that has been in existence for many years.

PESTLE involves examining a company's **external** environment to ascertain what pressures might be exerted and their potential effect on the business in general and on the situation around which the negotiation is taking place, in particular. It may be utilised with reference to your own organisation to help you ascertain and codify external pressures on your business as well as with respect to your supplier's business for the same purpose in that regard.

Subject Index